POLAR AVIATION

Aerial view of the North Pole (16,870 feet), showing an ice pack breaking up. The North Pole can only be located by the navigator and his special instruments, as the Magnetic Pole is located on a small island in the northern Hudson Bay area, and magnetic compasses are of little use.

THE WATTS AEROSPACE LIBRARY

POLAR
AVIATION

EDITED BY

Lt. Col. C. V. Glines, U.S.A.F.

Franklin Watts, Inc.,
575 Lexington Avenue • New York 22

ACKNOWLEDGMENTS

The selections in this book are used by permission and special arrangements with the proprietors of their respective copyrights who are
listed below. The editor's and publisher's thanks to all who made this
collection possible.

The editor and publisher have made every effort to trace the ownership of all material contained herein. It is their belief that the necessary
permissions from publishers, authors, and authorized agents have been
obtained in all cases. In the event of any questions arising as to the use
of any material, the editor and publisher express regret for any error
unconsciously made and will be pleased to make the necessary correc-
tion in future editions of this book.

True and Wilbur Cross, for "Last Balloon to Nowhere," by Wilbur Cross
with Thorleif Hellbom. Reprinted from the August 1962 issue of *True*.

Hutchinson Publishing Group for "Toward the North Pole by Airplane,"
by Lincoln Ellsworth. This selection is from the book MY POLAR FLIGHT,
by Capt. Roald Amundsen. Copyright © 1925 by Hutchinson & Co. Reprinted
by permission of the publisher.

Paul Reynolds & Son, and John Toland for "Flight of the Norge," by John
Toland. This selection is from the book SHIPS IN THE SKY, by John Toland.
Copyright © 1957 by John Toland. Published by Holt, Rinehart & Winston,
Inc.

Flying Magazine for "Air Pioneers Over Greenland," by Frank H. Ellis. Reprinted from the December, 1955 issue of *Flying* Magazine, copyright © 1955
by Ziff-Davis Publishing Co. Reprinted by permission of the publisher.

Harper & Row, Publishers, Inc. for "Exploring the Arctic," by J. Gordon
Vaeth. This selection is from the book GRAF ZEPPELIN by J. Gordon Vaeth.
Copyright © 1958 by J. Gordon Vaeth. Reprinted by permission of the pub-
lisher.

John Murray, Ltd. for "Balloon Ascent Over Antarctica," by Captain Robert
F. Scott. This selection is from the book, THE VOYAGE OF THE DIS-
COVERY, by Captain Robert F. Scott, copyright © 1909 by Captain Robert
F. Scott. Reprinted by permission of the publisher.

Foreword

THERE IS NO CHAPTER in the history of aviation more dramatic or more exciting than that written by the aerial polar explorers. To satisfy their curiosity for the unknown, brave men have traveled literally to the ends of the earth. In the quest for discovery and knowledge they have given their strength, frequently their health, and sometimes their lives.

World maps of a hundred years ago contained vast areas that were marked "Unknown" or "Unexplored." Yet, in the short span of a man's lifetime, the airplane has enabled explorers to investigate these regions with less hardship and in a fraction of the time of their earthbound colleagues. Today there are few areas that can be labeled unknown or unexplored. Indeed, because of the airplane, man has gone everywhere and in doing so has contributed to a prodigious growth in human knowledge.

Arctic exploration began not with a search for the North Pole but for the Northwest Passage to the Orient to gain access to the riches of Asia. The motive was commercial. The first to try, as far as historians know, was Eric the Red who sailed from his colony in Iceland and established a beachhead in Greenland in the tenth century. Eric's son, Leif Ericson, left Greenland and reached the coast of North America five hundred years before John Cabot and Christopher Columbus.

It was not until the first quarter of the nineteenth century that the quest turned from profit to a desire for knowledge. Men wanted to go to the top of the world — to the North Pole. Their real purpose was not always clear but their goal was.

The first organized attempt to reach the North Pole was made in 1827 when Sir William Edward Parry, sailing in the *Hecla* to Spitsbergen, formed a sledge-boat expedition. But the weather and the personal hardships were too great and he turned back after reaching 82°45′, a record latitude that was unmatched for forty-five years. In the spring of 1831, James C. Ross planted the British flag at the North Magnetic Pole, a first giant step to the ultimate goal.

After Ross, the men of a dozen northern hemisphere nations, including the United States, strove for three quarters of a century to be first to set foot on that magic geographical point from which all directions are south. The first to succeed, after six unsuccessful attempts, was Admiral Robert E. Peary. On April 6, 1909, he jammed the American flag in the ice and forever etched his name in the annals of polar exploration.

The history of Antarctic exploration is briefer than that of the Arctic. The first man to cross the Antarctic Circle was Captain James Cook, an Englishman, who sailed his ship, the *Resolute*, across this imaginary line on January 16, 1773. Some fifty years later, Captain Fabian Bellingshausen, a Russian, was the first to sail below the Antarctic Circle and discover land. But it was not until 1895 that a Norwegian, Carsten Borchgrevink, became the first man to set foot on the virgin Antarctic Continent.

The honor of being the first to reach the geographic South Pole went to another Norwegian, Captain Roald Amundsen who, with four companions, arrived there on December 14, 1911. They had traveled the incredible distance of 1,860 miles by dog sledge in ninety-nine days — a triumph of good planning, adequate transport, and a fortunate choice of the easier of two routes to the Pole from the Ross Barrier.

Amundsen's feat was duplicated four weeks later by Sir Robert F. Scott who traveled the more difficult route. Unfortunately, Scott and his men did not survive the return trip.

The hardships faced by those who braved the bitter cold, the utter loneliness, and the harsh perils of polar travel are unmatched in the history of human endurance. It was inevitable that the airplane, as soon as it reached a point of reliability, would become the primary means of transportation. The enormous difficulties experienced by ground-bound explorers, not only in finding a way over the snow and ice, but in the constant struggle against cold and starvation, could be avoided. Distances, which on foot would take weeks or even months, could be covered in mere hours. True, there were risks and dangers in the air, but they could hardly be greater than those on the ground. Although the Poles had been conquered while the airplane was in its infancy, men would continue to invade the forbidding white deserts in the quest for more knowledge. But now they would go by airplane for it alone provided the way and means.

The Turks have an ancient proverb which says, "The world belongs to the dissatisfied." This seems particularly applicable to the polar airmen who are drawn irresistibly to the magic spirit world that calls them and persuades them to forsake the comforts of civilization, to give up the warmth of home and hearth for the utter misery of basic survival in the coldest regions on earth. Their dissatisfaction with ignorance has led to great discoveries and added immeasurably to the sum of human knowledge. This has been done in spite of Apsley Cherry-Garrard's belief that "Polar exploration is at once the cleanest and most isolated way of having a bad time that has yet been devised."

This anthology represents the history of flight in the polar regions. It does not contain all the stories that could be told, but it does parallel man's progress as he first tried flight in balloons, then dirigibles, and finally airplanes to bring the inaccessible polar areas of the world within easy reach. Flights into these areas were first foolhardy, then daring, then routine.

Contents

PART TWO: CONQUERING THE ANTARCTIC
BY AIR

PART THREE: WAR BELOW ZERO

PART ONE

TO THE TOP OF THE WORLD

People, perhaps, still exist who believe that it is of no importance to explore the unknown polar regions. This, of course, shows ignorance. It is hardly necessary to mention here of what scientific importance it is that these regions should be thoroughly explored. The history of the human race is a continual struggle from darkness toward light. It is, therefore, to no purpose to discuss the use of knowledge; man wants to know, and when he ceases to do so, he is no longer man.

—FRIDTJOF NANSEN

Introduction

TRAILBLAZING has always been difficult. Every new geographic discovery has been preceded by disappointment, frustration, and failure. Exploration in the frigid zones of the earth is no exception. In fact, it has been the rule, because the men who first tried had no precedent, no maps, and no advice. These men had to find out for themselves how to survive, then how to travel and navigate accurately. Lack of knowledge and inadequate preparation caused the deaths of many of these pioneers.

As in all the history of human progress, failures do not deter brave men. The very fact that there were failures spurred others on for the honor or glory of accomplishing what their predecessors could not. Inevitably, someone did achieve the seemingly impossible and another milestone in human progress was passed.

The honor of being the first to attempt flight to the North Pole goes to Salomon August Andrée, a mechanical engineer, who was born in Grenna, Sweden, in 1854. Ironically, Andrée, the first to try, also became the first to die.

After graduation from the technical school, the equivalent of a modern engineering college, Andrée became an assistant professor, and later a chief engineer, in the Swedish Government Patent Office. His interest in things scientific drifted toward the science of "aerostation" or ballooning and aerial navigation. At the age of twenty-two, he made his first balloon ascent. The sheer exhilaration of the experience led him to make other flights, one of which almost cost him his life when he attempted a crossing of the Baltic and crashed on the reefs around the Isle of Goeland.

Accidents and mishaps did not stop Andrée from experimenting, and he tried steering his balloon by means of a guide rope and a sail. His successes, real or imaginary, are academic. Andrée is remembered, not for his balloon successes, but for his magnificent failure.

What really motivated Andrée to attempt to sail a flimsy silk-and-varnish gasbag to the most inaccessible point in the northern hemiphere will never be known. The only facts available today are the accounts of witnesses and the entries he made in his diary which was found clutched to his frozen, lifeless body thirty-three years later. His tragic disappearance convinced one and all that a free balloon was not the proper vehicle for a flight to the North Pole.

Last Balloon to Nowhere

Wilbur Cross with Thorleif Hellbom

SALOMON AUGUST ANDRÉE, a wiry, intense Swede whose system was constantly supercharged with energy, was only twenty-two when he tasted his first absorbing experience with balloons while working at the Philadelphia World's Fair. From that day on, he began to devote himself to the study of aeronautics. He was an individualist who could pursue one line of thought as tenaciously as a tightrope artist performing on the high wire. Old-line balloonists were astonished that a man so young and inexperienced could take to the air, in varying weather conditions, and never once exhibit any signs of fright.

His first craft was the *Svea,* which he had persuaded the publisher of *Aftonbladet,* an evening newspaper in Stockholm, to buy for him, "to promote public welfare and science." From that moment on, ballooning was his mistress, his religion, his entire life. In *Svea,* he made many significant weather observations, studied the speed and movement of sound, and took some remarkable aerial photographs. His greatest accomplishments in the early 1890's were several daring, and unprecedented, flights across the Baltic Sea. Then, in 1895, Andrée startled his associates by announcing:

"It is possible — and feasible — for a balloon to fly to the North Pole!"

Even the skeptics listened as Andrée passionately explained just why and how a balloon could forever outmode the plodding, laborious method of packing across the ice on foot or with dogs and sledges.

"The winds are steady," he pointed out. "From Spitsbergen, you can almost count on a northerly wind of two weeks' duration. It will carry a balloon across the roof of the world, and beyond to Alaska."

"But," came the objection, "how can a balloon stay aloft that long?"

Andrée had the answer to this question, too. "In the summertime, conditions would be ideal. Constant daylight would keep the temperature variation within a few degrees. Therefore, the gas would neither expand much nor contract. The result would be a minimum amount of leakage and no need to valve off precious gas because of expansion. By attaching a sail to the bag, a balloonist could increase the speed so that the distance would be covered well within the 15- to 20-day period of buoyancy his craft could have."

On May 31, 1896, after more than a year of preparation, the *First Andrée Polar Expedition* left Stockholm on a tidal wave of patriotic fervor. Andrée hit headlines all around the world as he left for Danes Island, Spitsbergen. Then, for six weeks, the world — and especially Sweden — waited expectantly while the expedition remained weathered in at the advance base.

The right wind and weather never came. On August 17, Andrée dejectedly gave up. The balloon was deflated and the expedition crept back to Stockholm in a state of abject depression. Almost overnight, the man who had been labeled a national hero because of his previous, daring flights became an object of criticism and ridicule. He was called a "fraud" by some journalists, a "publicity seeker" by others. Even the most sympathetic newspapers conceded that his

5

chances of ballooning to the North Pole were as limp as the deflated bag.

All that fall and winter Andrée brooded. Then, in the spring of 1897, buoyed by new hope and financially backed by the noted Alfred Nobel, inventor of dynamite and donor of the Nobel prizes, Andrée decided on a second attempt. This time, the Swedish government assigned a gunboat, the *Svensksund,* to accompany the expedition to Danes Island, with an expert crew to repair the balloon hangar, dig the gas apparatus out of the snow, and help with launching.

"We can *not* fail," said Andrée over and over with an almost pathological insistence, indicating that this time he would get his balloon, *The Eagle,* airborne at all costs.

Accompanying Andrée on the flight would be Knut Fraenkel and Nils Strindberg. Fraenkel was a civil engineer, with considerable Arctic experience. At twenty-seven, he was a mountaineer, gymnast, and railroad builder — a man in the tradition of the old Vikings. Though he had crashed twice while ballooning, he regarded the experience as "rare sport." Strindberg, twenty-four, was more of an intellectual, with a background as a university professor. He was strikingly handsome, a fact that brought the expedition a multitude of female well-wishers. A photographer, he had designed a special reflex camera, in a sealed case, to take pictures as the balloon soared over the polar ice.

By mid-June, 1897, Andrée was back at Danes Island with *The Eagle,* whose bag was 97 feet high and 68 feet in diameter, made from 600 pieces of pongee silk. Maker Henri Lachambre had personally tested all the pieces before stitching and cementing them together. Andrée, in his thorough, meticulous way, had even arranged for two engineers from the Nordenfelt Company to follow each step in the manufacture and to make regular tests. The upper two-thirds of the bag was three-ply, both for strength and reduction of leakage; and the lower third was two-ply. The finished bag was carefully varnished inside and out so that, though weighing a ton and a half because of this extra process, it was supposedly impervious.

More than 380 hempen cords formed a netting over the bag. On the underside, they were woven together to form a dozen ropes, which then passed through a bearing ring shaped from American elm and were secured to the basket. The basket was made of wicker and wood, and designed as a double-decker. On top, in an area about six feet in diameter, was the observation platform, similar to that on most balloons. Below was a compartment which had a mattress and sleeping bag of reindeer skins and was tight and solid enough in construction to serve as a darkroom. Andrée's idea was to develop photographs along the way, and send prints back by carrier pigeon and by cylinders dropped into the sea. In this way, a valuable record of the Arctic would get back to civilization, even if the expedition did not.

Around the walls of both decks were small compartments with the wide variety of equipment the three men had gathered: photographic supplies, food, extra clothing, navigational instruments, maps, books, utensils, and other items. Guns and ammunition were fitted into a space in the floor of the lower compartment.

The expedition had enough food for an estimated three and a half months. Included were special lemon lozenges to prevent scurvy, a concoction made of 55 pounds of chocolate and pulverized pemmican shaped into solid cakes, and two bottles of port presented to them by the king.

There were also 36 homing pigeons, in wicker cages, which had been trained in the Arctic and were supposedly capable of taking messages back to Spitsbergen from any faraway point along the route. Andrée, something of an inventor, had devised a sledge that would come apart to form two, a collapsible canvas boat, and other unique items of equipment. He had also devised a clever system of "automatic ballasting" that did not necessitate valving or throwing sandbags over the side. This consisted of a harness with three heavy coconut fiber ropes, each a little over 1,000 feet long. The ropes, waxed at the lower ends, were supposed to drag easily across the surface of water and ice, their combined weight being enough to pull the balloon down about 10 feet for each 20 feet of length the aeronauts hauled into the basket. In the standard trailing position, the ropes would hold *The Eagle* at about 600 to 700 feet as she rode.

Despite Andrée's foresight and attention to detail, the balloon had one dangerous flaw: she leaked. While in the shed being readied for flight, it was found that she lost about 35 cubic meters of gas per day. Andrée tried to stop the leakage by varnishing the seams, but without much luck. The advice of everyone, including the balloonmaker himself, was that the expedition should be postponed and the bag rebuilt.

"I do not have the courage to postpone the flight again," Andrée replied, remembering the ignominy of the year before. He was strongly supported by both Strindberg and Fraenkel, even though it had been demonstrated that *The Eagle* was losing a lift capacity of 99 pounds every twenty-four hours.

On July 11, 1897, at 2:30 in the afternoon, the flight order was given.

"Strindberg! Fraenkel!" The three men climbed into the basket, reaching out to give last handshakes to the men on the ground.

"Cut!" shouted Andrée. A sailor took his knife to the anchor rope.

"Oh, hell!" the man muttered as the blade nicked his finger.

Andrée leaned over the basket at the exclamation. "Hell — that is where we are going," he retorted as the balloon leaped skyward.

The Eagle wobbled erratically as the wind caught the sail, and headed northward. Passing over the shore, one of the three long trailing ropes caught on a rock. Snagged, the balloon dipped dangerously, so low that the bottom of the basket touched the water. Andrée and his companions struggled to maintain their balance. Then the balloon righted itself again, as the trailing line yanked free, losing a whole section of the end, and the bag began to rise. For almost an hour *The Eagle* could be seen against the gray north sky, growing smaller and smaller.

Then it vanished and was never sighted again.

In August of 1930, the curious discovery by the men on the little Norwegian sealer *Bratvaag* was slow in reaching the outside world. The skipper wanted to complete one of the most profitable fishing cruises he had ever enjoyed. So word of the find was shouted across to one Capt. Gustav Jensen, whose ship, the *Terningen,* was sighted a few days later. When Jensen reached port, his statements touched off a large journalistic bomb. Newspapers of all nations frantically began hiring small steamers to go to look for the *Bratvaag,* to get the first story. Radio appeals were made (the *Bratvaag* had a receiver, but no transmitter), pleading with the skipper to meet at a designated mid-ocean rendezvous and give the sender an "exclusive" for which his editors would pay a whopping price.

When two weeks went by with no contact, reporters began hinting that Captain Jensen of the *Terningen* had concocted the whole story for publicity. Or that the relics discovered had nothing to do with the Andrée expedition.

Finally, on September 3rd, *The New York Times* headlined the true significance of the story:

"BODIES OF AIRMEN LOST 33 YEARS FOUND NEAR WHERE BALLOON FELL IN ARCTIC."

The dream of Salomon Andrée to fly to the North Pole in a free balloon ended in tragedy. The first to try, he was the first to die. His balloon, *The Eagle,* is shown here fading away in the mist after leaving Spitsbergen, never to be seen again. It was over thirty years later before the fate of Andrée and his companions was known.
National Archives Photo

During the next few days, the story was patched together. There was no doubt that the relics on White Island were from the Andrée Expedition: the canvas boat, a sledge, some food, a rusty rifle, clothing, a cookstove, and a camera, still loaded with film.

Two skeletons had also been found, still dressed in furs. One was Andrée's, leaning against a supporting ledge of rock; the other was that of Strindberg. The bones of Fraenkel were not found until a few

9

weeks later, when further searches were made at White Island.

Most important of all, there was a diary.

Now the entire world waited to see whether the writing was still legible, after 33 years under the snow; and, if so, whether the pages contained a complete record of the struggle. Andrée, even in his dying hours, had fortunately practiced the same meticulous care that had been characteristic of his life. He had padded the diary in straw, then sealed it as tightly as possible in oilcloth. Even as he died, the book was clutched to his chest, inside the protective clothing he wore. Its recordings were as nearly complete as anyone could have wished.

All Sweden rejoiced that the greatest of all Arctic mysteries would be solved: How had the three men met death? But the mystery was not solved. If anything it was intensified. There was no reason at all why the explorers should have perished when and where they did, no more reason than had they been on a camping trip in the Kjolen Mountains of northern Sweden.

On July 11, 1897, three hours after the start of the flight, the three explorers were in high spirits. The barometer was rising, the wind steady, though with a slight drift to the east. Andrée was not worried about the drift. With proper handling of sail and trailing lines, *The Eagle* could be steered at an angle as much as 30 degrees to the right or left of the true wind direction.

Andrée decided, with his usual restlessness, that it was time to send some messages to the outer world. Consequently, he wrote four notes and tied them to four of his carrier pigeons. Later, he placed another message in a metal cylinder and dropped it over the side. It read:

> *Buoy No. 4. The first one dropped. July 11, 10 P.M. G.M.T. So far our trip has gone well. We continue at a height of about 250 meters, with a course at first north 10 degrees east, true, but later north, 45 degrees east, true. Four carrier pigeons were dispatched at 5:40 P.M. Greenwich time. They flew westward. We are now over ice, which is much broken in all directions. Glorious weather. Excellent spirits, Andrée, Strindberg, Fraenkel. Above clouds since 7:45, G.M.T.*

A second buoy, less than an hour later, showed that *The Eagle* had risen to about 1,800 feet and was at about 82 degrees of latitude and 25 degrees longitude east. The balloon's speed was remarkable.

Hour after hour passed, with a monotony that quickly replaced the initial exhilaration of the start. There was nothing to do but eat and sleep. Below, the Arctic wastes had a hypnotic sameness, one ice floe after another, sometimes jammed together by wind and currents, at other times broken up, with patches of dark water showing through. The three men wrote their observations and made notations about the temperature, the wind, the weather. But, with continual daylight and almost no change in weather conditions, there was little to record.

On the third day out, Andrée wrote another note and attached it to several carrier pigeons:

From Andrée's Polar Expedition to Aftonbladet, *Stockholm. July 13, 12:30 noon. Lat. 82 degrees, 2'. Long. 15 degrees, 5' East. Good passage each 10 degrees south. All well on board. This is the third pigeon post. Andrée.*

This was the only carrier pigeon message ever received.

That day, the men began to hear a disturbing sound: the crackling of ice, forming a thin veneer over the fabric and breaking off in small sheets. Slowly the weight increased, pushing the balloon lower—so low that finally the bottom of the basket touched the ice hummocks for the first time. Like a ball, the balloon bounced up to 500 feet, then slowly settled again.

The afternoon of the third day was the beginning of the "Hell" that Andrée had prophesied in his caustic final remark as the flight started. Hour after hour, *The Eagle* continued its exhausting cycle: rising, falling, dragging the gondola for long stretches over the choppy ice, then rising again as the men jettisoned ballast.

From later evidence, from correspondence with the explorer, Fridtjof Nansen, and from remarks he had made, Andrée had known for many weeks that the flight would be a failure. Perhaps he had pictured at least reaching the Pole and being able to send out one glorious message by pigeon and buoy before vanishing forever. But he had never anticipated trouble so soon.

It was ironic that the balloon carried a preposterous collection of entirely useless objects, many of which the three men clung to when all hope of flight had ended and they were forced to march across the ice. These included quantities of Russian and U.S. money in silver and gold, a white dress tie, an expensive porcelain bowl, the heavy silver base for a German vase, a white shirt in its original wrappings, a large collection of heavy towels, old newspapers, packets of personal letters, and two tickets to the Stockholm Exposition of 1897.

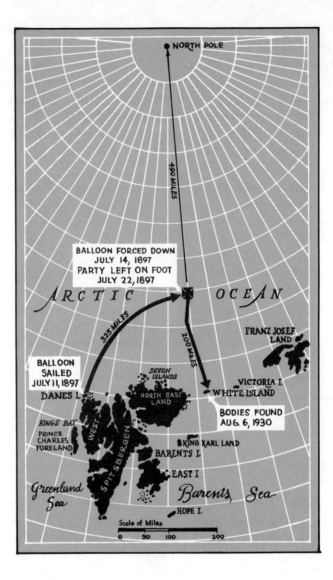

On July 14, *The Eagle* unaccountably rose for a few hours, perhaps because of a temperature change. But by afternoon, luck ran out. The constant jolting had loosened an escape valve and hydrogen could distinctly be heard hissing out above the heads of the three men. *The Eagle's* lifeblood was draining away, and nothing could be done about it.

By 7 P.M. that day, after a long, punishing drag over the sharp ice hummocks that threatened to rip the gondola to shreds and matchwood, Andrée gave the order which all three knew was inevitable: "Get ready to open the rip valves."

By 7:30 they were down for good, untangling the ropes on an ice floe, trying to furl the sail so it would not catch the wind, and despairingly watching the great bag grow limper and limper as it settled down into a great dark blob of fabric.

There was one small blessing: for the first time in four days, the men slept soundly, securely wrapped in sleeping bags and canvas.

For the next seven days, the men camped at the scene of the landing, sorting out their equipment, readying the sledge, and putting together the collapsible canvas boat. There was one great decision to make: which direction to march in? The men used the time in trying to determine the drift of the ice. The obvious course would have been to head south, and slightly to the west, toward North East Land off Spitsbergen and the Seven Islands, where there were known to be caches of food and supplies. Instead, for a reason that will never be known, they headed almost due east, toward the barren, and little-known, Franz Joseph Land.

Perhaps, since the wind had carried *The Eagle* much farther eastward than estimated, Andrée was convinced that the moving ice would also carry them east. On July 22, eleven days after the glorious start from Danes Island, Andrée, Strindberg, and Fraenkel began their laborious march across the ice pack.

The difficulties were overpowering. The men kept slipping into pools of melting ice; the sledge runners caught on hummocks; breaks in the ice made it necessary to go hundreds of yards out of their way to avoid open water; the constant glare of twenty-four hours of daylight made their eyes bloodshot and blackened their skin wherever it was exposed. To make matters worse, the general drift of the ice was now seen to be westward, taking them farther and farther from their objective each day.

"We will have to change the direction of march," said Andrée finally, not giving in to the elements until August 4. They had already abandoned a few things each day, and a whopping 220 pounds of baggage on July 27. "We will make for the Seven Islands."

On taking observations in his diary, he noted that they were then at Latitude 82:7 North and Longitude 22:43 East. During almost two weeks of plodding, therefore, they had progressed about 60 miles from the point of landing.

With feet cut and frostbitten, and arms bruised from many slips and falls on the ice, the men found it a relief to arrive at open water somewhere off North East Land. They stowed their gear in the canvas boat and set out with paddles and oars. Then the whims of the elements caught them again. Suddenly the current changed from westward to southeasterly. Again they saw their objective, the Seven Islands, fade away. From September 12 to 17 they drifted, partly on open water, but mostly encamped on floes. The days were beginning to shorten. The nights became pitch dark and brought bitter cold and dangerous squalls.

On September 17, they sighted the first land in 68 days — White Island. Working toward it frantically, on foot and by boat, they paused long enough to make two important kills: a seal on September 18, a bear (Andrée's diary refers to bears as "the wandering meat shops of the Arctic") on September 20. They also took time for as weird a celebration as has ever been recorded in polar history. The details were found in the remains of Strindberg's diary. This was a feast of "seal steak, seal liver, seal brains, seal kidneys, butter, and Swedish bread, *gateaux aux raisins,* with raspberry sauce, and port wine for dessert." The wine was the gift of King Oscar II, vintage 1836. With it, they drank a toast to the king, unfurled a small Swedish flag carried for the occasion (or any other that might arise), and made the Arctic wastes echo with the National Anthem, sung at the top of their lungs.

A day later, the triumph of approaching land was shattered when the ice beneath them suddenly started to break up. Part of their supplies were thrown into the water. A small hutlike shelter they had erected against the night's cold was torn apart. But somehow they all escaped alive, managed to salvage a good part of their equipment (Andrée had insisted on having sinkable items lashed, whenever possible, to floatable ones), and eventually reached land. Drenched, exhausted, and frozen, the three men began the last phase of their historic ordeal.

They actually reached White Island with enough food, shelter, and equipment to survive from that first week in October, when they set foot ashore, through the winter. They had already conquered the worst hardships — weathering out some 11 weeks on the dangerous, shifting ice. It only remained now to hold out until the winter ice became firm and they could sledge across some 50 miles to North East Land, where they would find natives and shelter.

For a week, the three men had been suffering stomach cramps,

14

diarrhea, and other intestinal upsets. They were badly weakened, constantly in pain, and often too exhausted to cook the rich polar bear meat they had saved from their recent kill. They had, however, a small primus stove, in such good condition and with enough fuel remaining that it was actually operated when found 33 years later.

Andrée's diary does give a clue to one death, that of Nils Strindberg who was the first to go. Shortly after the three men had pushed and tugged the sledge and the canvas boat across the rocky shores of the island, Strindberg was seized by what the other two men decided was a heart attack. He died within a few hours. The last entry in Strindberg's diary, on October 6, was "Resignation."

Andrée and Fraenkel lived about two weeks longer. The condition of the camp, with no real shelter constructed and with equipment strewn around, indicated that the two men were too weak to work. It was contrary to Andrée's nature that he should have left valuable instruments and ammunition in the canvas boat, where they were found by the *Bratvaag* sailors in 1930; or that he would not have used loose rock to construct a wall for protection against the wind and the cold.

And so the record fades away, rather than ends. For the last few entries in Andrée's diary are indecipherable, and the last recognizable date is October 17. Knut Fraenkel died in his sleeping bag, and Salomon August Andrée died propped against a rock. The Great Adventure had ended.

A decade after Andrée's fatal attempt to reach the North Pole, a flamboyant American newspaperman, Walter Wellman, took his three-engine dirigible the America *to Spitsbergen to try his luck. His first attempt, made in 1907, ended soon after takeoff when he became lost in a snowstorm. Wellman tried again two years later but was forced down on an ice pack 60 miles north of Spitsbergen. He made no further attempts when he learned that Peary had captured the honor sought by so many.*

The next dirigible pioneer to consider a polar flight was a German, Count Ferdinand von Zeppelin. In 1910, a group of German scientists traveled to Spitsbergen — which was to become a favorite launching point for subsequent attempts — to study the possibility of establishing a dirigible base there. While the scientists recommended that the German government should sponsor such an undertaking, the project died from lack of official enthusiasm.

When the airplane was born in 1903, few people believed it would be more than a passing fancy. It was believed that the airplane would prove to be as impractical as balloons and dirigibles seemed to be. Before the first decade of airplane flight, there is no recorded instance where anyone thought that, even if airplanes would become reliable, they would be used to explore the frigid zones of the earth. But curiosity and necessity know no bounds. In 1914, a Russian army officer by the name of Nagurski made the first airplane flight above the Arctic Circle from Novaya Zemlya in search of the missing Sedow expedition which was attempting to reach the North Pole by dog sledge.

Interest in flying toward the North Pole waned after Wellman's attempt — except for the interest of one man, Roald Amundsen, first man to arrive at the South Pole. In 1912, after his return from Antarctica, he began planning to conquer the North Pole by using an airplane. But he had to wait ten years before the proper airplane was available. His plan was to fly from Alaska over the Pole to Spitsbergen. In 1922, he purchased a small Junkers monoplane and took it by ship to Alaska. Unfortunately, the plane was irreparably damaged on a trial flight and the attempt was abandoned.

In 1925, however, the persistent Amundsen tried again, this time with the wealthy American philanthropist, Lincoln Ellsworth, and four others. Using Spitsbergen as the base, two planes were to be used, and the six pioneers came within 136 miles of success. In the failure, however, much was learned. It was now proven that not only could planes operate in the topmost latitudes but successful landings and takeoffs were possible.

In the following account, Lincoln Ellsworth gives his version of this epic flight.

16

Toward the North Pole by Airplane

Lincoln Ellsworth

PEARY was the first man with whom I ever discussed the matter of using an airplane for polar work. This was shortly before his death, and I was dining with him at his home in Washington. Peary believed in the use of airplanes in the Arctic.

My mind never did free itself for any great length of time of the airplane idea for Arctic service. In the autumn of 1924, Captain Amundsen arrived in New York for his lecture tour of the United States. He had already made public his belief that the Polar Sea could be successfully crossed in an airplane. Happening to be in New York when he arrived there, I looked him up. We had a long talk.

I told Amundsen of my freshened interest in the airplane idea since reading of his belief in it. We went over the matter together. I believed that my father could be induced to finance the attempt if he could meet Amundsen.

My father was enthusiastic after meeting him, and aided us to the extent of buying two Dornier-Wal flying boats, built in Pisa, Italy.

I sailed for Norway to join Amundsen and to get in touch with the Aero Club of Norway, the sponsor of the expedition.

We were given a tremendous reception in Norway by the officials and people generally, and a tremendous send-off when, on April 9, we sailed for Spitsbergen.

We spent five weeks at Kings Bay, assembling our planes and waiting for the weather to moderate. During this time the Kings Bay Coal Company was our host and did everything to make our stay enjoyable. Captain Amundsen and I spent all our mornings together studying navigation and perfecting ourselves in the use of the sun compass, the drift finder, and the sextant. In the afternoons we would take long ski trips.

Toward the end of May our meteorologists decided that it was time to get under way. We feared to start too early because of the effect of the cold on our motors — it would be at least ten degrees colder at the Pole — and it was a risk to start too late, because of the fogbanks that hung over the polar pack during the summer months.

May 21 was the day we chose for the start of our great venture. It was thrilling to think, when we came awake that day, that in a few hours we would be on our way into the unknown.

We boarded our planes. There were many fervent handshakes and quiet words of cheer from the immediate group; also many cheers from the people lining the wharves and shores of the bay.

We were carrying 7,800 pounds of dead weight in each plane. That is 1,700 pounds above the original estimate, but we could think of nothing that we could afford to leave behind. The skis, canvas canoe, collapsible sled for drawing the canoe, shotgun, rifle, and 300 rounds of ammunition, etc., were for emergency, in the event we would be grounded and have to abandon the planes and walk over the ice to Greenland. We were strongly urged to take along a radio outfit, a most useful thing in case we got into trouble; but the weight of it — 300 pounds — made us say no.

Each plane carried 90 kilos of provisions, sufficient to last three men one month at the rate of two pounds per day per man. Our daily ration list per man was: —

Pemmican	400 grams
Milk Chocolate	250 grams
Oatmeal biscuits	125 grams
Powdered milk	100 grams
Malted milk tablets	125 grams

At 4:15 all was ready for the start. The engines were turned over for a warming-up. At five o'clock the full horsepower was turned on. We moved. The *N.25*, Captain Amundsen navigator, led the way. Riiser-Larsen was the pilot, Feucht the mechanic. I was navigating the *N.24*, with Dietrichson for pilot and Omdal as mechanic. Six men in all — there was no room or duty for more than these.

N.25 trembled, went forward, hesitated, moved onward, dropped down off the bank onto the ice of Kings Bay. I was not conscious of our own takeoff. I was busily occupied arranging my instruments; when I did get time to look out to see how we were getting along — my notion being that we had only just left the earth — instead of the ice of Kings Bay that I expected to see beneath me, it was far out upon a majestic panorama, the mountaintops and glaciers of Spitsbergen, that I found myself gazing. It is rather a surprise to find yourself looking into eternal space, when it is solid earth you expect to see directly below.

Within a half hour after leaving Kings Bay we ran into a heavy bank of fog. We rose to 1,000 meters to clear the fog. Rising well above it we saw, outlined against the fog, a double halo. In the middle of the halo was a perfect shadow of our plane. Evanescent, phantomlike, these two multicolored halos seemed to be beckoning us enticingly into the unknown. During that first hour through rifts in the mist we caught glimpses of the open sea. Then followed an hour or so of an ocean with small, loose ice cakes, which indicated the fringe of the polar ice. "Then suddenly," as Captain Amundsen put it later, "the mist disappeared, and the entire panorama of polar ice stretched away before our eyes — the most spectacular sheet of snow and ice ever seen by man from an aerial prospective."

Hour after hour we sped on — driving, driving, always driving, knowing only that we must go on and on over that interminable sheet of ice.

When we left our base the sun had been at our left. It now hung low in the sky directly ahead of us. It was midnight, the time set for the end of our drive. Our dead reckoning showed that we had traversed a space of 1,000 kilometers. We should now be at the Pole. The Pole was under us, if nothing had checked our headway.

It was a sweet thought, but it could hardly be true; because of the fog which lay along the horizon we could not take a sextant shot at the sun, but we knew we had been bucking a strong northeast wind and we must have been carried to the westward of our course.

I felt certain that we could not yet be at the Pole and so I was surprised when I saw N.25 ahead of us begin to circle and then descend. Our petrol tanks were half empty. It was a strange thing that just then, as our petrol tanks were half empty, there ahead of us was the first lead of water large enough for an airplane to land in that we had seen in our whole journey of 600 miles over the ice. Why this should be the first open lead of any width in all the 600 miles we had flown, where it ended, just how wide it was, we never found out. We only had time to see that there it was for our landing.

It was at 1 A.M. on the morning of May 22 that we landed. From 500 meters in the air it was not such a bad-looking place to be dropping into, but it was an awful-looking hole, we saw, as we drew nearer to it.

19

We circled for perhaps ten minutes looking for a suitably sized spot of clear water to land in. There was no such space to be found. The lead was a choked-up mass of floating lumps of ice, as though someone had started to dynamite the ice pack and had given up the job when halfway through it. Ice blocks standing on edge or piled high on top of one another, hummocks and pressure ridges, was all that greeted our eyes. It was like trying to land in the Grand Canyon.

We came down in a little lagoon among the ice floes, taxied over to a huge ice cake, and, anchoring our plane to it, jumped out with our sextant and artificial horizon to find out where we were. Not knowing what to expect, I carried my rifle, but after our long flight I was a bit unsteady on my legs — I tumbled down in the deep snow and choked up the barrel.

We spoke to each other as we stepped out on to the ice pack — spoke but got no answers. Our lips moved, but no words issued therefrom. Eight hours at close quarters with our motors had left us temporarily deaf. We stared at each other. Our eyes, when we took off our goggles, showed themselves bloodshot.

It was a ghostly scene. It was one o'clock in the morning and the midnight sun hung low above the northern horizon — a pale red orb to look at, radiating a little light but no heat.

Observation showed that we were in latitude 87° 44'N., longitude 10° 20'W. This westerly drift of more than 20 degrees had cost us nearly a degree in latitude, and enough extra fuel to have carried us to the Pole. As it was, we were just 136 nautical miles from it. At the altitude we were flying just before descending, our visible horizon was 46 miles; which means that we had been able to see ahead as far as latitude 88° 30'N., or to within just 90 miles of the North Pole! Eight hours after leaving civilization we were able to see within 90 miles of the goal that Peary had expended 23 years to reach. Truly "the efforts of one generation may become the commonplace of the next."

When we had finished taking our observation we began to wonder where N.25 was. We crawled up on all the high hummocks nearby and with our field glasses searched the horizon. Dietrichson remarked that perhaps Amundsen had hopped off and gone on to the Pole. "It would be just like him," he said.

It was nearly noon of that day before we spotted N.25 from one especially high hill of ice. She lay in among a group of rough hummocks, not more than three miles distant.

It was rough-looking country everywhere, and the position of *N.25* was not cheering to behold. Her nose was pointing into the air at an angle of 45°. Just ahead of her was a huge cake of old Arctic blue ice that must have been 40 feet thick. From where we were it looked as if she had crashed into this great wall of ice.

Our own plane was in bad shape. We had torn the nails loose on the bottom of the plane when we took off from Kings Bay, so that she was leaking badly; even now the water was above the bottom of our petrol tanks. Also, only one engine was working — the forward propeller was out of commission. In short, we were wrecked. Things were so bad that it seemed as if only a miracle could ever get us out.

During that first day Dietrichson and I tried to reach *N.25*, Omdal staying behind in an effort to repair the damaged motor. We dragged our canvas canoe up over high hummocks and tumbled into deep crevasses until we were thoroughly exhausted. The snow was two to three feet deep over all the ice, and we floundered through it, never knowing what we were going to step into next. Dietrichson went down between the floes and only by hanging on to the canoe was he able to save himself from going in over his head. An open lead, whenever we found one, was always covered over with a scum of new ice just thick enough to keep us from using the canoe, but not thick enough to let us walk on it with safety. As a result we did not get far on that first day's trip to *N.25*. After half a mile we had to give it up and return.

We pitched our tent on top of the ice floe, moved all our equipment out of the plane, and made ourselves as comfortable as possible. But there was no sleep for us, and very little rest.

Omdal continued to work on the motor; Dietrichson and I took turns at the pump. Only by the most incessant pumping were we able to keep the water below the petrol tanks. While working the pumps we could not keep out of contact with the water. The temperature was −11°C.

On first sighting *N.25*, we had run up our Norwegian flag on top of a high hummock on our ice cake, hoping that her crew would see it; but they gave no sign of seeing us on that first day. We rigged our small inflated balloons that the meteorologists had given us wherewith to obtain data regarding the upper air strata, tied pieces of flannel to them, and turned them adrift. Our hope was that the wind would carry them over to our *N.25* comrades, and indicate to them in which direction to look for us; but it was a contrary wind: it blew them in the wrong direction or, drifting them too low, tangled them among the ice hummocks.

Throughout our first day the wind was from the north and we could see quite a few patches of open water; but on the second day the wind began to blow from the south, and the ice to close in around us. The closing ice pack was like the grasp of a great claw that was slowly but surely contracting.

On our third day, May 24, the temperature being −11.5 C., our pump continued to freeze up. We had to keep thawing it out. The heavy, high ice between us had now drifted out from between the two planes, leaving *N.25* in plain view.

On this day, using our flags in order to semaphore, we established a line of communication between the two planes; but it was tedious work and required two men, one with the flag, and the other with a pair of field glasses to read the signals. We then had to wait for their return signals before sending another message.

On this day also, after an exchange of messages, we decided to try to reach Amundsen; so we packed our canvas canoe, put it on the sled, and started across what looked to us like mountains of hummocks. After a few hundred yards we had to give up: the labor was too exhausting.

We now broke our load into packs of about 50 pounds, put on our skis, and covered our canoe with canvas, but after a few hundred yards we had to drop the canoe. We put our skis on most loosely, for there was no knowing when one of us might drop into the Polar Sea; and to drop in, or to get tangled up in loose slush and ice, with a pair of skis fastened to our feet, would be disastrous.

After traveling for two hours and fifteen minutes, we reached the wide lead which separated us from *N.25*.

New ice was forming on each side of the lead. We could see no way for us to cross. So, after a seven-hour trip, in which we covered perhaps five and a half miles in about the same length of time it had taken us to fly from Spitsbergen, we returned to our sinking plane.

At seven next morning the temperature was down to −9.4 C. It was still snowing, but the wind had shifted around to the west. We decided, if that space of clear water expanded to any extent, to try to get our plane on to the ice floe. In anticipation of that event, Dietrichson took to shoveling off a level space on our ice cake.

The whole floe was about 200 meters in diameter, with perhaps one level stretch of 80 meters. There were two feet of soggy wet snow

Lincoln Ellsworth

23

that had to be cleared away before we could reach the solid ice of the floe. It was laborious work for all, for we had only a homemade clumsy wooden shovel and our ice anchor to shovel the snow with. I loosened the snow by picking at it with the anchor, and Dietrichson shoveled it away.

Looking through our glasses at *N.25*, we could see her propellers going, and Amundsen pulling up and down on the wings, trying to loosen the plane from the ice, but she was immovable.

On the morning of May 26, *N.25* signaled us to inquire how we were making out with the salvaging of our plane. We replied that we had succeeded in getting her nose up on to the ice cake, but that with only one engine working, it was impossible to do more. She was safe now from sinking, but not from being crushed should the ice move in on to her.

Amundsen signaled back that as it did not look good for our plane, we had better come over to his camp and help save *N.25*. We signaled that we were coming. This was the fifth day of our separation.

The ice had been steadily shifting, until the two camps were now no more than half a mile apart. One wide, newly frozen-over lead, with a few high hummocks and some old piled-up ice directly in front of their plane, now obscured our view of their camp as we journeyed toward them. Not knowing whether we should be able to return, we had made up everything portable into packs. These packs weighed 80 pounds each. We were well aware of the chances we were taking in trying to cross the newly frozen ice with such heavy loads on our backs, but we saw nothing else to do. We must get all possible stores and equipment to *N.25*, if we were to be of any real help in the fight to get back to civilization.

With our feet shoved loosely into our skis, we shuffled along, slowly feeling our way over the new thin ice. Omdal was in the lead, Dietrichson in the rear, and I in between. Suddenly I heard Dietrichson yelling behind me. Before I knew what it was all about, Omdal, ahead of me, cried out also. With the cry, I saw Omdal disappear. The ice under me started to sag, and I jumped quickly sideways to keep from falling through. There happened to be a ledge of old ice just beside me. Lying down on my stomach, half on this ledge of old ice and half out on the new ice, I reached out a ski, and pulled Dietrichson over to where I could grab his pack, and partly pulled him out on to the firmer ice. He lay there panting, exhausted.

I turned to Omdal. Only his pallid face showed above water. As I

24

reflect on it now, it was strange that although these two Norwegians had been conversing almost wholly in their native tongue, Omdal was now yelling in English: "I'm gone, I'm gone!" And he was almost gone, too. He had been digging his fingers into the ice edge to keep from being pulled under, but the ice kept breaking under him. I reached him and drew him over on to the firmer ice before he could sink, and held him up there by his pack. I then called to Dietrichson to crawl over to me and hold up Omdal. Dietrichson came over and held Omdal, while I cut the heavy pack loose from Omdal. It took all the strength the two of us had left to drag him on to his stomach and up on the firm ice.

Throughout all this, the crew of *N.25* could not see us, and if they had been able to see us they could not have reached us because of the high ice which lay in front of their plane. They could hear our cries, but could not aid us — they could only wait, listening and wondering about the nature of our distress.

We hurried on to reach Amundsen's camp, where Dietrichson and Omdal got into dry clothes, drank hot cups of chocolate, and were ready for work again. Omdal's fingers were swollen and lacerated from digging into the ice; he suffered with them for a long while afterwards. Both men had lost their skis. In view of the probability of being forced to tramp to Greenland, the loss of the skis seemed a calamity.

It was good to be with our old companions again. We joined in the work of freeing *N.25* from her precarious position. She lay half on and half off an ice floe. Her nose was up on the cake, and her tail down in the sea. Her manner of landing had reduced her speed so much that she had run up onto this floe with comparative gentleness, and so saved herself from crashing into the heavy cake of blue ice which lay directly ahead; but whereas she had found sufficient open water for a landing now — only five days later — there was not sufficient clear water into which to launch a rowboat. The drifting ice had locked her in.

A most orderly routine was in force at the Amundsen camp. Regular hours for everything: sleep, eat, smoke, and talk; no need to warn these men, as so many explorers have had to do, not to tell one another the story of their lives, lest boredom come. These Norwegians have their long periods of silence, in which the glance of an eye or the movement of a hand takes the place of vocal expression.

One might have expected hurry and disorganization in the con-

ditions that confronted us, but it was just the reverse. We did everything as though we had oceans of time ahead of us. It was this calm,
cool, unhurried method of doing things that conserved our energy,
kept our spirits normal, and eventually got us out of a desperate
situation. It may seem strange that no one among us ever got completely depressed or blue, but so it was.

Captain Amundsen and I slept together in the pilot cockpit,
which we covered over with a canvas to darken it at night. I found
it difficult to get accustomed to the continuous daylight. The monotony of it was wearing. Omdal, Feucht, and Dietrichson slept on
skis stretched across the freight compartment, which served us for a
month as joint bedroom, dining room, kitchen, and living room.
Riiser-Larsen had the tail all to himself, and into this he had to crawl
on his hands and knees.

It took us one whole day to construct a slip and work the plane up
on to the ice cake. The work was exhausting on our scanty rations — a
cup of chocolate with three oatmeal wafers night and morning, and
at noon a cup of soup made from 80 grams of pemmican. We had
only the crudest of implements to work with — three wooden shovels,
a two-pound pocket safety ax, and an ice anchor. We lashed our
sheath knives to the end of our ski sticks to further the work.

The floe we were on measured 300 meters in diameter. A 400-
meter run would give us a fair chance to take off. Our best chance, of
course, would be to take off in open water, but the wind was still in
the south, and south winds did not make for open water.

As the days went by we gave up hope of open water; we would
have to depend on a takeoff from the ice. Riiser-Larsen was the most
tireless of all of us in a search for a floe of the right dimensions. If
any of us found an ice floe of sufficient area for a hop-off, we felt it
would be Riiser-Larsen.

We toiled on. By May 28 we had freed $N.25$ from the screwings of
the pack ice. On this day we took two soundings with our Bewhloth
Echo apparatus and got a depth of 3,750 meters. This depth corre-
sponds almost exactly to the altitude of Mont Blanc above the village
of Chamonix. Up to this day our only thought had been to clear the
plane and hurry on to the Pole; but now, if we were to save our lives,
we saw nothing for it except a return to Spitsbergen.

Our hope of reaching Spitsbergen rested in salvaging the petrol
from $N.24$. It must be borne in mind that we were continually ex-
pending petrol in our attempt to free the plane. By a circuitous route

Dietrichson, Omdal, and I, with our canvas canoe on a sledge, got across to *N.24* for petrol and the remaining supplies. It was cold, the temperature at 9° Centigrade below freezing.

We cut out one of the empty tanks, filled it from a full one, loaded it in our canoe, put the canoe on the sledge, and started back. We did not get back with the extra petrol — not that time. A large lead had opened up while on the way and we barely got across. We had to abandon the tank on the ice, but that same night the lead closed again, and Dietrichson and Omdal got the petrol over. The light sledge got broken among the rough hummocks. We now had 245 additional liters, 1,500 liters altogether — a margin of 300 liters above our estimate of the amount needed for *N.25* to fly back to Spitsbergen — to fly back, we amended, if, of course, we were ever able to get the plane into the air again.

On May 31 there were eight inches of ice in the lead, on the far side of the floe we were on. We decided to try to make a takeoff on that eight-inch stuff.

From our ice floe down on to this lead there was a six-foot drop, making it necessary to construct a slip on which to get our plane down on to the lead ice. We built the slip in accordance with standard road-making principles; first laying down heavy blocks of ice and solid snow above them, then smaller blocks of ice and tiny lumps; over all we spread a layer of loose snow which worked down into the crevices and solidified into a smooth surface. To construct the slip for our takeoff, to level off all the bumps and ridges thereon, took us two days.

On June 2, at 5 P.M., our slip was ready. We started up the motors, taxied across the floe and down the slip. With full speed ahead we started across the ice of the lead, but were hardly upon it when it began to sag beneath our plane. Soon we broke through. We plowed on through it for one thousand meters, but it was no use. The heavy ice clung to her sides; we could not get her into the air. We shut off the motors and let her rest for the night in the lead.

At midnight I was awakened from a sound sleep to hear Captain Amundsen calling out that the plane was being crushed. I listened. I could plainly hear the pressure against her metal sides. We pitched in and got everything out of her onto some solid ice. We then turned our attention to the plane itself.

The plane started leaking from the pressure of the ice, and we wondered how much more she could stand. We were gradually working toward *N.24*. After another day of labor and trial, we brought the two planes together.

How weather-beaten and forlorn my old *N.24* looked when we reached her! Her nose lay up on the ice floe, and she was listed to one side, with the ice frozen in all around her. The tip of one wing was frozen hard in the ice.

There was a long lane now of freshly frozen ice in front of *N.24*, but the old ice had so pressed in from both sides that parts of this lane had been pushed out into a curve. It was a narrow, crooked passage, but it offered an opportunity for a takeoff in *N.25*.

We tried it, taxiing *N.25* carefully down the crooked lane, and came very near to being wrecked. In trying to make the curve under reduced speed, her bow broke through the ice, she slowed down, lifted her tail into the air, came to a dead stop. We jumped out and hacked away at the ice until she settled on an even keel.

The main body of the pack was in motion under us. We would have to get out of there and get out quickly. At two o'clock in the morning we began work on an extension of our course and continued on throughout the following day, and on into the night.

The floe was covered with tightly frozen lumps and old pressure ridges of up-tilted ice cakes. Hacking away with our short-handled pocket ax and ice anchor as we stood on our feet was such backbreaking work that we changed over to going down on our knees to it, which position we did not like. Working on our knees there was danger of having our snow glasses broken by the flying pieces of ice, and without our glasses snow blindness was certain.

The sweat was rolling down my face, vapor was rising from the sweat while at this work of smoothing down the ice. I removed my glasses to clear them of the congealing vapor. I did not have them off for long, but it was long enough. That night I went badly blind in one eye.

On the morning of June 5 the ice wall pushed in upon our runway. When we woke up out of our sleep the runway was already destroyed. It was tough to be toiling over and over; tougher to see the vengeful forces of nature step in and finally crush, one after another, our efforts.

On the morning of June 6, Riiser-Larsen and Omdal started off to hunt up such a floe. Into the fog they strode, were swallowed up. We saw no more of them until evening, when out of the fog they emerged, assumed clearer shape before us. We searched their faces eagerly for what we might find there. And we knew, even before they spoke, that it was good news they were bringing.

They had found a floe!

They had searched through the fog, stumbled over discouraging ridges, when suddenly the sun burst through a rift above them and shone upon the tip of a floe of sufficient size. They hurried toward it, and found it, which proved to be all of 400 meters across.

This lifesaving floe was half a mile away, and there were two other floes between it and the floe we were camped on. It would be necessary to build a slip across these two floes and bridge the intervening leads of water.

We started the engines — it was now 7 P.M. We had to start them quickly. The main body of the pack had been moving down upon us — it was only ten yards away when the two patrols came in with the glowing report. Immediately behind the plane a huge ice wall was slowly advancing.

Fifteen minutes after starting up the engines, the solid ice closed in over the spot where our plane had lain.

Once more we were saved — for the time being. We worked our way slowly up to where we must begin to build the slip, sawing out the ice ahead where it was too heavy for the plane to break through.

After six hours of steady work we had constructed the slip and had our plane safe up on floe No. 1.

That night we slept, and early next morning began the stupendous task of cutting a passage through an ice wall 12 feet thick which separated floe No. 1 from floe No. 2, and then of bridging between the floes, which were separated from one another by a 15-foot channel of water. It was a hard job for men working on a short emergency ration and with our meager tools, but by the end of the second day the job was done.

When the time came, we turned the engines on full power and started across the ice bridge at full speed. Our only chance lay in going full speed; otherwise the plane would settle down and perhaps instantly stop on the other side where we had taken no time to level ahead — this because of our great fear that the ice floes, if we delayed too long at our work, would drift farther apart.

We made the passage! We were at last upon the big floe!

It had not been all mere straightforward toil up to the big floe. We were on floe No. 1, working away in the night, when a strong wind had set in from the south. Foreseeing all kinds of possible happenings, we began at once on the work of leveling a course for the plane across that floe, even though it was less than 300 meters across—desperately short for a takeoff for our heavy plane.

We leveled off and tried for the takeoff, but the wind had again shifted and our plane could not make it. The snow, cloggy and wet from the south wind, stuck to the plane and clogged her speed. Our plane, be it remembered, was really a heavy flying boat, with pontoons (or floats) on either side of the hull for landing on ice or in the sea. She bumped and slid along on the pontoons, unable to rise before open water was reached. We thereupon resumed and finished the work of getting her over the big floe, as already told.

It was June 9 when at last our plane lay safe upon the big floe. Now began the long grind of constructing the course upon which our final hopes must rest. If we failed now, there was nothing left.

We looked the ground over. There were two feet of snow covering the ice. We would have to remove all that heavy wet snow right down to the solid ice and then cut out a track 400 meters long, and the heavy wet snow would have to be thrown clear to 6 meters on either side so as not to interfere with the wing struts. After a few shovelfuls we stood weak and panting, and gazed disheartened at the work ahead. It may be worthwhile noting here that throughout all this terrible toil on half rations — emergency rations always — we felt at no time ravenously hungry; but we did have a feeling always of weakness. I have many a time felt much hungrier than I did on short rations up there in the Arctic, but never as weak as we were then; and we knew we were growing weaker.

One problem was how to taxi our plane through the wet snow and turn it at our starting point in the direction of our course; for as she lay, when first brought on to the big floe, she was pointed wrong. Even after we had dug down to the blue ice under the snow she would not turn, because with the removal of the blanket of snow the ice beneath became soggy and sticky. Fog rots ice rapidly.

We worked our skis underneath the plane in the hope that thus it would push more easily; but the weight of the plane split the skis, whereupon we had to give up that idea. Without our skis we would be helpless if it ever came to getting ahead on foot!

By the end of the first day we had managed to clear 50 meters of our needful 400; that is, a path 160 feet or more long and 40 wide. After that first day we thought of stamping down the snow with our feet and found that it served the purpose admirably!

We started our second day's work on the big floe. I began to wonder that day if we were to make the great sacrifice for our venture. The outlook was hopeless. Summer was coming on, the snow was soft, and the lead wouldn't open. The meager rations and the prospect, the meager tools we had to work with — it was a desperate outlook.

For four days now we had been stamping down the ice to smooth it.

On June 14 our 400-meters course, as we supposed it to be, was to our liking. Then that ever wakeful Riiser-Larsen paced the distance. "What's this!" he cried, and repaced it. "Four hundred meters, no! It was 500 meters!" he exclaimed, whereupon Captain Amundsen remarked that not one million dollars could buy that extra hundred meters from him. We all agreed that it was priceless.

And so it proved to be.

On the evening of June 14 we drank our chocolate. There was a tail wind — we decided to make a try for it.

But the plane only bumped over the course. A speed of 100 kilometers (62 miles) was necessary for our plane to leave the ground. For four tries the best speed we could make was 40 kilometers. On our fifth try we made 60 kilometers. Riiser-Larsen, pulling up at the edge of the floe, turned in his seat and said to me, as I jumped from my plane and stood on the ice:

"I hope you are not disappointed, Ellsworth. The wind was against us. I think we'll do better next time."

Stouthearted Riiser-Larsen, that calm, dispassionate embodiment of saving hope! In his brain was born the great idea that we should all get down on our hands and knees and with our sheath knives level off and smooth every little bump of ice we could find. We did that; and also we decided to discard everything that could possibly be spared, even the empty petrol tanks, to lighten the plane before we tried again.

The wind changed during the night, and in the morning was blowing lightly from the north, the second time since our arrival on the ice. (We had landed in a north wind.) It was favorable for our takeoff. The temperature was — 1.5 C., the snow was crisp and hard on top.

We threw away everything, including our heavy ski boots and parkas, and retained only half our remaining food supplies, as well as a canvas canoe and a shotgun.

We all took our seats, and the great moment came. The plane began to move. The wind was from the north, the first north wind since we landed. This wind was in our favor. Riiser-Larsen began to smile. She had gone 100, 200, 300 meters with constantly increasing

31

speed — Riiser-Larsen's smile widened. Four hundred meters she had gone, the end of the floe was there right before her. Were we going into the air or merely crashing over into the lead? But her speed was now 100 kilometers, and she was lifting, lifting. She stayed lifted.

We were off! It was a great moment when we looked down and back and saw that we were clear.

It took us two hours to fly through the fog. We could get neither above nor below it. During those two hours we flew solely by magnetic compass — a thing generally considered to be an impossibility in the Arctic.

Dietrichson dropped down for a drift observation as frequently as possible. As the fog still hung low, he had to fly close down to the floe — only 100 feet up above it for a time. Finally we rose above the fog, and from then on we steered by sun compass.

We were southward bound, homeward bound, back to where people live. I was sitting in the tail of the plane. We had been flying for more than seven hours, when Feucht looked back to me. "Land!" he shouted.

"Spitsbergen?" I asked.

"No Spitsbergen," he answered, in his imperfect English.

I wondered if it was Franz Josef Land, without caring overmuch just what land it was. It was land and any land is good. My immediate thought, everybody's immediate thought, was that all rationing regulations were off, and we could eat all we pleased. We all started in munching chocolate and biscuits.

Riiser-Larsen had been noticing that the stabilization rudders were becoming more and more difficult to operate. Finally they failed completely to move, and we were forced to descend a mile from the coast in a sea that was running fairly high. The waves washed over the plane, thoroughly drenching the pilot, compelling us all to seek shelter below.

I had eaten too freely of our rations before descending and it was my first solid food in nearly a month. My stomach rebelled; I became violently ill.

We had been flying 8 hours and 35 minutes, and had just 90 liters of petrol left, half an hour's supply of fuel, when we landed in that rough sea.

How remarkable all our escapes were! Again and again it looked as if life or death, we not knowing which, lay right beyond the hour. Said Captain Amundsen, "You can call it luck if you want, but I don't believe it."

How good that land looked again. The warm sun was shining on the rocks. I picked out a flat granite boulder and stretched out face up to the sky, as did all the others.

By and by we got out our sextant to find out just where we were. We were at that work when someone yelled: "A sail!"

It was a little sealer heading out to sea. We yelled, we waved our flags; she continued on her way to the open sea.

We were not going to let her get away. We jumped into our plane and taxied out to her. She was a little sealer and her name the *Sjöliv*, and she had been chasing a wounded walrus that had taken refuge in our bay. It was lucky for us, that pursuit of the wounded walrus; otherwise she and her crew would have been away long ago.

They were overjoyed to see us.

Three days later we landed back in Kings Bay.

We tried to tow our plane, but because of the heavy wind we had to leave her in Brandy Bay in North East Land, Spitsbergen. Later we returned with sufficient fuel to fly her the hundred miles to Kings Bay.

We placed the *N.25* on a steamer, and on June 25 sailed from Kings Bay for Norway. We landed at Horten, which is the naval base near Oslo.

On July 5, the stage being all set for us, we flew the *N.25* into Oslo. It was hard to realize that this plane under us was the same one that had so lately been battling the Arctic ice. Good old *N.25*!

The near success of the Amundsen-Ellsworth flight spurred others interested in polar aviation to consider the airplane more seriously. Commander Richard E. Byrd had gained some experience in the north when he commanded the aviation unit of the MacMillan Expedition to Greenland in 1925. It was on this expedition that Byrd met Floyd Bennett, a U.S. Navy mechanic, who turned out to be an excellent pilot. It was also on this three-month trip that Byrd gained the confidence to consider reaching the North Pole by airplane. He quietly set about planning his flight with Floyd Bennett. Taking leave from the Navy in January, 1926, the two of them raised the necessary funds from private sources and enlisted the aid of half a hundred naval and marine reservists. The Byrd Expedition sailed from the Brooklyn Navy Yard on April 5 aboard the steamer Chantier *for Spitsbergen. Also on board was a three-engine Fokker monoplane named the* Josephine Ford *in honor of Edsel Ford's three-year-old daughter.*

After several minor accidents unloading and testing the Fokker, final preparations were completed on May 8. Bennett and Byrd climbed in, warmed up the engines, and started down the runway that had been carved out of the ice and snow. But the load and the friction of the skis were too great. The Josephine Ford *jolted roughly over the ice hummocks and came to rest in a snowbank. Fortunately, no damage resulted.*

Shortly after midnight, after taking off as much equipment as they dared and smoothing out the runway, the two men decided to stake their lives on one final try. This time they would either get off or crash under full power at the end of the runway in the jagged ice....

Success at Last!

Richard E. Byrd

WITH A TOTAL LOAD of nearly 10,000 pounds we raced down the runway. The rough snow ahead loomed dangerously near but we never reached it. We were off for our great adventure!

Beneath us were our shipmates — every one anxious to go along, but unselfishly wild with delight that we were at last off — running in our wake, waving their arms, and throwing their hats in the air. As long as I live I can never forget that sight, or those splendid fellows. They had given us our great chance.

For months previous to this hour, utmost attention had been paid to every detail that would assure our margin of safety in case of accident, and to the perfection of our scientific results in the case of success.

We had a shortwave radio set operated by a hand dynamo, should we be forced down on the ice. A handmade sledge presented to us by Amundsen was stowed in the fuselage, on which to carry our food and clothing should we be compelled to walk to Greenland. We had food for ten weeks. Our main staple, pemmican, consisting of chopped-up dried meat, fat, sugar, and raisins, was supplemented by chocolate, pilot bread, tea, malted milk, powdered chocolate, butter, sugar, and cream cheese, all of which form a highly concentrated diet.

Other articles of equipment were a rubber boat for crossing open leads if forced down, reindeer-skin, polar-bear and seal fur clothes, boots and gloves, primus stove, rifle, pistol, shotgun and ammunition; tent, knives, ax, medical kit, and smoke bombs — all as compact as humanly possible.

If we should come down on the ice the reason it would take us so long to get back, if we got back at all, was that we could not return Spitsbergen way on account of the strong tides. We would have to march Etah way and would have to kill enough seal, polar bear, and musk-ox to last through the Arctic nights.

The first stage of our navigation was the simple one of dead reckoning, or following the well-known landmarks in the vicinity of Kings Bay, which we had just left. We climbed to 2,000 feet to get a good view of the coast and the magnificent snow-covered mountains inland. Within an hour of taking the air we passed the rugged and glacier-laden land and crossed the edge of the polar ice pack. It was much nearer to the land than we had expected. Over to the east was a point where the ice field was very near the land.

We looked ahead at the sea ice gleaming in the rays of the midnight sun — a fascinating scene whose lure had drawn famous men into its clutches, never to return. It was with a feeling of exhilaration that we felt that for the first time in history two mites of men could gaze upon its charms, and discover its secrets, out of reach of those sharp claws.

Perhaps! There was still that "perhaps," for if we should have a forced landing disaster might easily follow.

Lt. Cdr. Richard E. Byrd was an excellent navigator. He is shown here at Spitsbergen, Norway, practicing with a sextant before his historic North Pole flight in 1926. On the left is Floyd Bennett, pilot of the plane *Josephine Ford.*

It was only natural for Bennett and me to wonder whether or not we would ever get back to this small island we were leaving, for all the airmen explorers who had preceded us in attempts to reach the Pole by aviation had met with disaster or near disaster.

Though it was important to hit the Pole from the standpoint of achievement, it was more important to do so from that of our lives, so that we could get back to Spitsbergen, a target none too big. We could not fly back to land from an unknown position. We must put

36

every possible second of time and our best concentration on the job of navigating and of flying a straight course — our very lives depended on it.

As there are no landmarks on the ice, Polar Sea navigation by aircraft is similar to that on the ocean, where there is nothing but sun and stars and moon from which to determine one's position. The altitude above the sea horizon of one of these celestial bodies is taken with the sextant. Then, by mathematical calculations, requiring an hour or so to work out, the ship is located somewhere on an imaginary line. The Polar Sea horizon, however, cannot always be depended upon, due to roughness of the ice. Therefore we had a specially designed instrument that would enable us to take the altitude without the horizon. I used the same instrument that we had developed for the 1919 transatlantic flight.

Again, should the navigator of a fast airplane take an hour to get his line of position, by the time he plotted it on his chart he would be a hundred miles or so away from the point at which he took the sight. He must therefore have quick means of making his astronomical calculations.

We were familiar with one means of calculation which take advantage of some interesting astronomical conditions existing at the North Pole. It is a graphical method that does away largely with mathematical calculations, so that the entire operation of taking the altitude of the sun and laying down the line of position could be done in a very few minutes.

This method was taught me by G. W. Littlebales of the Navy Hydrographic Office and was first discovered by Arthur Hinks of the Royal Geographic Society.

So much for the locating of position in the Polar Sea by astronomy, which must be done by the navigator to check up and correct the course steered by the pilot. The compass is generally off the true course a greater or lesser degree, on account of faulty steering, currents, wind, etc.

Our chief concern was to steer as nearly due north as possible. This could not be done with the ordinarily dependable magnetic compass, which points only in the general direction of the North Magnetic Pole, lying on Boothia Peninsula, Canada, more than 1,000 miles south of the North Geographical Pole.

If the compass pointed exactly toward the Magnetic Pole the magnetic bearing of the North Geographical Pole could be calculated

Richard E. Byrd and his friendly rival, Roald Amundsen, are shown above inspecting emergency supplies being stowed aboard the *Josephine Ford* before Byrd's North Pole flight. Two days later, Amundsen, in the dirigible *Norge,* accompanied by Lincoln Ellsworth and piloted by Umberto Nobile, flew from Spitsbergen to Alaska via the North Pole.

mathematically for any place on the Polar Sea. But as there is generally some local condition affecting the needle, the variation of the compass from true north can be found only by actual trial.

Since this trial could not have been made over unknown regions, the true directions the compass needle would point along our route were not known. Also, since the directive force of the earth's magnetism is small in the far north, there is a tendency of the needle toward sluggishness in indicating a change in direction of the plane, and toward undue swinging after it has once started to move.

Nor would the famous gyroscopic compass work up there, as when nearing the Pole its axis would have a tendency to point straight up in the air.

There was only one thing to do — to depend upon the sun. For this we used a sun compass. The same type instrument that had been invented and constructed for our 1925 expedition by Albert H. Bumstead, chief cartographer of the National Geographic Society. I do not hesitate to say that without it we could not have reached the Pole; it is even doubtful if we could have hit Spitsbergen on our return flight.

Of course, the sun was necessary for the use of this compass. Its principle is a kind of a reversal of that of the sundial. In the latter, the direction of north is known and the shadow of the sun gives the time of day. With the sun compass, the time of day is known, and the shadow of the sun, when it bisects the hand of the 24-hour clock, indicates the direction after the instrument has been set.

Then there was the influence of the wind that had to be allowed for. An airplane, in effect, is a part of the wind, just as a ship in a current floats with the speed of the current. If, for example, a 30-mile-an-hour wind is blowing at right angles to the course, the plane will be taken 30 miles an hour to one side of its course. This is called "drift" and can be compensated for by an instrument called the drift indicator, which he had also developed for the first transatlantic flight.

We used the drift indicator through the trapdoor in the plane, and had so arranged the cabin that there was plenty of room for navigating. There was also a fair-sized chart board.

As exact Greenwich time was necessary, we carried two chronometers that I had kept in my room for weeks. I knew their error to within a second. There seems to be a tendency for chronometers to slow up when exposed to the cold. With this in mind we had taken their cold-weather error.

As we sped along over the white field below I spent the busiest and most concentrated moments of my life. Though we had confidence in our instruments and methods, we were trying them for the first time over the Polar Sea. First, we obtained north and south bearings on a mountain range on Spitsbergen which we could see for a long distance out over the ice. These checked fairly well with the sun compass. But I had absolute confidence in the sun compass.

We could see mountains astern gleaming in the sun at least 100 miles behind us. That was our last link with civilization. The unknown lay ahead.

Bennett and I took turns piloting. At first Bennett was steering, and for some unaccountable reason the plane veered from the course time and time again, to the right. He could glance back where I was working, through a door leading to the two pilots' seats. Every minute or two he would look at me, to be checked if necessary, on the course by the sun compass. If he happened to be off the course I would wave him to the right or left until he got on it again. Once every three minutes while I was navigating I checked the wind drift and ground speed, so that in case of a change in wind I could detect it immediately and allow for it.

We had three sets of gloves which I constantly changed to fit the job in hand, and sometimes removed entirely for short periods to write or figure on the chart. I froze my face and one of my hands in taking sights with the instruments from the trapdoors. But I noticed these frostbites at once and was more careful in the future. Ordinarily a frostbite need not be dangerous if detected in time and if the blood is rubbed back immediately into the affected parts. We also carried leather helmets that would cover the whole face when necessary to use them.

We carried two sun compasses. One was fixed to a trapdoor in the top of the navigator's cabin; the other was movable, so that when the great wing obscured the sun from the compass on the trapdoor, the second could be used inside the cabin, through the open windows.

Every now and then I took sextant sights of the sun to see where the lines of position would cross our line of flight. I was very thankful at those moments that the Navy requires such thorough navigation training, and that I had made air navigation my hobby.

Finally, when I felt certain we were on our course, I turned my attention to the great ice pack, which I had wondered about ever since I was a youngster at school. We were flying at about 2,000 feet, and I could see at least 50 miles in every direction. There was no sign of land. If there had been any within 100 miles' radius we would have seen its mountain peaks, so good was the visibility.

The ice pack beneath was crisscrossed with pressure ridges, but here and there were stretches that appeared long and smooth enough to land on. However, from 2,000 feet pack ice is extraordinarily deceptive.

The pressure ridges that looked so insignificant from the plane varied from a few feet to 50 or 60 feet in height, while the average thickness of the ice was about 40 feet. A flash of sympathy came over me for the brave men who had in years past struggled northward over that cruel mass.

We passed leads of water recently opened by the movement of the ice, and so dangerous to the foot traveler, who never knows when the ice will open up beneath and swallow him into the black depths of the Polar Sea.

I now turned my mind to wind conditions, for I knew they were a matter of interest to all those contemplating the feasibility of a polar airway. We found them good. There were no bumps in the air. This was as we had anticipated, for the flatness of the ice and the Arctic temperature were not conducive to air currents, such as are sometimes found over land. Had we struck an Arctic gale, I cannot say what the result would have been as far as air roughness is concerned. Of course we still had the advantage of spring and 24-hour daylight.

It was now time to relieve Bennett again at the wheel, not only that he might stretch his legs, but so that he could pour gasoline into the tanks from the five-gallon tins stowed all over the cabin. Empty cans were thrown overboard to get rid of the weight, small though it was.

Frequently I was able to check myself on the course by holding the sun compass in one hand and steering with the other.

I had time now leisurely to examine the ice pack and eagerly sought signs of life, a polar bear, a seal, or birds flying, but could see none.

On one occasion, as I turned to look over the side, my arm struck some object in my left breast pocket. It was filled with good-luck pieces!

I am not superstitious, I believe. No explorer, however, can go off without such articles. Among my trinkets was a religious medal put there by a friend. It belonged to his fiancé and he firmly believed it would get me through. There was also a tiny horseshoe made by a famous blacksmith. Attached to the pocket was a little coin taken by Peary, pinned to his shirt, on his trip to the North Pole.

When Bennett had finished pouring and figuring the gasoline consumption, he took the wheel again. I went back to the incessant navigating. So much did I sight down on the dazzling snow that I had a slight attack of snow blindness. But I need not have suffered, as I had brought along the proper kind of amber goggles.

Twice during the next two hours I relieved Bennett at the wheel. When I took it the fourth time, he smiled as he went aft. "I would rather have Floyd with me," I thought, "than any other man in the world."

We were now getting into areas never before viewed by mortal eye. The feelings of an explorer superseded the aviator's. I became conscious of that extraordinary exhilaration which comes from looking into virgin territory. At that moment I felt repaid for all our toil.

At the end of this unknown area lay our goal, somewhere beyond the shimmering horizon. We were opening unexplored regions at the rate of nearly 10,000 square miles an hour, and were experiencing the incomparable satisfaction of searching for new land. Once, for a moment, I mistook a distant, vague, low-lying cloud formation for the white peaks of a faraway land.

I had a momentary sensation of great triumph. If I could explain the feeling I had at this time, the much-asked question would be answered: "What is this Arctic craze so many men get?"

The sun was still shining brightly. Surely fate was good to us, for without the sun our quest of the Pole would have been hopeless.

To the right, somewhere, the rays of the midnight sun shone down on the scenes of Nansen's heroic struggles to reach the goal that we were approaching with the ease of an eagle at the rate of nearly 100 mph. To our left, lay Peary's oft-traveled trail.

When I went back to my navigating, I compared the magnetic compass with the sun compass and found that the westerly error in the former had nearly doubled since reaching the edge of the ice pack, where it had been 11 degrees westerly.

When our calculations showed us to be about an hour from the Pole, I noticed through the cabin window a bad leak in the oil tank of the starboard motor. Bennett confirmed my fears. He wrote: "That motor will stop."

Bennett then suggested that we try a landing to fix the leak. But I had seen too many expedition fail by landing. We decided to keep on for the Pole. We would be in no worse fix should we come down near the Pole than we would be if we had a forced landing where we were.

When I took to the wheel again I kept my eyes glued on that oil leak and the oil-pressure indicator. Should the pressure drop, we would lose the motor immediately. It fascinated me. There was no doubt in my mind that the oil pressure would drop any moment. But the prize was actually in sight. We could not turn back.

At 9:02 A.M., May 9, 1926, Greenwich civil time, our calculations showed us to be at the Pole! The dream of a lifetime had at last been realized.

We headed to the right to take two confirming sights of the sun, then turned and took two more.

After that we made some moving and still pictures, then went on for several miles in the direction we had come, and made another larger circle to be sure to take in the Pole. We thus made a nonstop flight around the world in a very few minutes. In doing that we lost a whole day in time and of course when we completed the circle we gained that day back again.

Time and direction became topsy-turvy at the Pole. When crossing it on the same straight line we were going north one instant and south the next! No matter how the wind strikes you at the North Pole, it must be traveling north, and however you turn your head you must be looking south, and our job was to get back to the small island of Spitsbergen which lay somewhere south of us!

There were two great questions that confronted us now: Were we exactly where we thought we were? If not — and could we be absolutely certain? — we would miss Spitsbergen. And even if we were on a straight course, would that engine stop? It seemed certain that it would.

As we flew there at the top of the world, we saluted the gallant, indomitable spirit of Peary and verified his report in every detail.

Below us was a great eternally frozen, snow-covered ocean, broken into ice fields or cakes of various sizes and shapes, the boundaries of which were the ridges formed by the great pressure of one cake upon another. This showed a constant ice movement and indicated the nonproximity of land. Here and there, instead of a pressing together of the ice fields, there was a separation, leaving a water lead which had been recently frozen over and showing green and greenish-blue against the white of the snow. On some of the cakes were ice hummocks and rough masses of jumbled snow and ice.

At 9:15 A.M. we headed for Spitsbergen, having abandoned the plan to return via Cape Morris Jesup on account of the oil leak.

The reaction of having accomplished our mission, together with the narcotic effect of the motors, made us drowsy when we were steering. I dozed off once at the wheel and had to relieve Bennett several

43

Lt. Cdr. Richard E. Byrd and Chief Petty Officer Floyd Bennett were the first men to fly over the North Pole. Above, the *Josephine Ford* turns on the final approach for a landing at Spitsbergen after their historic flight of May 9, 1926.
Library of Congress Photo

Shown here is the trimotored Fokker, *Josephine Ford,* after its successful flight to the North Pole. In the background is the hangar of the dirigible *Norge*. While this photo was being taken, the *Norge* was en route to Alaska via the North Pole.
Library of Congress Photo

times because of his sleepiness.

I quote from my impressions cabled to the United States on our return to Kings Bay:

"The wind began to freshen and change direction soon after we left the Pole, and soon we were making over 100 miles an hour.

"The elements were surely smiling that day on us, two insignificant specks of mortality flying there over that great, vast, white area in a small plane with only one companion, speechless and deaf from the motors, just a dot in the center of 10,000 square miles of visible desolation.

"We felt no larger than a pinpoint and as lonely as the tomb; as remote and detached as a star.

"Here, in another world, far from the herds of people, the smallnesses of life fell from our shoulders. What wonder that we felt no great emotion of achievement or fear of death that lay stretched beneath us, but instead, impersonal, disembodied. On, on we went. It seemed forever onward.

"Our great speed had the effect of quickening our mental processes, so that a minute appeared as many minutes, and I realized fully then that time is only a relative thing. An instant can be an age, an age an instant."

We were aiming for Grey Point, Spitsbergen, and finally when we saw it dead ahead, we knew that we had been able to keep on our course! That we were exactly where we had thought we were!

But, to our astonishment, a miracle was happening. That motor was still running. It is a hundred to one shot that a leaky engine such as our means a motor stoppage. It is generally an oil lead that breaks. We afterward found out the leak was caused by a rivet jarring out of its hole, and when the oil got down to the level of the hole it stopped leaking. Flight Engineer Noville had put an extra amount of oil in an extra tank.

It was a wonderful relief not have to navigate any more. We came into Kings Bay flying at about 4,000 feet. The tiny village was a welcome sight, but not so much so as the good old *Chantier* that looked so small beneath. I could see the steam from her welcoming and, I knew, joyous whistle.

It seemed but a few moments until we were in the arms of our comrades, who carried us with wild joy down the snow runway they had worked so hard to make.

45

After their first attempt to reach the Pole by airplane failed, Amundsen and Ellsworth concluded that the dirigible was a better vehicle for polar travel because it could remain aloft for longer periods. They contacted Umberto Nobile, the Italian dirigible expert, and contracted with him to buy the N.1, to be renamed the Norge, *and have him pilot it to the Pole in the spring of 1926. Proceeding in their plans independently of Byrd, the Amundsen-Ellsworth-Nobile team agreed that the ideal weather would exist in Spitsbergen from mid-April to mid-May.*

Nobile modified the Norge *and flew it to Spitsbergen via Russia in early May. The plan was to make preparations quickly at Spitsbergen and proceed over the Pole to Alaska rather than to return to the takeoff point. The Byrd party was already in place when the* Norge *arrived at the fog-enshrouded airport at Kings Bay but Amundsen was not concerned. He was convinced that the heavy Fokker could not take off in the thick snow, which almost proved to be right. However, in spite of Byrd's successful flight of May 9, preparations continued with the* Norge. *On the morning of May 11, Nobile ordered the restraining ropes cast off and the giant dirigible rose slowly and majestically upward. An aerial voyage of incredible distance was begun.*

Flight of the Norge

John Toland

IN ALL there were sixteen men and one dog aboard. Riiser-Larsen was almost constantly at his navigation desk, assisted by Ellsworth, who was glad to do the most menial jobs aboard. In the radio room were Birger Gottwaldt and Storm-Johnsen. In the navigation chair the Norwegian journalist Ramm was scribbling dispatches for the operators to relay to Kings Bay. Weatherman Malmgren stood at Ramm's side, studying the fog that was beginning to close in threateningly.

The sixteenth man was Amundsen. He sat alone on an aluminum water tank, his sunken eyes fixed on the ice pack as it slowly disappeared in a swirl of fog. He was thinking, "I wonder what I shall see next."

At 10:30 the little *Norge* was enveloped in dense fog. Ice began to form on all the metal parts of the ship. The celluloid windows of the control car were encrusted in rime ice like thick wool. Nobile ordered Wisting to bring the ship up to 2,130 feet. There was no improvement. Nobile called for more altitude. At 3,160 feet the ship stuck its nose out of the fogbank. The temperature had now sunk to 12 degrees below zero.

Suddenly a shout came from the radio room. Storm-Johnsen and Gottwaldt came forward. Beaming happily, Gottwaldt held a radiogram in his hand. The King of Norway had just decorated him with a Gold Service Medal. Everyone shouted congratulations.

Soon latitude 87 degrees, 43 minutes, was reached. Amundsen peered down at the ice hummocks. A year ago he had spent 25 days at this spot. He grimaced. "Not this time, dear friend, not this time," he said to himself. Ellsworth caught his eye and the two men smiled. They were both happy to be in a safe dirigible this trip.

At 6:00 P.M. the port motor coughed and stopped. Caratti heaped insults on his engine. He discovered that water had got into one of the pipes and had frozen, stopping the gas supply. The starboard engine, idle till now, burst into action and the ship went on without losing its momentum. At 7:55 P.M., after almost two hours of explosive tirades, Caratti again had his motor in operation. Omdal then shut down his.

Soon it began clouding. By 11:25 the fog was a thick wall ahead. Since the ship was only 100 miles from the Pole, the two regular compasses were behaving erratically. The *Norge* was sent up to 3,000 feet so that Horgen could steer by sun compass, a device that caught the midnight sun in a periscope and cast its reflection on a glass plate marked with a calibrated wire cross.

It was Riiser-Larsen's job to see that the axis of the periscope was always parallel with the axis of the earth. Once, while engrossed in other duties, he forgot the sun compass, and Horgen unwittingly steered the *Norge* in a complete circle.

At midnight there was a second celebration. It was Ellsworth's forty-sixth birthday. Except for the mechanics on duty, everyone crowded into the control car. Nobile brought out a flask of eggnog. Every man took a swig and shook hands with Ellsworth.

"It isn't often," said Amundsen, his arm over the younger man's shoulder, "that you can fly over the North Pole on your birthday."

As the ship neared the Pole, the excitement mounted. At 1:00 A.M. the sky, to everyone's relief, began to clear. It would have been a bitter disappointment to fly over the roof of the world without seeing it.

At 1:15 A.M. Riiser-Larsen, bulky as a bear in his suit, knelt on

47

The dirigible *Norge,* piloted by the Italian, Umberto Nobile, passed over the North Pole two days after Byrd's successful flight in a trimotored plane. Continuing on to Alaska, the *Norge* landed at Nome after covering 3,400 miles in 70 hours. The *Norge* is shown being guided into its hangar at Spitsbergen.

Library of Congress Photo

Capt. Umberto Nobile, skipper of the *Norge,* is shown looking out the observation window shortly before takeoff from Spitsbergen. Two years later, Nobile again successfully flew to the North Pole to become the first man to reach that geographical point twice. However, his airship, the *Italia,* was forced down and several crewmen were lost. Nobile was saved but was blamed for the accident.

Library of Congress Photo

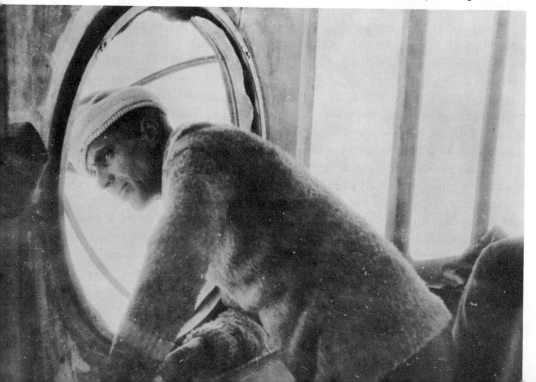

the floor near a starboard window. He was squinting at his sextant, which had been set at the height and declination the sun should have at the Pole at the date. The reflection of the sun and the bubble of the artificial horizon drew closer and closer.

"Ready with the flags!" he called.

Amundsen opened a window and stuck out the Norwegian flag. Its staff was weighted and pointed at the end so that it would stick in the ice. Ellsworth was ready with the American flag sent him by President Coolidge. Nobile called up to Alessandrini on the keel to get the Italian flag.

"Hurry up, Alessandrini!" he shouted. When the rigger finally arrived with the flag, it was hastily fastened to a spear.

Riiser-Larsen grew tense. "Now we are there!" he cried suddenly.

It was exactly 1:30 on the morning of May 12, 1926. Amundsen flung out his flag. The men watched it spin down to the sunbathed polar basin. Now, through the hazy atmosphere, they could see that the ice below was broken up in a mass of small floes. The end of the flagpole stuck in the ice. Amundsen, his throat choked with emotion, turned. He clasped Wisting's calloused hand. Neither spoke. Both were thinking that not quite fifteen years before they had planted a similar flag at the South Pole.

Nobile ordered the motors slowed down. Horgen steered the ship in a circle. Next, the American flag went over the side. A moment later Nobile excitedly tossed the Italian flag overboard. It glided, caught in the drift gauges, and finally fell.

The men all shook hands. It was a moment of unqualified triumph for everyone.

Now began the hardest and most important part of the expedition — to navigate the unexplored territory that lay between the Pole and Point Barrow, Alaska. Peary had thought he had seen mountains beyond the Pole. It was Amundsen's dream to find out if there actually was land in that bleak area.

"You're forty-five again," someone told Ellsworth jokingly. Since the time at Point Barrow was about eleven hours later than Kings Bay time, as soon as the Pole was crossed the morning of May 12 had become the afternoon of May 11. And every direction was south.

"Your birthday lasted only an hour and a half," said Amundsen sympathetically.

"Yes," Ellsworth said. "But I'll have another one in a few hours."

The men in the control car crouched down for the only hot meal of the trip. Horgen was ousted from his thermos-jug seat; mugs were filled with meatballs and hot grease. The sandwiches, by now, were stale and the tea and coffee ice-cold.

For hours they floated over the monotonous glittering ice, rifted by wind and tide into cracks and occasional leads of open water. Then the ice became a solid, formidable mass.

"We are at the Ice Pole," announced Riiser-Larsen. Again everyone shook hands. The center of the polar ice mass was the least accessible spot in the world.

Fog drifted in from the east. Riiser-Larsen was the only one who welcomed it, for it gave him a chance to sit down for the first time since leaving Kings Bay. He napped for half an hour while the ship plowed ahead. Now the sluggish English aperiodic compass, which reacted so slowly it seemed stuck, was being used alternately with the quixotic German Ludolph compass, which oscillated wildly at the slightest provocation.

At 5:19 that evening an excited cry rang out. In the west a mountain ridge reared up out of the fog. Amundsen, his heart beating wildly, rushed to a window. Peary was right! There was land in the "empty" Polar Sea! Nobile ordered the ship steered toward the mountain. The suspense was greater now than during their approach to the Pole.

Then Amundsen began to laugh, almost to himself. "It's just a Cape Fly-away!" he said. Even as he spoke the mirage mountain dissolved into nothingness. The men were familiar with the phenomenon, but they felt the disappointment keenly.

At 5:30 they were back on course, skimming over billows of fog. Then the fog rose. So did the ship. But then the cloud roof above them began to drop. Soon the two banks met, surrounding the ship completely. Since they were already at 3,500 feet, Nobile couldn't go higher without valving precious hydrogen. After a conference with Riiser-Larsen, Nobile decided to go down to see if the fog reached the ice. The dirigible sank slowly, so that the air ballonets could be filled to compensate for the contracting gasbag.

Ice began to form on the ship. Malmgren was called into the conference. It was decided to go up again. The situation was becoming grave. The sun compass, which was mounted on an outrigger, was frozen to a solid block of ice. The guy wires were covered with an inch of ice. As these wires quivered, ice broke off, and some of it was falling into the propellers. Then, like small projectiles, the ice would be driven through the canvas into the keel, often making holes in the ballonets. Each time an ice "bullet" pierced the canvas it sounded like a gunshot. Then Cecioni would propel his bulk into action, quickly mending the holes with rubber patches.

For hours the fog had prevented speed or drift measurements. Soon after the ship had passed the Ice Pole, the ship's aerial was encased in thick ice and the radio had gone dead. Riiser-Larsen was navigating on instinct alone.

Now icicles hung from all the projections of the gondolas and along the radiators and gangways. Even the propellers were ice-coated. Everyone remembered the prophecies of experts that the *Norge* would eventually be forced down by the weight of ice and snow.

The tension grew as ice continued to fly into the keel, narrowly missing the gasbag itself. Occasionally a patch of the ice pack appeared underneath, but never long enough for Riiser-Larsen to take an observation. No sign of life was seen — no birds, not a seal or walrus or polar bear.

Early in the morning of May 13, the fog began breaking up. At 3:20 the sun shone through long enough for a reading. It was found that Riiser-Larsen was almost on course. He calculated that land should be sighted between six and eight.

At 6:30 the navigator noticed some dark spots off the port bow. He blinked his eyes, afraid he was seeing another "Cape Fly-away." To avoid setting the men up for another bitter disappointment, he said nothing, In 15 minutes Riiser-Larsen had no doubts.

"Land ahead on the port bow!" he cried.

The men — in the air for almost two days — forgot their exhaustion and the numbing cold. The good word ran from gondola to gondola. Soon little gravel pits appeared ahead. At 7:25 A.M., 46 hours and 20 minutes after leaving Kings Bay, the *Norge* crossed land a few miles from Point Barrow. Beyond the gravel pits lay snow-covered flatland, stretching out as far as they could see.

Once again Nobile passed around the flask of eggnog. To Riiser-Larsen it felt like fire going through his body. Then Nobile, overwhelmed with joy, leaned far out of a cabin window. His face tingled in the cold wind.

The helmsman followed the Alaskan coast for an hour. Suddenly Amundsen cried out, "Look!"

Below, an Eskimo was dancing on the ice, waving his arms. His dogs were howling in terror.

A few minutes later a group of shacks appeared, then a reindeer training field and a small house with a red roof.

"It's Wainwright!" shouted Amundsen, leaning forward. He pointed at a house that grew larger. It was Maudheim, built by Amundsen and his home for two years. People stood on the roof of Maudheim and waved at the explorers.

Instead of landing, the *Norge* continued its voyage. In spite of fatigue, every crew member wanted to push on to Nome, the announced goal. Several hours later they began to regret their enthusiasm. A violent gale came up from the north and blew the ship sideways in and out of massive clouds of fog. The ship, its flexible keel bending in the wind, was driven almost to the Siberian coast. Then, falteringly, the *Norge* fought its way back across the rough, foaming waters of the Bering Strait.

Fog closed in.

At last, an hour later, a slight opening appeared below. The ship sank tentatively. The rugged, mountainous coast of Alaska jutted up at them. Nobile ordered Horgen to follow a narrow mountain ravine southward. Jagged hills, reaching above the fog, were on both sides of them. A gale-force wind began to blow across the ravine, rolling the little ship sickeningly. The windows fogged up. Titina, Nobile's terrier, began to move restlessly in the cabin. Nobile, taking the elevator wheel from Wisting, told Riiser-Larsen to lean out the window and shout if they came to a rise. The ship moved slowly through the blinding white billows. Everyone in the control cabin peered ahead, straining his eyes to see the danger before it was too late.

Riiser-Larsen suddenly shouted back a warning. Nobile jerked the wheel to the right and the nose of the *Norge* shot into the air. The black wall that had leaped in front of them dropped away.

"Did it knock off the rear gondola?" asked Nobile, his face pale.

A moment later the message came forward that Pomella was safe. His gondola had dropped so low he felt he could have touched the hilltop.

Now, high in the fog again, they were lost again. Nobile lowered the ship carefully until the ravine could be seen, then resumed the perilous job of threading a trail through the hills. Riiser-Larsen again leaned out the window. A second time his alert warning saved the ship. By four in the afternoon they all agreed it was suicide to continue at that altitude.

Nobile decided to climb above the fog so Riiser-Larsen could take a reading of the sun. The engines were slowed down and the ship rose quietly. At last, above the 3,000-foot mark, the ship came into sunlight. But the sun was so high that no observation could be taken from the control cabin; from every angle the gondola was in the shade. A reading would have to be taken from the top of the ship. The navigator climbed up the steep bow ladder onto the top of the pitching dirigible.

At last Riiser-Larsen finished the reading and started down the ladder. But the gasbag, exposed to the sun's rays for a long time, began to swell dangerously. The hydrogen had expanded so rapidly that Nobile couldn't control it by opening the gas valves. Titina, silent until this moment, skittered back and forth in the gondola, howling and whining.

Since the ship was cruising at low speed, it was impossible to drive her down. Nobile, watching the hydrogen gauges shoot up, knew he had to act quickly.

"Run fast to the bow!" he shouted in English to the Norwegians in the control car. They looked at him quizzically. "Run to the bow!" he cried, gesturing. Three Norwegians finally understood and scrambled up to the keel. They ran to the bow, tipping the nose down.

By this time all three motors were at full speed, and the ship nosed even further down. Nobile watched the hydrogen gauge waver at the danger point and then drop. In a minute pressure was back to normal. For the time being, the danger was over.

Hours passed. There was no coffee or tea. The sandwiches were frozen to the consistency of wood. The meatballs were frozen into ice crystals. Amundsen, no stranger to tedium, told humorous stories to shorten the hours. He gave everyone the feeling that if the worst happened and they were forced to the ice, he would take over and lead them to safety.

At 1:30 in the morning radio signals from Nome could be heard distinctly. Gottwaldt tried to reach the station but got no response.

A few minutes later a winding river could be seen through the fog. "It's the Serpentine!" cried Amundsen.

Now there was no further need for navigation: it was necessary only to fly low and follow the coast. Riiser-Larsen took over the watch from Nobile, who hadn't been relieved for sixteen hours. The exhausted commander slumped into their only armchair to get a few minutes' sleep before tackling the tricky landing maneuvers.

As they drew near mountains to the leeward, the balky port motor sputtered. The ship began to drift toward a crag. Riiser-Larsen ordered the idle starboard motor started up, so the *Norge* wouldn't have to risk rising into the fog. But there was no response on the annunciators. Riiser-Larsen quickly signaled the aft gondola for full speed. His order was executed, and the ship moved safely ahead.

There had been nothing wrong with the starboard engine. Cecioni heard the bell and saw the indicator on the big disk move. But he was so weary that he couldn't grasp the meaning of the signal. The efficiency of the whole crew was impaired by dulled reflexes and diminished powers of concentration.

At 4:30 A.M. a tiny dot was spotted. Amundsen thought it was Sledge Island. Nobile was awakened.

"We're near," Riiser-Larsen told him. "In half an hour we should be over Nome!"

Nobile leaned out a window to refresh himself. The sea was somber, rough, foamy. The skies were an ashy gray, striped with black clouds. Every few minutes a snow squall would cloud the windows. The ship was constantly buffeted by furious gusts of wind.

"Prepare landing ropes!" called Nobile to Alessandrini on the keel above.

Riiser-Larsen began writing out directions for the landing party, and the men off duty went to work folding up the sleeping bags on the keel. Wisting, his eyes red from fatigue, was at the rudder wheel. Amundsen, his old comrade, stood next to him. Together they tried to pick out familiar landmarks. A cluster of shacks appeared on the snow. Then they spied an abandoned three-masted steamer lying on her side in the middle of the ice.

Now the wind began blowing so hard that the *Norge* was brought to a standstill. Nobile ordered all three motors speeded to 1,200 revolutions. Still the ship made little progress against the gale. It was obvious that an even greater storm was building up. The sky had become black, the *Norge,* tilted at an angle of 30 degrees, was pitching heavily.

Amundsen and Wisting shook their heads. They didn't recognize the little community, and no one knew where Nome lay from the village. The three leaders had a quick discussion.

Everyone agreed that the men had reached the end of their endurance, that it would be insane to fly on with a great storm threatening to strike, that an immediate landing should be attempted even though the ship was bouncing crazily in the wind.

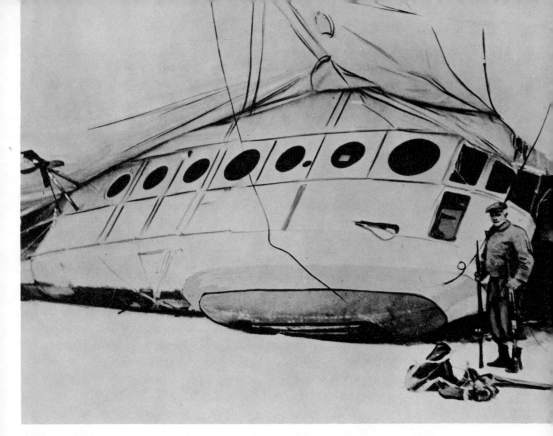

The landing of the *Norge* near Nome, Alaska, after the flight from Spitsbergen via the North Pole, completed a flight of seventy hours. The huge bag was deflated and the ship dismantled. Shown above retrieving his gear from the slowly collapsing *Norge* is Roald Amundsen, who, with Lincoln Ellsworth, organized the flight. The pilot of the *Norge*, Umberto Nobile, later flew the *Italia,* another dirigible, to the North Pole and became the first man to make a second flight to the top of the world.

Library of Congress Photo

Riiser-Larsen feared that they were in for a crash landing. He suggested that the panels of the control cabin be kicked out. It was a trick of the British, he explained.

Nobile objected heatedly. Amundsen sided with Riiser-Larsen. But Nobile refused to be panicked. He headed the ship down.

"Look!" cried Riiser-Larsen to Amundsen as the ground loomed into detail. "There's plenty of help! I see a lot of cavalry down on the shore."

Smiling, Amundsen shook his head. The "cavalry" was merely irregular brown stripes in the coastal sand.

A mooring line was dropped. Eskimos and traders rushed from the village to grab it. One Eskimo boy thought the ship was a giant flying seal. He called to his father, told him to take his gun and shoot the animal.

Riiser-Larsen leaned out a window and shouted directions in Norwegian.

"You must speak English here," said Amundsen in amusement. The navigator had not oriented to their arrival on the other side of the world.

Abruptly the gusts of wind stopped. During this momentary lull the *Norge* approached the ice with cautious haste. The big air fender under the main gondola touched ground, and the ship bounced a yard in the air. Then, at exactly 7:30 on the morning of May 14, she settled serenely. It was a perfect landing.

The men staggered out onto the ice. Their legs were wobbly, their eyes glazed. Amundsen went up to Nobile, who was ordering the crew to deflate the gasbag quickly, before the strong wind started up again. The great Norwegian explorer thanked Nobile warmly for bringing them safely through the long storm.

Ellsworth wrung the Italian's hand gratefully. "My house in New York is yours!" he cried. "My villa at Florence is yours!"

At that moment no one thought of personal glory or national pride; to a man they were simply relieved — relieved that the intolerable tension was at last over. The Norwegians went into the village, led by the impassive natives.

Now the *Norge* was shrinking fast. The control car was dragged under the retreating folds. Then the engine gondolas disappeared under the empty rubber envelope.

Now only Alessandrini and Nobile stood watching their beloved airship. The two men looked at each other. At this moment of great triumph, they both had a strange feeling of sadness.

The aerial successes of Byrd and Amundsen brought forward more candidates who wanted to join the fraternity of polar airmen. Next to achieve fame was Capt. George Hubert Wilkins (later Sir Hubert Wilkins), an Australian, who had been a prominent member of Vilhjalmur Stefansson's Canadian Arctic Expedition in 1913-18. Convinced that the airplane, with its greater speed, was the best vehicle for flying the Arctic regions, he planned to explore the regions north of Point Barrow, Alaska.

Since Wilkins was not a pilot, he sought out Lt. Carl Ben Eielson, well known in Alaska for his knowledge of flying in the frozen north country. All he needed, he thought, was a good pilot and a good airplane. But the venture was not as simple as that. There was a third element — money — that was also a prerequisite.

Wilkins approached the North American Newspaper Alliance, National Geographic Society, and interested individuals who formed the Detroit Arctic Expedition which included a Board of Control and various Committees to plan the operation. The modest intention of Wilkins turned into a hopeless muddle of organization. The original purpose of exploring the Beaufort Sea area 300 miles northeast of Point Barrow was enlarged to culminate in a flight from Point Barrow to Spitsbergen as a grand finale.

Two Fokkers were purchased by the organization: a small single-engine named The Alaskan *and a large trimotor christened* The Detroiter. *Another pilot, an Army Air Service major, Thomas G. Lanphier, was added to the "staff" and operations began.*

In quick succession, a number of accidents marred the exploratory flights. A newspaperman was killed when he walked into the propeller of The Detroiter, *and both planes were severely damaged in landing mishaps. The bad luck persisted but so did Wilkins, and after more crashes and more forced landings, Eielson and Wilkins took off from Point Barrow in March, 1927, in a new Stinson biplane for a point 550 miles away. Their intention was to land on the pack ice and take soundings to determine the thickness of the ice. After a successful landing and takeoff, the Stinson's engine malfunctioned and a crash landing was made 65 miles northwest of their destination in the dark. Their plane wrecked, Eielson and Wilkins were confined to its cabin for four days by a violent snowstorm. Thirteen days later, the two determined, bedraggled men arrived at Point Barrow on foot; the only aftereffect was the loss of one of Eielson's little fingers.*

Refusing to give up, even though financial support was withdrawn after the Stinson crash, Wilkins still planned on the flight to Spits-

57

bergen. He sold the two Fokkers and the remaining Stinson and pur-chased a new Lockheed Vega. In the spring of 1928, Wilkins and Eielson were at Point Barrow ready to duel the fates again. On April 16, the skies cleared and they decided to go . . .

A Prayer of Thanksgiving

Capt. George H. Wilkins

"Switch off?" to Eielson.

"Switch off," he answered.

"Gas on?" I asked.

"Gas on," he said.

I swung the propeller sharply through three or four turns to suck gas into the cylinders, placed the blade at an angle marked previously to show when one piston was in firing position, then shouted:

"All clear?"

"All clear," Eielson answered and snapped on the switch. He swung the booster magneto and as she had done each time we asked her to start, the engine coughed once, kicked back, coughed again and then emitted a steady purr. My heart swelled with thankfulness. The engine sounded fine and though the direction of the wind was not perfect it was still very good.

The weather forecast, as I understood it, was in our favor for the greater part of the journey. We must chance what we might find at Spitsbergen. The only regret was that five gallons of gas I had in-tended to pour into the tanks before starting had leaked out during the night. There was no more on the field and without time to send back to the hangar we were forced to leave with the tanks not quite full. However, I felt we would have sufficient to cover our flight.

I climbed into the navigator's cabin and shouted, "Let's go!" to Eielson. The Eskimo men yawed the tail of the machine and we slid off the boards we had placed beneath the skis to prevent them from freezing to the snow. Away we went quickly gathering speed as we passed down the runway. The floor of the track was slightly un-dulating and as our speed increased Eielson had a difficult task to keep the fast-moving plane within a width of fourteen feet. Thirty, forty, fifty miles an hour, we gathered speed as we progressed, the machine behaving like a proud horse tugging at a load. From the cabin window I could see the tail planes swaying and missing by no more than a foot first one bank and then the other. I marveled at Eielson's skill and courage. An error of a few pounds pressure on the rudder, a swing of a few inches one way or the other, and we would have hurtled into the snowbank, our skis would have buried themselves beneath the blocks we had thrown from the runway, and disaster would have surely followed.

Eilson kept his nerve. I prayed. Sixty, seventy miles an hour. We lifted, swung sickeningly, touched the ice again—then soared smoothly into free air. Never has there been a more fervent prayer of thanksgiving than the one I uttered.

Our greatest danger was passed. The regular hum of the engine assured me all was well with it. The machine climbed beautifully — no squashing along with the tail down to give one the feeling that at any moment she might drop plummetwise to destruction. No. No! She was a thing of life; buoyant, swinging out with a manner true and straight, seemingly matching her will to ours. I thanked God for the understanding of the man who designed her; for the honest, conscientious men who had built her, and for the skill and wisdom of the man at the controls. I was conscious of the great privilege of guiding her on her course.

I passed a note to Eielson: "Wonderful takeoff. How's everything?"

"Everything's great!" he shouted through the speaking tube. "She handles fine. Engine turning seventeen twenty-five. Temperature hundred and twenty."

We had previously discussed the first leg of our course in relation to the sandpit at Point Barrow so Eielson could swing and take up his departure from that point. I fixed the articles in the cabin, all of which had been piled up forward to gain the best advantage in the takeoff. As soon as the compass was clear I got observations for drift and ground speed.

Ground speed was 108 mph. Drift ten degrees to the left. Wind at low altitude was slightly north of east, a little against us, but that I did not mind. We were by that time 30 miles over the Arctic Ocean and I was sure that the wind would soon change. The horizon to the north and east was as clear as clear could be. The ice, after we had skimmed over the lagoon and crossed the rough high-pressure ridge near the shore, was badly broken and much open water was in evidence.

59

On April 16, 1928, Capt. George H. Wilkins (later Sir Hubert Wilkins) and Carl Ben Eielson made an incredible 2,200-mile flight from Point Barrow, Alaska, to Spitsbergen, Norway. En route, they were forced down by a severe blizzard and had to remain in the plane's cabin for five days before being able to continue their flight. Shown here before their ski-equipped Lockheed *Vega* are Wilkins (left) and Eielson.
National Archives Photo

For the first 50 miles these conditions prevailed. The wind by that time was lighter and south of east, but I was cheered by the fact that the loose ice was no longer drifting in the sea. It was stationary or if moving at all was going against the wind. This indicated that the wind from the east would soon be over. It would swing to the southeast, south, and southwest and because of this we would be assured of fine weather for the first few hundred miles. Then we would meet a calm, probably some fog, and again clear weather toward Grant Land. There was no guessing at that time what it would be like further on.

We flew on and on and I was busy as a bird dog for the first few hours, settling everything in the cabin. I put out my charts, tested both sextants for index error, and put them in order. I tried the gas pump to see that it was clear, made sure the dump valves were free should we have occasion to use them; set the wireless aerial, testing its note to get the best resonance; made sure the drift indicator was registering true, and changed it from side to side. I discovered my stopwatch would not function if left in the cold cabin and had to keep it in my pocket.

I had little time to write my notes or closely examine the ice, but I had plenty of time to notice that a forced landing anywhere during the first three quarters of an hour would have been our last. There was no ice smooth enough or fields large enough for a machine to land, so badly broken was the pack ice. I had supreme confidence in our machine and in finding good landing fields further out to sea.

For the first hundred miles we flew at an altitude gradually rising from five to eight hundred feet. From that distance to the ice pack we could see every detail clearly. About a hundred miles from shore the ice became heavier and ridged. The ridging seemed to be the result of heavy packs coming from the northeast and, moving against the shore, pressed the lighter ones moving west. The direction of the icefalls indicated the direction with the greatest pressure.

My long experience in traveling over the ice on foot, watching it grind and pile itself in ridges, of finding my way by the direction of snowdrifts, here proved useful many times. In earlier years I had stood upon the ice and watched it squirm and pile in jumbled masses. I had listened to it groan under the pressure of high winds and swift-moving currents. At the beginning of pressure the edges of two packs would come together with a dull, rasping sound, increasing to a groan as the pressure mounted. When under great force the huge blocks of ice issued sounds like the sobbing and wailing of a suffering child. To stand in their midst, uncertain of safety, not knowing whether the ice on which one stood would, at the next moment, rise and tilt or spew one into the seething mass had been awe inspiring.

An hour or so before, I had watched with interest the sky behind us darkening. High in the air over an area that had been beneath a clear canopy when we passed, long stratus clouds had formed. First scarcely visible, then darkening, the cloud bank we were rapidly approaching announced its presence by a peculiar grayness above the horizon. If the air is calm right to the limit of vision, the sky seen from the altitude at which we were flying touches the distant earth rim in almost steely blueness. The cloud bank we crossed over was probably the result of a comparative calm between winds in the vicinity at that time.

Meeting low cloud at that interesting point of the journey was exasperating. Land in that particular vicinity would best serve our meteorological plans — enabling us to complete a ring of stations on fixed points almost equidistant in longitude and at about 80 degrees North Latitude. My great desire had been to find an island at that point and when we came there the surface was cloud-ridden.

We had been in the air 11 hours. It was past midnight local time but the sun — now almost due north — had been well above the horizon all of the time, yet for an hour or so it had been almost impossible to get even a reasonably accurate sextant observation, probably because of the refraction. My sights of the sun would differ so greatly as to vary its position by two degrees. It was almost beyond me as we sped along to keep the sun centered on the bubble of my sextant; I had to take many readings and take their mean. This difficulty did not present itself earlier in the day nor did it have to be contended with later when the sun was higher above the horizon. Around midnight, from an altitude of 3,000 feet, we observed with the naked eye the dull red orb dance and skip like the mast light of a distant ship rising and falling with the waves.

About this time Eielson, who could see the gas gauges and the tachometer which I could not, handed me a note reading: "Engine been turning about sixteen fifty. We are using approximately eighteen gallons an hour. Now about forty gallons left in wing tanks. Oil temperature hundred and five." This showed that our gas consumption so far was high. We should soon be consuming less gas as our load was getting down to normal. By rough calculation I figured that if we could get the consumption down to even 12 gallons an hour on the last quarter of the journey we should have enough to complete 20 hours' flying. We were averaging more than 100 mph over the ice. The distance over our course without deviation was about 2,200 miles. We had seesawed over the clouds and we would probably seesaw again. We had also, from my observations, swung a little to the right on one leg of our journey and a little too much to the left on the next leg. It was not possible to keep accurate within a mile or so. I felt certain that if my interpretation of the meteorological conditions were right we should have no violent head winds and that we could make it, but I knew it would mean piloting with strict attention to the job and most careful navigation.

I was confident in the comparative accuracy of navigation so far and was cheered by the fact that we were obviously over comparatively near-shore ice. By near-shore I mean within 100 miles or so of shore. It is not difficult to differentiate between ice frequently on the move, pressed by the winds against the stubborn resistance of shallow water and the ice far offshore. Ahead high clouds of a nature observed only in the neighborhood of land, rose to considerable heights. Far, far away in the very distant eastern sky, pillars of high storm clouds hung like wraiths under the pale blue zenith. They were perhaps 150 or 200 miles away and seen only with the aid of clear high atmosphere and the advantage of 6,000 feet altitude above the ice. Beneath these vaporous pillars was a grayish white darkening toward the horizon. From north and south long, gray stratus clouds streaked toward the storm center.

I was then certain of the Greenland storm and as certain also of a following wind for many miles. We might have swung northward to clear the high clouds which barred the way on a direct course, but it had been my hope to check absolutely our position by actually sighting Grant Land in the distance. With the cloud interference, a distant view was not to be had and when Eielson, to avoid a towering cloud mass, swung to the south I acquiesced. There was no real reason for this move as we could be at no point other than north of Grant Land. The clouds spoke of the mountains they covered, but it is only human to want the assurance of actual vision. I wanted to see rocks and soil.

To the south the clouds rose steeply, higher and higher. Eielson swung more to the right to avoid them and I hurriedly passed him a note: "You must not go west of south. Turn east or north if necessary to avoid cloud." Faithfully Ben banked the ship and swung into the north.

Vision ahead was bad. We plowed through several cloud banks. I was hastily writing a note to inform Eielson of my estimate of the exact position, and to say that we could not afford to go into the cloud to look for Grant Land and suggest that he wing due north to clear the cloud, when I heard him shout. I looked out of the window and saw slightly to the right and not far — perhaps less than 20 miles away — the rugged mountaintops of Grant Land piercing the clouds. It was a fleeting glimpse we had, but it served to stir deep emotion in our hearts.

As we swung clear of clouded Grant Land we saw what Peary named *The Big Lead*. It stretched from a few miles north of the neighborhood of Cape Columbia toward Greenland until lost from view in the distant haze.

As we passed onward and north of Greenland the ice below us was much fractured. Much of the area was covered with ice too thin to land on and sledging travel hereabout, on the day we passed, would have been impossible. Not long after clearing the clouds near Grant Land the snowdrifts showed the wind to have been variable throughout the season. North of Grant Land the wind had been frequently if not constantly from the north or slightly northeast. Our course was somewhat north of east and as we gained a more northerly latitude we slipped from the edge of the Greenland windstorm into still-cold, 48-below-zero weather. For the first time during the flight my feet and hands were slightly chilled, but not cold. The oil temperature in the engine decreased to about 60 degrees Fahrenheit and from time to time Eielson had to climb the machine steeply or advance the throttle in order to increase the temperature of the engine.

Soon our course trended south of east and as we approached Latitude 84 from the north, we again came within the influence of the wind. Southward and more south our flight continued and as we swung in that direction the wind swung also, speeding us on our way. Three hours after leaving Grant Land one lone peak on the most northerly point of Greenland showed dimly in the cloud tops far to the south-by-west.

I was now positive that the low temperature and the high northwest wind would lead to trouble where it met the warmer air near Spitsbergen. Already on the far horizon we could see the ashen grayness that, when seen from a distance, indicates high Arctic winds and storms. But the north wind had us in its paw, and, as Peary said of his return trip from the Pole, we were sliding down the North Pole Hill in fine shape.

The edge of the Greenland storm and the cloudy conditions near Spitsbergen seemed to meet in the far south but for a couple of hundred miles our way was clear. Then we could see before us high, curling cumulus clouds rising to heights even greater than our now lightly loaded plane could reach. As we approached the clouds Eielson climbed the machine steadily up, up to seven, eight thousand feet and the clouds were still high above us. It was useless. We could not hope to get above them and if we were to conserve our gasoline it was not advisable to go any higher. We must thread our way through the cloud lanes — and keep our course as best we could.

From my cockpit the sun, which had swung steadily on our left until after passing Grant Land, was now obscured by the right wing of the plane. Just before entering the clouds I asked Eielson to vary from the course for a moment while I made an observation to locate our position as nearly as possible.

The sun at the time was about 16 degrees above the horizon. By coming east we had met his Solar Majesty halfway round the world. Several sights gave me the needed information. We were approximately 200 miles northwest from Spitsbergen and slightly east of our course. The wind from a little west of north was drifting us eastward but I was not inclined to alter my calculated compass course at that moment. There would be no telling the force and direction of the wind when we reached the clouds and I considered it wiser to be too far east over land than too far west over the Greenland sea from where we would have had to fight our way in a crosswind to make the coast of Spitsbergen.

We made sure that all the gas the pumps would carry was in the top tanks. It appeared that we had gas to last four hours at least and perhaps more. At an altitude of 8,000 feet we entered the cloudy area. Eielson selected the lanes between the feathery masses, cleverly compensating for his deviation without my aid. The air was turbulent and unstable. At rare intervals we saw in the dim distance beneath us dark streaks of water between scattered ice. For an hour and a half we flew through cloud lanes, very occasionally seeing patches of almost ice-free water, but these glimpses were too fleeting to enable us to get an observation for drift and speed. We could see the sun at times and at others it was hidden behind high clouds but these infrequent flashes enabled us to check our compass course.

As one would naturally assume, our compass during that period was less reliable than at any other time of the flight. Frequent and sudden changes to avoid cloud formations and to follow lanes swung our compass back and forth, giving it no time to steady. To keep our course we had to rely on our sense of direction, a study of the tilt of the cloud tops and occasional sights of the sun, rather than place any reliance on the compass.

We figured that if the wind had held in our favor — and we believed that it had — we must be nearing the mountains at the north end of Spitsbergen. But even the highest mountaintops would be covered with cloud if there the clouds continued as high as those among which we were flying. The clouds also appeared to extend down almost to the water so that we dared not go beneath them for fear of running directly into the mountains.

Our engine had functioned splendidly all the way, but it was reaching the end of a grueling trip and the gas in the tanks was getting low. Now in the moisture-laden atmosphere there was greater danger that the carburetion of gas and air might fail and let us down into the icy water. If we turned east to make sure of being over land, we would have — assuming we could make a safe landing in the mountains — a most tedious journey over deep snow and glaciers.

The air was turbulent above the clouds; beneath them it was boisterous. Our now almost empty plane was tossed like a cork on a stormy sea. Loose things in the cabin tumbled and rattled. With nothing to get a grip on, I tumbled too, if I didn't rattle.

Right then Eielson's valuable training and cool skill demonstrated their worth. With the plane nosed down and with engine full on she bucked like a broncho but Eielson, never losing the upper hand, held and guided her splendidly around the rugged mountaintops. We came down to within a few feet of the ice-strewn water near the coast where the surface wind was furious and the salt spray, whipped from the sea, filled the air. Over the land the snow drifted high and thick, precluding a judgment of distance.

A patch of smooth, snow-covered land was passed in an instant's flash and dead ahead loomed a mountain. With an adroit swerve of the machine Eielson avoided it by a narrow margin. We could see that it would be dangerous to follow the coast too closely so we swung broadside to the wind and crabbed our way out to sea. But the sea held for us no haven of rest or safety unless, forsooth, it should be a long, long rest. It soon became evident that what we had missed was a small mountainous island; also that it was useless for us to remain out over the water. Back we turned toward the land only to be re-warned by the steep mountains. We were like an imprisoned bird beating against a windowpane.

We knew we were running short of gas and must land soon or be without enough to move again if we came down. We had no choice but to endeavor to relocate that one smooth patch of white of which we had caught but a glimpse. The windshield before Eielson was almost totally obscured with snow and frozen oil; his vision restricted to the little he could see through the small open windows, and by

66

looking first on one side and then the other. The windows of the cabin, flush with the fuselage, were clear of snow, providing me with a fairly clear outlook.

We hawked about this way and that. I passed note after note to Eielson as fast as I could write them:

"Turn right."

"Now to the left."

"A bit more."

"No, we have passed it."

"Turn back."

"Turn back."

"Keep as close to the land as possible."

"There it is on our right."

Eielson had little time to read my notes. Indeed, I marveled that he could even spare time to grasp them, let alone follow their meaning, so busy he must have been with the controls of the machine.

We were past the place I meant, almost as he saw it, so he swung once more out to sea in a narrow circle and heading into the wind came low into the teeth of the snowdrift. It was a right anxious moment for both of us. My face was hard against the windowpane as I tried to learn if the surface was smooth or covered with broken ice. It was impossible for Eielson to see but with steady nerve braced for all eventualities he leveled the ship and lowered her gently until lost in the swirling snow.

We came smoothly to rest. Because of the high wind our ground speed, gliding with engine dead, was necessarily slow, perhaps 20 or 30 mph. Even on the ground we could not judge accurately the force of the wind because of the blinding snow but it must have been unusually high and was such that the machine moved scarcely 30 feet beyond where the skis first touched. Once on the ground we could see no more than a few feet to each side of the machine. I flung the engine covers and an empty oil can from the cabin and struggled forward to empty the oil tanks before the oil should freeze.

"Open the tap," I shouted to Eielson and held the can under the drainpipe but nothing happened. Again I shouted my request as loudly as possible. But Eielson was temporarily stone-deaf as the result of the constant throb of the engine. He could not hear a word, and only when by signs I was able to make him understand, the oil flowed. The wind continued with hurricane force and high drifts soon formed. We stamped the snow about the skis so that it would

67

freeze and prevent the ship from swinging or turning over.

Promptly as could be managed we threw the covers over the engine; first the one of canvas, then the waterproof, and tied them tightly.

We could convey our meaning to each other only by signs at first but, as had been the case last year when we had fallen through a dark, raging blizzard 5,000 feet to the pack ice, there was nothing we needed to discuss immediately. Silently we climbed into the cabin of the machine and brushed the snow from our clothing. "Thank God the machine's safe," I screamed in Eielson's ear. He nodded solemnly. The minds and hearts of both of us were too full of thankfulness for conversation even if hearing had been easy.

The plane rocked and trembled in the gusty wind. I reached for the remainder of the lunch provided for our use during the flight and we munched dry biscuit, chocolate, and pemmican. There was still enough hot coffee in my thermos bottle for a swallow each. Ben had a few cigarettes in his pocket and after a smoke we settled down to rest. Neither of us, I think, was physically tired but the strain of the last two hours had told on our nervous systems. Sleep for a while was impossible.

It is interesting now, some time after the event, to compare our mental state at that time with what our attitude had been the foregoing year when, after our forced landing, we faced a long walk home. Last year in our machine when we were plugging wearily onward hoping our gas would last until we reached our base or the land at least, our engine had suddenly quit. For 20 minutes we floated down through utter darkness, a gray forbidding darkness. Not black like a winter's night but a nerve-racking, sense-dulling density. Beneath us lay what? Rough ice we knew and perhaps a lane of open water. Injury, minor or fatal, seemed imminent but we were resigned — helpless in the hands of our Maker, his to dispose of without effort on our part. There was nothing we might do to help ourselves.

But for the landing we made this year on Spitsbergen, we had to fight. Fight every inch of the way, anxious, uncertain, never quite helpless but ever against tremendous odds. We had, as we sat in the plane, reached a position of safety not only for ourselves but for our plane. I cannot say which year, this or last, our prayer of gratitude was more earnest. Both times it was sincere.

The remarkable flights of Byrd and Bennett and Wilkins and Eielson by airplane and Amundsen, Ellsworth, and Nobile by dirigible were significant milestones in aviation progress. These brave pioneers who planned and concluded their flights so well led the way for the many who followed. While these early flights did not produce much information of scientific value, they did prove that polar aerial travel was feasible. Since it was the shortest way from the Old World to the New, air routes should be developed over the Great Circle Route via the northern latitudes — Labrador to Greenland to Iceland to the British Isles and the Continent. Bert ("Fish") Hassell, Oliver Paquette, and Parker ("Shorty") Cramer, members of that rare breed of visionaries, foresaw that such a route was not only possible but practical. On August 16, 1928, Hassell and Cramer left Rockford, Illinois, in a single-engine Stinson monoplane named The Greater Rockford *to prove it.*

Air Pioneers Over Greenland

Frank H. Ellis

WHEN Bert R. J. "Fish" Hassell and Parker D. "Shorty" Cramer decided to attempt an Atlantic flight in 1928, they planned differently than those before them. Their search was to survey the most feasible route from the United States to Europe, via Canada, Greenland, and Iceland. They believed this to be a more practical procedure in view of available aircraft than the nonstop projects then in vogue.

The two airmen left Rockford, Illinois, on August 16, 1928, in a single-engined, wheel-equipped, Stinson Detroiter, *The Greater Rockford,* named for the city where $30,000 had been raised to finance the undertaking.

Six hours and 40 minutes after takeoff, they landed at Cochrane, Ontario. Weather was bad and they remained two days. Continuing on August 18, their flight carried them nonstop to Greenland, establishing the first west-to-east flight from the American continent to the Danish possession. Mount Evans, base camp of the University of

Michigan Expedition in Greenland, was their objective. The camp was on Stromfjord Arm, about halfway up the west coast of Greenland.

At first a very accurate course was kept. The pair flew over the Hudson's Bay Company post at Rupert House, on James Bay, and circled the buildings to check their whereabouts.

Local storms about which they had no previous knowledge now beset them, and they were obliged to abandon the prearranged route. Their radio did not transmit but simply gave out automatic, long buzzing sounds to operators receiving signals on the ground. Suited only as an approximate check to follow their whereabouts in flight, it became useless for such a purpose once an arranged course was abandoned, so from Rupert House onward, they discontinued its use.

When the short northern night settled over the wilderness, they were winging over the Quebec hinterland, heading for Ungava Bay. Daylight caught them crossing Hudson Strait, with Cape Chidley astern. This enabled the airmen to check their position correctly before they attempted the 550-mile overwater hop of Davis Strait — destination, Greenland.

Upon arrival over Greenland's inhospitable coast, visual identification of landmarks was their only resource, as their compass was useless, due to the proximity of the Magnetic Pole. Greenland was clear of fog when they made landfall, but they had no idea of their exact position. The expedition's base, christened Camp Lloyd, they knew to be located at the end of a sound, clearly marked on their map, but "where was the sound?" Aimlessly they flew, seeking to spot it, finally flying far up one long arm of the sea in an endeavor to locate any suitable landing place, as fuel was running low.

At last they chose a smooth-looking spot on the ice cap itself, and set the Stinson down safely with 2,400 miles behind them since departure from Cochrane.

Alone and lost, they still had a good map of the area. After careful check, the explorers believed they could pinpoint their position, and thought to reach the expedition's base in a day's walk. Bitter disappointment awaited. The expected short trek stretched to 15 lean and weary days.

Hiking the tundra along the edge of the cap, times without number they negotiated deep crevasses, and frequently had to backtrack many miles before a crossing could be accomplished. Shortage of rations soon became a threat to survival. They were reduced to five

One of the air pioneers over Greenland, Parker D. "Shorty" Cramer.
Wide World Photos

ounces of pemmican each, per day. Ptarmigan were encountered, but the pilots were able to shoot only a few. Several times they had no alternative but to strip off their clothes and swim glacial streams with the bundles tied to their heads.

Thus the two airmen slogged along, following the edge of the ice cap as closely as possible. Once on level tundra, Cramer became mired in quicksand, being rescued with great difficulty by Hassell, who made a rope from clothing tied together.

The two airmen knew that the expedition they sought was scheduled to vacate its base on September 1, and were desperate when that date found them on a side hill of a wide fjord. As they pondered the idea of swimming rather than losing precious hours walking around, they spotted a speck on the distant sea. It appeared to be a small boat. A fire was quickly lighted to send up a smoke signal in hope of attracting attention, but the little craft soon vanished from sight behind a headland. After an hour's vigil, another moving object was seen on the water, and they risked one of their precious shells as a signal shot. It was a boat all right, powered with an outboard motor, and when it reached them, the airmen were greeted by Elmer Etes and Duncan Stewart of the expedition's staff, who informed Hassell and Cramer that several Eskimos had spotted their smoke signal, and informed Professor Hobbs, chief of the venture.

With no possibility of salvaging the Stinson, the pilots returned with the expedition to the United States. Hobbs had planned to leave not later than the 4th, so the rescue came only in the nick of time.

During World War II, a vast amount of flying was accomplished over Greenland by military airmen. During one reconnaissance flight in 1944, an American army pilot spotted the upside-down wreckage of a plane on the ice cap, and photographs were taken of it.

A real mystery developed. Prints showed the airplane to be the wreckage of a type no longer in use. Eventually the discovery came to the attention of the commanding officer of the Air Force base at Goose Bay, Labrador — Lt. Col. B. R. J. Hassell. One look at the photos, and he knew the answer. Buffeted by winds on the ice cap for 16 years, his old Stinson lay a lonely derelict — gallant monument to the first attempt to fly from the United States to Europe, via Greenland.

After such a brush with disaster, it might have been expected that further attempts to fly to Europe via Greenland would have been abandoned. However, Cramer, less than a year later, was on the wing again heading in the same direction with two companions, this time in a twin-engined Sikorsky amphibian flying boat.

Sponsored by the Chicago *Tribune* the project had every earmark of success. Pilot on the new venture was Robert H. Gast, Cramer being copilot and navigator. Their passenger was Robert Wood, Aviation Editor of the *Tribune*. The publishers of the newspaper gave the machine the name of *'Untin' Bowler*, why, it is hard to judge, but the title refers to a type of headgear worn in England for foxhunting.

Berlin was the planned destination, via Canada, Greenland, and Iceland. The three voyagers took off from Lake Michigan, at 8:45 A.M. on July 3, 1929. A brief stopover was made at Milwaukee, before continuing into Canadian territory via Saulte Ste. Marie to refuel. The same day they carried on to Rupert House, a Hudson's Bay post on James Bay.

July 4 brought poor weather, but they set off in hope of making a good showing. A dense overcast spread over the land. The *'Untin' Bowler* flew up the coast to Great Whale River, at the southeast end of Hudson Bay, and there was held by weather until the 7th. On the wing again, the plane carried on over the Quebec wilds and Ungava Bay, heading for Port Burwell at the entrance of Hudson Strait. The crew had difficulty locating the tiny Hudson's Bay post, and their first landing along the coast was on a desolate tickle (cove), where weather grounded them until the 9th. An anxious time resulted when drifting ice floes endangered the hull of the Sikorsky with each change of tide. When they finally reached Burwell on the 9th, the flyers learned to their chagrin, that they had flown right past the place on the 7th, and that residents had clearly heard the sound of their engines as they went by.

Weather held bad, and the craft was anchored offshore at Burwell to await improvement. On the 13th, a tremendous storm blew up from the north, driving before it great masses of ice from the open strait. As it increased in violence, huge floes smashed against the amphibian's hull, and the strenuous efforts of the three airmen with the help of several Eskimos were of no avail in trying to keep the ice clear of the craft. The unequal fight finally came to an end when the anchor rope parted, and the crew was obliged to abandon the craft to its fate. Heaving floes soon stove in the side of the *'Untin' Bowler*, and she sank several miles offshore. The disheartened trio was obliged to return to Chicago by ship, and train, and thus Cramer's second attempt to fly to Europe via Greenland had a dismal ending. "Shorty" might have been forgiven if he had tossed in the sponge, but not him. He was going to Europe via Greenland, so for a third time he had a go at it. Arrangements were completed in 1931.

By this time, officials of various commercial aviation organizations, both American and British, were beginning to view the Atlantic with real interest from the standpoint of regular mail and passenger flights. They had been watching long before this, but not until July, 1931, did plans formulate for an actual survey flight to take place.

Backed by Trans-American Airlines Corp. — a subsidiary of Thompson Aeronautical Corp. of Cleveland, Ohio, a new Bellanca seaplane was purchased for the project. Powered with a Packard Diesel radial engine, it was something new in Atlantic endeavor. All previous aircraft, successful, or otherwise connected with ocean flights, had been equipped with conventional motors using gasoline.

No prior publicity was given this flight, and the Bellanca had no special name, being designated simply, Survey Plane No. 1.

Once again into the Atlantic flying picture came "Shorty" Cramer as pilot, his navigator and radio operator being Oliver Paquette. The latter, a Canadian, was born and raised at Sudbury, Ontario. Paquette already had been associated with several ground survey trips in the north, in the employ of the Canadian government and he was "on loan" to Trans-American Airlines, due to a special request from Cramer, who had made his acquaintance at Cochrane in 1928.

The place of departure of Cramer's third attempt was Detroit, with Copenhagen, Denmark, the ultimate goal.

After the two airmen set off from the Detroit River on August 28, 1931, their first stop was unscheduled. A landing was made on Abitibi Lake, near Lowbush, Ontario, to enable Paquette to pay a brief visit to his wife and parents, then living in nearby Cochrane.

The following day the airmen flew on to reach the Hudson's Bay post at Rupert House, continuing on the 30th to make the post at Great Whale River. On the 31st, they made the long hop over the Quebec hinterland to Wakeham Bay, on Hudson Strait.

After an overnight stop, the flight continued across the sea to the north shore of the strait, landing at Pangnirtung, on the coast of Baffin Island.

Overwater hops held no fears for them in their float-equipped aircraft, and the long trip across Davis Strait to Greenland went off as scheduled with a landing at Holstinborg.

Here the Diesel engine was given a thorough check in readiness for the flight over the Greenland cap. This historical "first" the airmen made on September 5. They went over the vast ice fields in five hours' flying time, cruising at 9,500 feet, and landing on the east coast of Greenland at Angmagsalik.

Now faced with the overwater trip to Iceland, the intrepid pair held every expectation of success, a belief which came true when they made the 450 miles to Reykjavik on the 7th. Not satisfied with that, they quickly refueled, and were off again for the Faroe Islands, arriving there late in the afternoon, to land on the sea off Thorshaven, Sidero Island.

Peril, however, beset them on this lap. They were forced to land on the open Atlantic with a cracked cylinder. Cramer put the craft down safely, and after makeshift repairs, took off again despite huge swells which were running. He was indeed a master of his trade.

Early on the 9th, the daring pair were off again, reaching Lerwick, in the Shetland Islands, by 10:00 A.M. Now they were in a hurry, and refueling, were off on the last sea lap to the Norwegian coast; then south to Denmark, and Copenhagen.

But it was not to be. Weather reports were bad, and almost immediately after the pair left the Shetlands, storms of terrific violence converged along their route. A radio message from Paquette at noon divulged the news that they had sighted the Norwegian coast, and expected to arrive at the Danish capital around 4:30 P.M.

That was the last message the waiting world ever had from them. Time wore on, and a great throng of people who had gathered at the Copenhagen airport to greet them was finally obliged to disperse. A huge celebration had been planned to welcome the airmen from the New World, and a medal from the Danish Aeronautical Society was in readiness for presentation to Cramer.

The hours extended into weeks. Late in September the British trawler, *Lord Trent,* sighted and salvaged the battered remnants of the Bellanca, but the sea never gave up the gallant airmen.

In March, 1932, a strange aftermath occurred, proving that the ocean does relent a little at times. The crew of a Danish trawler spotted a soggy bundle afloat several miles off the Orkney Islands. The sea was calm, and salvage was easy. When turned over to the consul at Amsterdam, the package was found to contain personal papers of Cramer and Paquette, including the former's flying license, and a letter he had written to his parents. The precious belongings had been tightly wrapped in a piece torn from an oilskin coat, which also contained a number of buoyant flying instruments and a tightly sealed empty Thermos bottle, which had kept the pathetic relics afloat for over seven months.

The stress and difficulty of accomplishing that final act, with their aircraft disintegrating amidst tremendous seas, while their minds were assailed with the heartbreak of defeat and death, stamps those two men as heroes extraordinary.

Although they lost the fight, the names of "Shorty" Cramer and Oliver Paquette will not fade.

The successful flight of the Norge, captained by General Umberto Nobile, convinced many doubters that the airship might be the best vehicle for polar flying. Nobile himself returned to Italy a national hero and immediately began planning to take a new, improved dirigible to the North Pole — the Italia. The success of his previous flight had to be shared with a Norwegian and an American. Nobile, with the encouragement of Mussolini, wanted to be the first man in history to fly over the North Pole a second time.

A few weeks after the flight of Eielson and Wilkins, Nobile arrived at Spitsbergen; on May 23, 1928, he began his second and last flight in the Arctic. This time, however, the venture ended disastrously. Nobile succeeded in crossing the North Pole but on the return trip to Spitsbergen, the giant airship crashed. A Swedish scientist and six crewmen in the ship's gondola were lost as it broke loose and were never found. Nobile and the rest of his crew were eventually rescued in the greatest search operation ever attempted up to that time. Nobile's former colleague, Amundsen, and the crew of his French plane were lost, and Nobile came home to be condemned by his people for his failure. He was officially censured and held completely responsible for the crash.

The tragic end of the Italia did not shatter the faith of the lighter-than-air proponents in the possibilities of the dirigible for long-range flight. Count Ferdinand von Zeppelin had by now become world-renowned for his successful airships. In 1910, he had inaugurated the world's first regular commercial airline service between Friedrichshafen and Düsseldorf. During World War I, the Zeppelins had brought a new dimension to warfare with their bombing raids until they met their match in the airplane.

After the war, Zeppelin continued to build and improve his airships. On August 29, 1929, his favorite dream came true for it was on that date that his biggest and best airship, named the Graf Zeppelin in his honor, completed the first and only circumnavigation of the globe ever attempted by airship.

The Graf Zeppelin began transatlantic service and made many trips without accident. Meanwhile the tragedies that had occurred to English, French, and Italian airships cast a pall over the airship world. To help counter the antidirigible propaganda that sprang up, Dr. Hugo Eckener, pilot of the Graf Zeppelin, decided to make a second spectacular voyage — this time to the North Pole. Spurred by the interest of Sir Hubert Wilkins, the two of them conceived a sensational scheme. Wilkins would navigate a submarine under the polar ice field. At the North Pole, he would push his way

77

*through the ice and meet Eckener who would have meanwhile
steered the* Graf Zeppelin *to the same spot overhead. Mail and
passengers would be exchanged to prove that the rendezvous had
been made.*

Plans progresssed but Wilkins had trouble with his submarine, the
Nautilus, *and Eckener decided not to wait. Instead, he modified his
own part of the plan to include aerial mapping as a by-product of
the flight and arranged to meet a Russian ship, the* Malygin, *in a bay
off Hooker Island in the Franz Josef Land area. The flight was to
proceed from Friedrichshafen to Leningrad, then follow the route
the* Norge *and* Italia *had taken across the Barents Sea to the rendezvous spot. By the summer of 1931, Eckener was ready. His flight was
to mark the last use of lighter-than-air craft in Arctic exploration.*

Exploring the Arctic

J. Gordon Vaeth

MIDMORNING on July 24 — the day that Count Zeppelin had always called his lucky day — the 127 took off to begin the fulfillment
of one of his greatest ambitions, a flight into the Far North.

First stop was Berlin, where the ship remained overnight, taking
on additional fuel and supplies. Here it was that some of the scientists
first tried out their sleeping bags. In the warm summer weather, they
weren't too enthusiastic about them. And getting in and out of the
bags left them covered with reindeer hairs, a nuisance which they
pulled, plucked, and picked off themselves for hours afterwards.

The next day the ship went on to Leningrad, flying a course that
took it there by way of the Swedish island of Gotland, the Estonian
seaport city of Revel (now Tallin), and the Finnish capital of Hel-
sinki.

At Leningrad a great and enthusiastic crowd of a hundred thousand greeted the expedition. Large banners had been unfurled:
"Welcome *Graf Zeppelin,* Conqueror of the North." Russian and German flags were flying everywhere. The reception committee of military men and political commissars spoke glowingly of the flight in
terms of international good will and scientific progress. The festiv-
ities were so exhausting and the food and vodka so profuse that
Eckener had trouble getting everyone rounded up for the early take-

off scheduled for the following morning. While the Russians tried to swamp the ship's galley with still more things to eat and drink, he finally managed to get away. It was 9:00 A.M. and he was hours late. "I guess I'm lucky even to get started this soon," he remarked.

One of the things which helped delay the departure was a request to deliver a package. The address was the most unusual of all the cargo ever carried by the LZ-127: Latitude 78 degrees, 29 minutes, and 58 seconds North; Longitude 91 degrees, 7 minutes, and 56 seconds East!

This strange request came from the wife of a Russian scientist named Urzaneff. He'd been away for over a year on an expedition of his own. Hearing of the *Graf's* projected trip, he had written his wife and asked her to try to arrange for the dirigible to drop him some books which he needed. Eckener grinned and assured Mrs. Urzaneff he'd deliver the package if he could find her husband. The professor's wife had seen fit to add some other things, too. There were fresh strawberries, apples, and potatoes from their garden, things he'd be sure to appreciate in the frozen Arctic wastelands.

Heading northwest from Leningrad, the *Graf Zeppelin* moved slowly across Lake Ladoga, the largest freshwater lake in Europe. Its water looked clear and cold, a picturesque sight to those aboard the airship. That summer's day its surface gave no hint that it is iced-over seven months out of the year, that when it freezes, it freezes so solidly that Russians can build a road across it, as they did in World War II.

After Ladoga came Onega, another lake and second largest on the continent. Like Ladoga, its southern shores were relatively flat and its northern edge rocky and ragged. Lake Onega abounded in small islands, the sites of old monasteries. One of the Russians explained its formation: "Its bed was dug by a glacier of the Ice Age. That's why it runs in a northwest-southeast direction. It's not very deep, about 105 feet on the average. But it's still big and deep enough to be an important link in our transportation system."

Three hundred miles further on, after crossing over countryside that became more and more sparsely settled, they reached the point where the Dvina River empties into the White Sea. A city lay there, the city of Arkhangelsk. Called by many the greatest lumberyard in the world, the Dvina's mouth was blocked with a great brown mass that was drifting timber, a sign of the immense natural wealth inside the Soviet Union. As they cruised above this northerly coastal city, Russia's only seaport until the early 1700's, the photographers aboard

79

looked for the eighteenth-century monastery to the Archangel Michael, the monastery that gave the great and busy port its name. So far the *Graf Zeppelin* had covered only 450 miles from Leningrad, yet the cameramen had snapped better than 500 pictures.

From Arkhangelsk the ship headed due north and out over the White Sea. The coastline was sprinkled with timber. In places it was thick with logs. Fishing boats dotted the surface, searching for herring and cod. Other vessels, too, were about, busily hauling wood.

It was seven that evening when the dirigible crossed the imaginary line of the Arctic Circle, a crossing celebrated by a dinner of ham, sausage, cheese, and cake washed down by liberal quantities of wine.

Beneath lay the curving neck of water connecting the White Sea with the Arctic Ocean. To the left was the desolate tip of the Kola Peninsula, and to the right, the equally barren spur of the Kanin Peninsula. And ahead lay a cold front. The *Graf*'s bow shoved its way into the darkish clouds. They parted before the monstrous snout to let the ship go through.

Despite its ugly appearance, the front wasn't severe. The temperature dropped rapidly, however. Over Arkhangelsk it had been 68 degrees. In the front it fell to almost the freezing point. A cold rain beat for a while against the hull. Then it stopped. Strong head winds began to blow from out of the cold northwest.

For most of the night — which wasn't night at all in those high altitudes — the *Graf Zeppelin* made its way over greenish waters. It was headed for Franz Josef Land, a group of about 70 islands and a favorite goal of explorers since its discovery by Austrians in 1873. It had a rendezvous to keep at one of those islands, a meeting with the Russian icebreaker *Malygin*.

Progress toward the north was slow. Although he had left Leningrad with 105 hours of Blaugas and 21 hours of gasoline on board, Eckener stopped one of his engines to conserve fuel. "I see no reason to fight this wind at high speed," he explained to the scientific group as they checked their instruments and made out their logs in the lounge. "We'll take our time and give these tight isobars a chance to move on."

The 30-mph head wind did slacken, only to have fog, at first intermittent patches and then a solid bank of it, form beneath the ship. Otherwise the second day was a beautiful one. The sun was shining and a happy bright blue sky looked down upon the *Graf Zeppelin*'s silvery cover. From midmorning to midafternoon the fog continued. When at last it began to dissolve, its curtain of gray opened to disclose the sea and long white strips of ice which grew thicker and more abundant the farther toward the Pole the airship flew.

A few minutes before 6:00 P.M. they arrived over Hooker Island. The 1,620-ton *Malygin* lay at anchor a quarter of a mile offshore in front of a steep and rocky cliff. Slowly Eckener circled the island's weather station, in existence only two years and the most northerly such station anywhere in the world. Then, satisfied that the sea was calm and the wind not gusty, he nosed his airship down.

A hundred feet above the cold and mirror-like bay, canvas buckets and a sea anchor were dropped. The buckets filled with water, then were pulled upward by the crew, thus adding to the dirigible's weight. Slowly it settled to the surface. There were gentle splashes as air-inflated rubber pontoons under the main gondola and the aft engine car entered the water. The *Graf Zeppelin* had come to rest on the Polar Sea.

The ease with which Eckener had carried out this Arctic landing amazed the geographers and scientists on board and the 40 or so passengers who had watched the maneuver from the deck of the *Malygin*. "You'd have thought he did this every day" was the universal reaction.

It was an incongruous sight, this enormous dirigible riding to a sea anchor in the isolation of Franz Josef Land, while a tiny pullboat slowly made its way over from a dwarflike, ancient-looking icebreaker.

The boat approached the gondola. One of the men in it stood up. He was wearing a fur cap. Lehmann recognized him through his binoculars. It was Umberto Nobile, the Italian who had piloted Amundsen and Ellsworth across the Pole in the *Norge* in 1926 and who had failed the time he tried to repeat the feat on his own with a similar airship, the *Italia*, two years later. That was when he had crashed on the ice and been rescued by one of the most intensive Arctic searches in history, a search in which Amundsen had disappeared, not to be seen again. Mussolini, disgusted with Nobile's failure, had practically ordered him out of the country. Now he was in Russia, a special adviser to the Soviets on airship construction.

"Ellsworth," Lehmann called. "Look who's out here!"

The American millionaire went to the window. He knew that his Norwegian friend had come out of retirement and given his life to try to save this man. Nobile knew it too. Filled with emotion and

81

To counter antidirigible propaganda caused by the many airship tragedies, Dr. Hugo Eckener, skipper of the *Graf Zeppelin,* decided to fly to the North Pole. At the same time, Sir Hubert Wilkins planned to navigate a submarine under the ice and emerge through the ice to effect a spectacular meeting with Eckener. Passengers and mail were to be exchanged to prove that a rendezvous had been made. The trip never came off but the *Graf Zeppelin* did make a notable flight to Franz Josef Land and met a Russian freighter. En route, the *Graf Zeppelin* landed at Staaken Airdrome, outside Berlin. It is shown here maneuvering for a landing while policemen look on.

U.S. Information Agency Photo

hardly knowing what to say, the two shook hands.

While more than 50,000 postcards and letters were being trans-ferred between the *Graf* and the *Malygin*'s boat (the Russians com-memorated the rendezvous with a special postal issue), the airship showed signs of beginning to drift. Eckener's watchful eyes reflected concern. He had practiced this type of water landing on Lake Con-stance and at the mouth of the Elbe River in Germany. He wasn't worried about the actual landing and takeoff. He was disturbed, how-ever, that the ship was shifting into an area of heavy floes. "Watch out for that ice!" he called from the control-car window. "If it punc-tures our flotation gear, we'll be in real trouble."

For a moment he watched the cold white danger come closer. Then he suddenly snapped: "Finish that mail transfer as fast as you can! Prepare for takeoff!"

To the surprise of everyone, particularly those in the icebreaker's boat, the last mailbags were abruptly yanked aboard. Some orders were shouted in German. Water splashed as the canvas dip buckets were emptied. The sea anchor was retrieved. The *Graf Zeppelin* was suddenly in the air again. It had all happened so fast that the boat crew, who had hardly heard a word of good-bye, sat dumbfounded as the long, slim hulk rapidly diminished in size above their heads.

Aloft once more after its less-than-an hour rest on the water, the dirigible prepared to begin its scientific work in earnest. Some ob-servations had of course already been recorded. Using a special instru-ment loaned by the Carnegie Institution of Terrestrial Magnetism in Washington, measurements had been made of the earth's magnetic field every four hours since leaving Leningrad. The "observatory" for these readings was the first cabin on the port side of the main gondola, a cabin which had been stripped of everything steel or iron. But now the time had come for the geographic surveying to begin, for the photogrammetric equipment to be put to use.

These automatically recording cameras had to have a fixed starting or reference point. This was provided by the Hooker Island weather and radio station. From an altitude of 3,000 feet the mapping of Franz Josef Land was begun.

Numerous errors were found in the maps and charts then available of that little-known region. Islands were represented as peninsulas. Peninsulas as islands. Often the shapes of the land masses were dis-torted. Two shown in the hydrographic publications — Albert Ed-ward and Harmsworth — couldn't be found at all. Slowly and methodically a camera survey was completed of Alexandra, Prince George, and Prince Rudolf, three of the largest and most important islands in the group.

Prior to leaving Friedrichshafen, Eckener had received a letter from a clairvoyant asserting that he would find the missing Amundsen's body in a bay in Franz Josef Land. While putting little stock in this improbable prediction, the expedition kept its eyes open for such a discovery. It found nothing.

About midnight they rounded Cape Fligely, the tip of Prince Rudolf Island. Here was the northernmost point of the flight. Latitude 81 degrees, 50 minutes North. Only 490 nautical miles from the Pole!

The weather was clear, the winds favorable, and the airship in excellent operating condition. But instead of going farther north, Eckener headed east.

"Why?" he was asked on his return, "why didn't you take advantage of the conditions you found and make straight for the Pole? It was a chance of a lifetime. Why did you muff it?"

The old airshipman would smile, a knowing look writing itself in the lines of his tough and weatherbeaten face. "I had my reasons," was his usual unrevealing reply.

Years later the answer came to light. Insurance! According to one who made the trip, they had all wanted to proceed from Cape Fligely to the much-sought-after north end of the axis of the earth. But the insurance policies covering the flight had prohibited it. Above 85 degrees North latitude or thereabouts, the premiums had become so costly that Aeroarctic couldn't afford them. A less cautious man might have taken the ship to the Pole, policies or no policies. But not Eckener. It wasn't in his makeup to let enthusiasm get the better of his judgment.

Leaving Franz Josef Land behind, they gradually descended from their 3,000-foot mapping altitude to a cruising height of 1,000. Their course was toward North Cape, the northernmost extremity of Severnaya Zemlya. Despite the assemblage of geographic talent and knowledge on board, no one knew its exact location. At the time it was one of the least-explored places in the Arctic, having only been discovered in 1913, when it was named Czar Nicholas Land. Naturally the Red Revolution had changed that. It was now Severnaya Zemlya, or North Land.

Three hundred and seventy miles unrolled beneath the hull, 370

84

miles of water and drift ice. Sometimes this ice was colored. Brown. Yellow. Even a tinge of green. At first the color came in isolated spots. Then more and more of it rose up from over the horizon. Increasingly extensive were these patches, finally becoming so numerous that they changed the overall Arctic landscape from its usual white to a patchwork of deep-toned colors. "They're from plant life," one of the experts told von Schiller, "plant life that has blossomed in open areas of thaw water only to be frozen over again."

While the track chart showed continued progress toward the east, Professor Moltschanoff began his special tests. He had devised an ingenious device, a balloon-borne weather reporter. It was a box containing instruments to measure the temperature, pressure, and humidity of the air. In the box was also a tiny battery-powered radio which would transmit this information back to the *Graf Zeppelin*. The idea was to hang these instruments and transmitter from a balloon, release the balloon from the ship, and then record the signals sent by the apparatus as it climbed up through the atmosphere. Moltschanoff calculated that the balloon would rise to about 40,000 or 50,000 feet before it burst.

This, one of the first radiosondes, was launched by the director of the Aerological Observatory of Slutsk between Prince Rudolf Island and Severnaya Zemlya. Since it had to be inflated on the lower catwalk and launched from a hatch in the belly, getting it out of and clear of the hull and propellers was no easy task. It was done by hanging a weight on the balloon to make the rig fall clear. Then a device released the weight, and the balloon, its sensing instruments, and its radio, were free to climb. Moltschanoff would launch a total of three of these weather-sounding balloons before the flight was over.

When the west coast of Severnaya Zemlya came into view, it was 5:30 A.M. Full of curiosity and looking like a big bulky bear in his great woolen sweater, his navy-blue watch cap, and his sun goggles pushed up over his brow, Eckener climbed to 4,000 feet and crossed to the eastern side, parts of which stayed hidden under low-hanging clouds. These were Arctic sights never before seen by man. There were mountains, glaciers, and powerful streams, 200 or 300 feet across, bringing to the sea the water from the melting snow and ice above. Strange and forbidding was the fog-shrouded unpeopled coastline along which they flew.

The airborne expedition was nearing Professor Urzaneff's address, the one given by the professor's wife in terms of latitude and longitude. But a blanket of blinding fog lay over the region. They couldn't see him. Comrade Asberg tried to raise him by radio. No success.

The ship headed south to continue its scientific reconnaissance. Leaving North Land behind, it crossed a stretch of open water. This was Vilkitski Strait, which separated the island of Severnaya Zemlya from the Siberian mainland on the other side, the part of the mainland that is called the Taimyr Peninsula.

Steering a southwesterly course, Eckener then paralleled the Taimyr coastline for about 300 miles. When they reached the mouth of the Yenisei, the great river which the *Graf Zeppelin* had crossed much farther to the south on its world flight of two years before, they saw signs of human habitation. At the river's mouth was a tiny settlement named Dikson, site of a government weather station.

Cruising low, they could see three small trawlers anchored in the river and a Dornier flying boat pulled up on the shore. Eckener knew that this was the time of year the little outpost was being provisioned for the long Arctic winter a few months ahead. "Let's give these fellows a surprise," he said. He called the chef. A few minutes later, bread, fresh vegetables, a large sausage, and a bundle of three-day-old newspapers dropped by parachute from the gondola to the meteorologists and radio operators below. They waved their appreciation and stood longingly outside their primitive shacks, watching the airship disappear into the northwest.

In the early morning of July 29 the LZ-127 came to Cape Zhelaniya, the northern tip of Novaya Zemlya. Here, as usual, it climbed and began to cruise along the coast, using its mapping cameras as it did. What looked like a permanent ice sheet covered the northern island. There was glaciation everywhere. And as the ship made its way along the eastern coast, a great chunk of ice broke off, fell into the sea, and began to drift. An iceberg had been born. But an iceberg wasn't an uncommon sight in that area. A hundred or more were seen drifting along the coast. Icebergs of all sizes. Icebergs of all shapes.

Moving south, the Zeppelin came to Matthew Strait, the body of water separating the northern and southern islands. The latter had no permanent ice sheet and bore primitive vegetation like mosses and lichens, the same type of life, in fact, that is believed to exist in the cold climate of the planet Mars. Twice the ship cut across this habitat of polar bear, reindeer, walrus, seal, and fox. Then, satisfied that this island extension of the mainland's Ural Mountains had been adequately covered, the captain set a return course for Arkhangelsk.

Except for a pass over Leningrad at three the following morning to return Professor Urzaneff's books, and except for a brief stopover at Berlin's Templehof Airport to acknowledge a reception in the *Graf Zeppelin*'s honor, Eckener took "our brave old ship," as he called it, straight for home. He arrived there shortly after 4:00 A.M. on the 31st.

The flight had discovered new islands and new mountains. It had brought back photographs to correct the charts of the north polar regions. It had recorded data on the temperature, pressure, humidity, and electrical potential of the Arctic air. And it had measured the earth's magnetic field in previously inaccessible northern latitudes.

The expedition did something else, however. It proved to Eckener's satisfaction that it was no more difficult to operate a large airship over the central Arctic Ocean than over more temperate waters.

This was a surprising discovery indeed.

The Russians have long been interested in polar exploration and had used airplanes for rescue work in the Arctic as early as 1914. But their natural reluctance to divulge their knowledge was mixed with the desire to exploit their successes for propaganda purposes. Whatever their failures, their successes have been laudable and significant. The shortest way to America from Russia lies over the North Pole. This fact of geography is indisputable. Any knowledge gained of this area, whether used for peaceful or warlike purposes, is important.

Soviet interest in Arctic aviation grew gradually through the late twenties and early thirties. But it was not until 1937 that their achievements attracted world notice and were revealed as extremely competent undertakings. The first significant achievement was the establishment of a floating ice station which was conceived and organized by Professor Otto Schmidt, a brilliant scientist whose name was later dropped from Russian history books because of his "deviationist" political views. Schmidt's plan was to use four four-engine ANT-6 (TB-4) aircraft to fly nine tons of supplies from an advanced base to the Pole. While his personal interest was primarily in the realm of the scientific observations to be made on the ice island, the feat of navigating to and landing four heavy planes on the ice at the exact geographical pole was a remarkable achievement.

In 1939, Schmidt published a booklet entitled "The Conquest of the Arctic." It is a significant document in the history of polar aviation.

We Landed at the North Pole

Otto Schmidt

THE EXPEDITION to the North Pole in 1937 was the culmination of work that had been carried on for many years. Having been appointed to lead the expedition, I, together with my assistants, headed by the well-known polar explorer, M. I. Shevelev, worked hard for a year and a half preparing for it. We had the powerful assistance of the Soviet government and enjoyed the constant attention of Comrade Stalin who was the inspirer of the expedition. This enabled us to make very careful preparations.

Others had reached the North Pole before us. In 1909 Robert Peary, traveling with a dog team, had crossed on the ice from the northern tip of America to the Pole. The intrepid American had been limited in his opportunities for investigation. With a dog team as his means of transportation, he could take along but an extremely small load and could not stay more than one day at the Pole. He had established that there were no islands at the North Pole, but only a deep ocean covered with ice. But he had not even been able to measure the depth of the ocean. He had sunk all the cable at his disposal to a depth of 7,544 feet, but had not reached bottom. Neither could Peary ascertain whether the ice was moving and in what direction. It had been still less possible for him to find out anything definite regarding the weather in the region of the North Pole — it is obvious that one day could not be sufficient for this purpose.

The magnificent exploit of the famous American indicated the necessity of continuing his work and enlarging upon his experience. However, for nearly 30 years nothing had been done along these lines. True, flights to the Pole had been made during this period by Byrd, Amundsen, and others. But since no landings had been made at the Pole these flights added little to what we had already known from Peary. It had become clear that a different technique was needed; that it was not sufficient just to fly over the Pole, but that what was required was to land at the Pole and stay on the ice long enough for extensive scientific observations. This was the task we had set for ourselves.

There were great technical difficulties to be surmounted. Authorities throughout the world considered that it was impossible to make a landing on moving ice with land planes, and we could not think of using seaplanes, because fissures between the ice are very rare at the Pole, and the few that may be found are too small and not constant. A poll, taken by the Moscow *Izvestia* among the best authorities on the Arctic throughout the world, elicited the universal opinion that a flight like the one we planned could not be realized. Still we were firmly convinced of the successful issue of our undertaking. Our conviction was based on the knowledge of the Arctic which we had gained during the preceding years of scientific study and investigation.

Personally, I had no doubt that we would find comparatively smooth ice fields in the vicinity of the North Pole. My conviction proceeded from the idea that fissures and hummocks are formed in the ice when in its movement it meets obstructions in the shape of land or shoals. At a distance from the shore such phenomena are also possible, but they are likely to occur more rarely and would be smoothed away by time.

It had also been suggested that only a small plane be sent or that a landing be made with parachutes. As is universally known, the technique of such landings has been highly perfected in our country. However, we made our flight in four heavy four-engine planes. We had to use heavy airplanes because our instructions called for the setting up of a regular scientific station at the Pole, with proper living quarters, a radio plant with a wind-driven motor, complex scientific apparatus and instruments, and a food supply and fuel to last for a year and a half.

The four heavy planes, accompanied by a number of smaller ones, assembled on Rudolf Island, which is the northernmost of the Franz Josef group. On May 21, 1937, the first of these airplanes, piloted by the famous polar flyer, M. Vodopyanov, landed at the North Pole. In addition to the crew, this plane carried the four members of the staff of the future scientific station and myself. We flew above the clouds at an altitude of over 2,000 meters (about 6,500 feet). When our astronomical coordinates indicated that we were above the Pole we began to descend. Our suspense was at its highest; would there be an end of the clouds, would we see the ice before we hit it? And what kind of ice would we find — smooth, or full of fissures and hummocks? At an altitude of 500 meters (1,640 feet) we came out of the clouds and we saw under us vast ice fields stretching to the horizon, with fissures far between, each ice field extending over an area of several square miles — a number of landing fields prepared by nature itself. Our theory was thus substantiated.

The pilot, M. Vodopyanov, made a perfect landing on an ice floe amid the silent vastness of the central polar region. Several days later the other airplanes landed at the Pole and we rigged up a radio station. After having spent 16 days at the Pole we took off on our homeward journey, leaving our four comrades to carry out the difficult exploit that had been assigned to them.

Papanin, Shirshov, Fyodorov, and Krenkel — the four comrades who were left at the Pole — immediately made themselves at home. From the very first day the scientific instruments were put to work. The depth of the ocean was ascertained. In the course of nine months these comrades were regularly engaged in collecting extremely valuable scientific material pertaining to meteorology, magnetism, gravimetry, the study of the currents, the physics and chemistry of the sea, geology, etc. As had been foreseen by Soviet polar experts, the drifting of the ice carried the station toward the shores of America, at first slowly and then at an ever increasing velocity, until, in January, 1938, the ice floe reached the shores of Greenland where it broke apart. The courageous four did not lose their self-possession and continued their work on the remaining 100-foot fragment of the ice floe until the arrival of the icebreakers that had been sent to their rescue. On February 19, 1938, the celebrated explorers had reached latitude 70°54′ north.

In 1937, four Russian ANT-6 four-engine planes landed at the North Pole to claim the honor of being first to land at the top of the world. The ANT-6's, shown here, were the commercial or cargo version of the TB-4 bomber used by the Soviet air force in the middle thirties. Nine tons of supplies were flown to the North Pole and four scientists remained on the floating ice island after the planes left. Nine months later, after the ice floe had drifted to Greenland, the men were rescued by icebreaker.

The year 1937 was a banner year in the history of Soviet polar aviation. While the four scientists of Schmidt's party were drifting on the ice station, an announcement was made from Moscow that commercial air service between Russia and the United States was being contemplated. Trial flights were planned and the first was made in June by Chkalov who piloted a single-engine monoplane from Moscow to Vancouver, Washington — 5,300 miles nonstop via the North Pole. Two more flights were planned — one in July and the last in August. The second flight was also successful and set a world's record for distance when Mikhail Gromov piloted his single-engine plane to San Jacinto, California. The third flight by Sigismund Levanevsky, flying a four-engine T-4, ended in disaster. No trace of his plane or crew has ever been found.

The second flight was highly publicized. Gromov wrote a narrative of his flight which, like Schmidt's, was translated from the Russian in 1939. It is a rare document and the significance of his closing words is now fully realized.

Across the North Pole to America

Mikhail Gromov, Soviet Air Force

THE IDEA of flying to America across the North Pole occurred to me long ago. It attracted the interest of a number of Soviet airmen. Sigismund Levanevsky, hero of the Soviet Union, was the first to moot the idea of a transpolar air route between the U.S.S.R. and the United States publicly in the press. After this, Soviet flyers began to study the problem seriously.

The shortest distance between the Soviet Union and America is across the top of the earth. The suggestion of establishing such a service is a striking instance of the endeavor of aviation to be independent of land routes. It is said that an airplane, like a bird, can fly straight to its destination, undeterred by mountains, forests, and seas. But in practice, as we know, this is far from the case.

There are quite a number of extensive areas of the globe over which no plane has yet flown. Until recently it was believed (especially abroad) that flying in the Arctic was impossible. However, the development of polar aviation has shown that to Soviet planes and Soviet airmen the stern North is no insuperable barrier. The Chelyuskin epic, the numerous flights undertaken in the Arctic for the purpose of reconnoitering the ice and tracing the movement of fur animals, and finally, the brilliant operation of 1937, when four heavy planes were landed at the North Pole itself, all testify to the successful conquest of a region of the globe which perhaps offers more difficulty to flying than any other.

The flight of the squadron of planes to the very Pole, their splendid landing on a drifting ice floe, and their return to the mainland without damage or untoward incident was a great event in flying. It changed and expanded our ideas of the potentialities of aviation.

Long-distance nonstop flying has interested me for a long time. The flight to America across the North Pole was the fifth of my long-distance flights. Fourteen years ago a group of Soviet airmen, including myself, flew from Moscow to Peking. The plane I used was an R-1, the first airplane designed and produced in the Soviet Union. The flight took us 33 days. On arriving in Peking we learned that the French airman Arrochard had flown an equal distance in three days. A year later, I started out on another big flight. I made the circuit of Europe in a Soviet all-metal plane in three days. Arrochard's feat proved to be within the scope of Soviet pilots. Three years later I made my third long flight, again the circuit of Europe, this time on a triengined plane, *Wings of the Soviets*.

I made my fourth long-distance flight on an RD plane in 1934, beating the world distance record in a closed circuit. My comrades on this flight were Spirin, navigator, and Filin, engineer. It was our good fortune to demonstrate that Soviet planes and Soviet engines were among the best in the world. We remained in the air for 75 hours and covered a distance of 7,707 miles. Our record was not officially registered because the U.S.S.R. was not yet affiliated to the International Aeronautical Federation.

In 1935 this same crew applied for permission to make a nonstop flight from Moscow to America across the North Pole. We were unable at that time to put our plan into execution, but I was determined to continue my efforts in the sphere of long-distance flying. In this I was interrupted by protracted illness and my work on testing new airplanes, but I did not give up hope. My ambitions brought me into close contact with Yumashev, a splendid airman and inter-

ACINTO

MOSCOW

1937 was a year of several remarkable aviation "firsts" for the Russians. In June of that year, Chkalov piloted a Russian-built ANT-25 from Moscow to Vancouver, Washington, via the North Pole — a distance of 5,300 miles. The next month, Gromov piloted a similar type plane from Moscow to San Jacinto, California — a world-record distance of 6,302 miles. Left to right above are Yumashev, copilot; Gromov, pilot; and Danilin, navigator.

After flying for 62 hours and 17 minutes, Gromov set the huge single-engine monoplane down in a rough field with enough gas left for another six hours of flight. With its long wingspread (112 feet) and slender fuselage, it bears a striking resemblance to the American U-2 reconnaissance plane of today. Shown here shortly after landing, it was later dismantled and returned to Russia by ship.

National Archives Photo

national record holder, and Danilin, who in my opinion is the best navigator in the Soviet Union. We planned several long-distance flights, one of which was particularly interesting; from Moscow to Brazil, across the Black Sea, the Mediterranean, the Sahara Desert, and the Atlantic Ocean. Careful preparations were made for this flight, but for a number of reasons it had to be deferred.

Yumashev worked out the details of several other interesting flights, one of them from Moscow to Australia. I was interested in initiating an air route from the U.S.S.R. to America across the Atlantic Ocean; I also worked out in fairly great detail the route for a record distance flight from Moscow to Mexico, via New York.

But, of course, what interested us most was the plan for the flight from Moscow to America across the North Pole, which had been temporarily postponed, but to which we returned again and again.

We worked on the details of this flight for two years. This may seem a long time. But the result was that many problems which had formerly seemed insoluble now became perfectly clear to us. We had a complete picture of the details of the proposed flight. This gave us great satisfaction. We proposed to use a plane which I had been testing for nearly two years, RD No. 25-1.

It was a monoplane of the classical type with underslung wings, and at that time was undoubtedly the most suitable craft in the world for long-distance flying. RD No. 25-1 was the embodiment of the most up-to-date innovations in aircraft construction. A machine of this type had been displayed in 1936 at the World Aviation Exhibition in Paris and had profoundly impressed the connoisseurs.

We did everything we could to reduce the weight of the machine. We removed the rubber chambers which enabled the plane to keep afloat on water, adapted the engine covers to serve as sleeping bags, decided to do without brandy and firearms and reduced the food supply from a 2 months' to a $1\frac{1}{2}$ months' ration. We thus managed to lighten the load by nearly 400 pounds. We accordingly increased the supply of fuel, oxygen, and water for the engine by this amount.

Having increased the potential range of the plane by lightening its weight and increasing the supply of fuel, we turned our attention to the selection of the propeller. This absorbed a great deal of time and energy. We made a large number of test flights to ascertain the expenditure of fuel and the ways of economizing it.

Two wireless apparatus were installed.

The original range of the RD No. 25-1 was 4,350 miles. But when

95

a geared engine was installed, the range was increased to 6,200 miles. Experiments showed that the corrugated surface should be replaced by a smooth surface, and this increased the range by roughly another 1,250 miles. Finally, after covering the anterior edge of the wing with a polished surface, we were able to fly 7,700 miles without a stop. The installation of metal propellers still further increased the range.

We made a thorough and careful study of our craft. It had to be ascertained what height and speed should be maintained as the flying weight of the plane changed with expenditure of fuel. Finally, enough material was collected to enable us to know exactly in advance what distance could be flown in calm weather. But inasmuch as calm weather could not be expected along the whole of the long flight we were contemplating, we had to discover the laws which would tell us how to fly to achieve the maximum distance.

In the end, we had at our disposal extensive charts showing what speed and elevation to maintain under various conditions. This clarity on all questions proved to be one of the most important factors determining the success of our nonstop flight. We had a good knowledge of the flying qualities of our plane. The engine was not only economical but absolutely reliable, and in this respect was unequaled.

What caused us most uneasiness was the meteorological aspect of the problem. The comparatively small margin of stability of the plane in the early hours of the flight (owing to excessive load) demanded calm weather at least during this period. After that the only serious danger to be feared was the formation of ice on the propeller and wings. For two years we had been studying everything published at home and abroad on the reasons for this phenomenon so as to find a means of combating it. We finally arrived at the conclusion that the lower the temperature, the less the chances of ice forming, and that in clouds at a high altitude this danger was entirely precluded. At a temperature below $-20°$C. the danger of ice forming was very slight. It was therefore necessary, in the event of the danger of ice forming, that our plane should be able to reach an altitude where the temperature was below $-20°$C.

Thus some of the most difficult problems of the flight were settled before the actual takeoff.

I had known Yumashev and Danilin, my comrades in the flight, for a fairly long time. They had performed no "miracles," but they were capable of any exploit. I had had repeated opportunities of convincing myself of this. There was every reason to think that the composition of the crew was such as to ensure a successful issue to the flight.

Before the start an event occurred which rather altered the character of our task. Chkalov, Baidukov, and Belyakov made their splendid flight to America. This altered the situation somewhat. It was no longer enough to fly to any point in the U.S.A. It must now be our purpose not only to confirm the possibility of a transpolar air route, but to attain the maximum distance of flight.

Such being the case, weather conditions assumed cardinal importance. In this respect the year 1937 was generally unfavorable for flying in the Arctic. On the eve of the start we were told by prominent meteorologists that we must expect head winds and unfavorable weather. However, time did not permit us to wait for better weather. Moreover, we calculated that even with such unfavorable weather conditions we could beat the world distance record. All that was needed was to adhere strictly to the altitude charts, to maintain a definite regime for the engine, and not to deviate from our course under any circumstances. We must not turn aside to avoid cyclones or other meteorological obstacles, for that would considerably reduce our range. We would have to fly in a straight line. Of course we knew that some deviation from the ideal schedule, and consequent loss of distance, were inevitable; but we decided to reduce them to a minimum.

I must have been born under a lucky star. During my 20 years as a pilot I have had to make several big flights. And they have all ended successfully.

Every time I was assigned a big flight I experienced a sense of real happiness. Just before the takeoff, however, I would be greatly agitated; but no sooner was I in the air than I recovered complete composure. Usually I was so agitated before a flight as to lose all appetite; I could take nothing but hot tea. But calm having returned after being in the air for 10 or 15 minutes, I would develop a wolfish appetite.

So it was this time: first a feeling of pleasure, then profound agitation, and then that wonderful composure and confidence.

We took off on July 12, 1937. The start was an unusually difficult one.

It may be said with certainty that if the plane had carried another 200 pounds the runway would have been too short for the takeoff.

The end of the runway was startlingly near, and I had to lift the plane steeply to keep the wheels from touching the rough ground beyond its edge. We were hardly off the ground when we began to retract the landing gear. I repeat, never have I had to make so difficult a takeoff.

We had barely reached an altitude of 1,100 feet when the earth was veiled from our sight by mist. We mounted to 2,620 feet, and then flew in a corridor between two layers of clouds. Only two-and-a-half hours later, at a height of 3,610 feet, did we emerge clear of them. On the right, the sun broke through a bank of feathery clouds.

After five hours of flight, Yumashev took my place at the controls, and I addressed myself to some refreshment. We did not see land again until we reached Kolguev Island. On the basis of the speed and time of flight, Danilin calculated that we were approaching the island. Yumashev brought the plane down below the clouds and we saw Kolguev Island beneath us. We descended to about 650 feet. The plane was buffeted violently. At this height we passed over the spot where the referee of the Central Aeronautical Club of the U.S.S.R. was to register our transit. Had it not been for this, of course, we would not have descended so low and subjected our craft to the risk of being smashed by the heavy jolting. Yumashev lifted the plane to its former altitude. I replaced him at the controls.

Down below, the blue waters of the Barents Sea were visible. We were heading for Novaya Zemlya. We first spied it at a distance of 60 miles. As we approached within 30 miles of it, a picture of unusual beauty and mystery opened before us. From afar, Novaya Zemlya looked like the sunlit shore of a southern sea, with long sandy banks of vivid hue, reminiscent of sunshine and warmth.

A layer of strato-cumulus cloud approached from the left and concealed the sea. Over Novaya Zemlya we twice descended to a level of 1,000-1,300 feet to have our flight registered. We then slightly altered our course to hit the 120th meridian at the spot where it led straight through Rudolf Island to the North Pole and then on to California. Here we again rose above the clouds.

A white veil appeared on the horizon and covered the sky. This was an approaching cyclone. Several hours passed. Yumashev informed me that he had detected some dark spots below which must be Franz Josef Land. Soon we spotted the snowy summits of the archipelago. We could feel the breath of an approaching cyclone.

Strata of black cloud and humpy cumuli again floated by. The scene was again overcast.

The only way we could avoid cyclones was to rise above them. We firmly stuck to our determination not to depart from our schedule unless absolutely necessary, and not to diverge from our course under any circumstances. Only forward, and only along a straight line, was our motto.

We had already reached an altitude of over 13,000 feet; the temperature had fallen to −16°C. Clouds barred our way. Nothing was to be seen. We kept our course by the radio signals from Rudolf Island, which now lay behind us. We flooded the propeller with liquid to prevent ice forming.

We continued to ascend. I noticed that the windows of the cockpit were covered with a crust of ice. Only at a height of 14,700 feet, where the temperature was −21°C., did they become transparent again. We nosed our way through high cumulus clouds. Then again flew blindly.

It suddenly grew lighter and the plane emerged from the clouds. Below us lay a white sea of feathery cloud. The sun shone brightly. We breathed freely.

Fighting our way through two cyclones, we approached the North Pole. We had already been in the air 24 hours. During this time all we had seen of the earth was the stretch between Shchelkovo and Zagorsk — two towns lying close to Moscow — a patch of Kolguev Island, the peaks of Novaya Zemlya, and about 125 miles of sea. All the rest of our route had been covered by clouds. We had flown either above them or through them.

As we passed in the vicinity of Papanin's camp on the drifting ice floe, we could not refrain from radioing a message of greeting to the explorers. This was on July 13 at 2:07 A.M. Here is the message:

"Greetings to the conquerors of the Arctic, Papanin, Krenkel, Shirshov, and Fyodorov, from the crew of the RD No. 25-1, Gromov, Danilin, Yumashev."

An hour later, to be exact, at 3:14 A.M., we passed over the North Pole. We were then at an altitude of 8,850 feet and were making a speed of 100 mph. The temperature of the air was −8°C. The crew were in excellent spirits.

Yumashev was at the controls. I went to lie down. I slept soundly for an hour and awoke with a keen appetite. I had hardly taken a bite when I observed a dark bank ahead of us. Here was a cyclone waiting for us on this side of the Pole. I took my place at the second controls to help Yumashev; but the cyclone proved to be feebler than its predecessors, and in half an hour the fight was over.

The weather cleared and we flew beneath a bright polar sun. From time to time, through breaks in the clouds, we saw the ice beneath us, traversed by fissures. The scene was grand but monotonous. The icy wilderness seemed endless.

After a while we perceived some dark patches against the clouds on the horizon. The nearer we approached, the more distinct they became. Suddenly we saw they were cliffs. Land! This was Patrick Island.

The breaks in the clouds became more frequent. The sea between the islands and the mainland was covered by white humpy ice, spattered with emerald and blue patches. The sun became dimmed. Clouds passed over us from time to time. All this lent the scene a mysterious and oppressive, yet majestic air.

The Canadian tundra appeared. The sky cleared. Unknown land stretched beneath us: numberless lakes of varying size and shape, bogs, rivers, and scrub, gradually passing into forest. This monotonous landscape stretched as far as the Rocky Mountains, which well deserve their name.

While over Canadian territory we heard for the last time the signals of the Moscow radio station which had been maintaining contact with our plane. We were at that moment at a distance of 3,725 miles from the capital of the Soviet Union.

The Rockies were covered with clouds. Keeping our course along the 120th meridian, we gradually ascended and successfully negotiated the mountain peaks. Beyond the Rockies we flew hemmed in by clouds. Ice suddenly began to form on the plane. Both the speed indicators failed. We descended, and only at a height of 9,800 feet did we emerge from the danger zone.

Shifting our course 10° or 15° to the right, we reached the shores of the Pacific in the vicinity of Seattle. An hour later the clouds above the hills evaporated, but the shore and sky were still veiled. Ahead of us, a splendid blue sky could be seen. This gave us hope that we would have fine weather during the night.

The first real night of the flight began. This was between Seattle and San Francisco. We espied the shore through breaks in the clouds. Below us gleamed the beacons of flying fields, and the lights of cities and villages. We flew beneath a clear sky. To the right lay the Pacific, veiled by clouds; down below lay the land. From our height of about 10,000 feet we could distinguish a chain of lighthouses. A head wind blew; it seemed as if we would never reach San Francisco.

We felt the effects of fatigue. The gas indicator was very encouraging. As we approached San Francisco, we saw that we could fly farther, and inquired of other flying fields whether they could receive us. We were informed that the flying fields in Los Angeles and San Diego would be covered by mist in the morning. We were referred to other flying fields, which were not easy to discover on the map.

However, our gas supply would permit several more hours of flying, so we radioed: "Have passed San Francisco; are continuing our flight." Yumashev and Danilin asked whether we ought not to inform the Soviet government that we had beaten the world distance record; but I had firmly made up my mind not to give way to jubilation, and not to send any messages until our flight was over and our plane safely landed.

It was late in the night when we reached the midway point between San Francisco and Los Angeles. The line of beacons swerved to the left. We kept straight on. Dawn was already breaking when we crossed the Cordilleras, which were not very high at this point, and flew over San Jacinto. We left Los Angeles behind us to the right, and headed for San Diego.

We were out of luck. The Mexican border was too near to permit us continuing our flight to the south and thus increasing our distance record.

The flying fields in the southernmost part of California and the whole strip, 30 miles wide, between coast and mountains were covered by morning mist. We were therefore obliged to turn back. We circled around for half an hour in search of a suitable landing place.

When I decided to land there was still enough fuel in the tanks for another six hours of flying. Anyhow, we had already beaten the world distance record some 200 miles north of San Francisco. After a careful scrutiny of the flying ground at Marchfield, we searched around for a somewhat larger landing place, for our now lightened plane demanded a good approach and would require a rather lengthy running space before coming to a standstill. We selected the only large, although rather uneven field, in this semiwilderness, and 62 hours 17 minutes after the takeoff in Moscow we made a successful landing some three miles from San Jacinto, California.

Reckoned in a straight line, we had flown 6,302 miles. Our plane was severely shaken and jolted on landing because of the hard, rough ground, but neither it nor the equipment suffered the slightest damage.

Danilin, our navigator, was the first to alight. There was not a soul to be seen, but a minute later he noticed an old and dilapidated automobile bounding over the hummocks toward us. A young man jumped out and addressed Danilin in English. We had provided for such an emergency in Moscow and had had the following note written for us in English: "We are Soviet airmen flying to America from Moscow across the North Pole. Please inform the Soviet Ambassador in Washington, the local authorities, and the nearest flying field that we have safely landed."

The young man leaped into his car and dashed to the telegraph office. A moment later the field was invaded by people and automobiles. Learning that we had flown from Moscow, the inhabitants of San Jacinto at once began to assail us with requests for our autographs. A military airplane arrived from March Field. The major placed a guard on our plane and bore its crew off in an automobile to March Field. There referees were appointed to examine our barographs and gas tanks and to determine the coordinates of our landing place.

After this we were no longer our own masters. We were visited by not less than a hundred press reporters and photographers daily. After our long journey we were allowed only three hours to rest in, although our obliging hosts of the American Air Force at March Field did everything in their power to make us comfortable. They even forbade all flying in the neighborhood during the three hours we were asleep so as not to disturb our rest.

Telegrams came pouring in. I was already awake when congratulations arrived from Comrade Stalin and from the leaders of the Communist party of the Soviet Union and of the Soviet government. What could we reply to such a mark of attention? My comrades and I sent a return message to the Kremlin in Moscow containing the assurance that we would be happy to perform any other commission for the benefit of our beloved country.

If we were asked what part of our journey from the U.S.S.R. to America seemed to us most dangerous, we would say that it was the route from San Diego to New York. . . . We were deafened by the shouts of welcome, rendered hoarse by the speeches we delivered at banquets, and blinded by the endless magnesium flashes of the ubiquitous reporters and photographers.

The Americans are great admirers of technical progress. I think that the cordial reception we were accorded by the authorities and the enthusiastic welcome we were given everywhere by the American people must be chiefly regarded as a tribute to the technical achievements of Soviet aviation. Our flight was not undertaken for sensational purposes; our aim was a technical one — to establish the shortest air route between the U.S.S.R. and the United States. There was a fairly large amount of fuel left in our tanks when we landed, and had we desired we could have continued our flight still farther.

We flatter ourselves that our flight has helped to strengthen the ties of friendship between the two countries. It has also performed no little service in respect to exchange of experience between the aircraft industries of the two countries. We have still a lot to learn from the Americans in regard to flying and the making of flying machines.

It is with a feeling of warm regard and gratitude that I recall my meetings with Upton Sinclair, with Ernie Smith, the famous pilot who was the first to make a long-distance flight from San Francisco to Honolulu, and with many other Americans.

We were very cordially received by Mr. Roosevelt, President of the United States.

Mr. Roosevelt impressed us by his vigor, energy, and vitality, and by his simplicity of manner. Our meeting with him will always remain one of the most significant recollections of our American visit.

To sum up, it may be said that the great Land of the Soviets has made considerable progress in the sphere of aeronautics. Its designers and industry are producing excellent planes and motors. Splendid airmen are being turned out by its flying schools and by the Red Army. The U.S.S.R. is a flying country. There can be no doubt that in the near future new and striking records will be established in height, speed, and distance. I myself have no doubt that the Soviet Union will not lag behind other countries in this respect; if anything, it will outstrip them. It has all the potentialities for it.

PART TWO

CONQUERING THE ANTARCTIC BY AIR

Aviation cannot claim mastery of the globe until the South Pole and its vast surrounding mystery be opened up by airplane.

—RICHARD E. BYRD

Introduction

THE HISTORY of aviation in the Antarctic is short compared to that of the Arctic. The remoteness of that area, its lack of importance from a strategic point of view, and the greater difficulties involved in supporting operations there logistically contributed to this difference.

The first flight in the Antarctic was in a captive balloon. No free balloons or dirigibles have ever been used. The interval between the first flight and the next in an airplane was more than a quarter of a century. The lessons learned in the Arctic were put to good use; there were no fatalities in flying over the Antarctic continent for more than 50 years.

The first man to make an ascent in the Antarctic was Capt. Robert Falcon Scott of the British Navy. Commanding the British National Antarctic Expedition, Scott's interest was strongly scientific, which made his efforts the most important up to that time.

Scott departed from New Zealand on December 24, 1901, and reached Cape Adare on January 8, 1902, in his ship the Discovery. *After coasting along the mountain scarp of Victoria Land, his expedition arrived at Granite Harbor on January 20. Here Scott turned eastward and skirted the Ross Ice Barrier. Later he discovered King Edward VII Land, but, finding no suitable winter quarters, decided to return to McMurdo Sound. En route at "Balloon Bight" on February 4, 1902, Scott made his ascent in a tethered balloon and verified the existence of vast glaciers extending in all directions to the south. His associate, Ernest Shackleton, also ascended and took photographs — the first aerial shots ever taken in the Antarctic.*

Scott made many other significant discoveries in the three years he spent on this first expedition. He wanted to be first to reach the South Pole and almost made it on his last expedition of 1910-13. However, he was beaten to the prized goal by Roald Amundsen who had arrived there only a few days before. The brave explorer and scientist and his four companions died on the return journey. While he had not been first to the Pole, he had achieved another "first." As he himself said it, he had earned "the honor of being the first aeronaut to make an ascent in the Antarctic Regions." It was the first and last time that lighter-than-air craft were used in the Antarctic.

Balloon Ascent Over Antarctica

Captain Robert F. Scott

IT WAS SIR JOSEPH HOOKER who first suggested the carriage of a balloon for obtaining a view over the great southern ice-wall, and when, after much difficulty, the necessary funds for this equipment had been raised, we had decided that the best thing for our purpose was one of the small captive balloons used by the army for lifting a single observer.

Thanks to the sympathy of the War Office we had been enabled to purchase a complete equipment of this description, consisting of two balloons, which, when neatly folded, occupied very little space, and a quantity of hydrogen gas, carried in steel cylinders at high pressure, which occupied a great deal. Indeed, it had been a great problem where in our small ship to stow these cylinders, of which there were more than 50 containing something over three fills for the balloon, and it was only by placing them on top of the deckhouses and by utilizing every other space about the deck that we had managed to solve it.

And as it was of little use to carry such a costly outfit without a knowledge of how to employ it, before leaving England I had taken advantage of the kind suggestion of the chief of the ballooning department at Aldershot, Colonel Templer, R.E., and had sent two officers and three men to receive some instruction at his hands.

I now found that although officers and men had regarded their short course as a most excellent diversion, they had picked up most of the wrinkles and had learned to proceed about their work in the most businesslike maner.

First a large sailcloth was spread on the snow, and a number of cylinders carried out and placed nearby. Then the balloon was taken out with tender care, laid on the sailcloth and connected to the cylinders with many small pipes. As the gas gradually inflated the empty case, the sticky folds were carefully straightened out until the time came for the process of "crowning" the balloon, when the gradually filling carcass was centralized and covered with its net, well weighted with sandbags.

The contents of cylinder after cylinder were added, until gradually our balloon became a thing of life swaying about in the gentle breeze; but the temperature was down to 16°, and owing to the contraction of the gas, wrinkles were still visible on its surface after it had absorbed its correct allowance of 16 cylinders containing 500 cubic feet apiece, and it was not until we had brought out and emptied three additional ones that its name "Eva" could be read on a smooth, unwrinkled surface.

The honor of being the first aeronaut to make an ascent in the Antarctic Regions, perhaps somewhat selfishly, I chose for myself, and I may further confess that in so doing I was contemplating the first ascent I had made in any region, and as I swayed about in what appeared a very inadequate basket and gazed down on the rapidly diminishing figures below, I felt some doubt as to whether I had been wise in my choice.

The honor of being the first man to go aloft over the Antarctic Continent goes to Capt. Robert F. Scott. Shown here looking for pack ice through a telescope, Scott ascended in a captive balloon on February 4, 1902, and verified the existence of vast glaciers extending in all directions to the south.
National Archives Photo

Meanwhile the balloon continued to rise as the wire rope attached to it was eased, until at a height of about 500 feet it was brought to rest by the weight of the rope; I heard the word "sand" borne up from below and remembered the bags at my feet; the correct way to obtain greater buoyancy would have been gradually to empty these over the side of the car, but with thoughtless inexperience I seized them wholesale and flung them out, with the result that the *Eva* shot up suddenly, and as the rope tightened commenced to oscillate in a manner that was not at all pleasing. Then, as the rope was slackened, I again ascended, but, alas! only to be again checked by the weight of the rope at something under 800 feet. Our wire rope was evidently too heavy to allow greater altitude, and the only lighter one we possessed seemed not quite within the bounds of safety should the wind increase.

But, as it was, my view was very extended, and probably afforded as much information as would have been obtained in a loftier position. The following I take from my diary:

"Here the nature of the barrier surface toward the south could be seen well. South of the rising slope ahead of the ship I had expected to see a continuous level plain, but to my surprise found that the plain continued in a series of long undulations running approximately east and west, or parallel to the barrier edge; the first two undulations could be distinctly seen, each wave occupying a space of two or three miles, but beyond that, the existence of further waves was only indicated by alternate light and shadow, growing fainter in the distance. In the far south a bank of cloud had all the appearance of high land, but such indications are now too well known not to be received with caution, and even as I looked through my glasses, faint changes in outline were perceptible. Far over the snow expanse a small black dot represented our sledge party; they must have been nearly eight miles away, and their visibility shows how easily a contrast can be seen on the monotonous gray of the snow."

When I again descended to the plain, Shackleton took my place, armed with a camera, and to this we are indebted for the photographs, which, whilst they constitute a record of the incident, naturally fail to give the faint differences of light and shadow which indicated the barrier undulations. One gives a good idea, however, of the inlet in which we lay, and another is remarkable for its reproduction of the patchy nature of the snow surface. This exhibits one of the types of surface over which we had to drag our sledges for so many weary miles. I had hoped that in the afternoon other officers and men would have been able to ascend, and especially our engineer, Mr. Skelton, and those of his department who had so successfully inflated the balloon, but the wind was gradually increasing, and our captive began to sway about and tug so persistently at its moorings that it became necessary to deflate it.

After Robert F. Scott's ascent by balloon in 1902, no further use of any type of aircraft was made until a decade after World War I. However, Sir Douglas Mawson, the first man to use wireless in Antarctica, planned to take a Vickers monoplane with "a special sledge runner undercarriage" with him on his Australasian Expedition of 1911-14. Because of an accident in Australia before departure, the wings were detached and the craft was converted to an "air-tractor sledge."

In 1920, J. L. Cope and Sir Hubert Wilkins planned to use aircraft declared surplus by the Royal Air Force to survey King Edward VII Land, but the project died for lack of public support. Sir Ernest Shackleton purchased a small Avro seaplane for his 1921-22 expedition but because of a change in itinerary, the plane was not shipped from Capetown. Its pilot, Maj. C. R. Carr, did arrive with Shackleton to become the first fully qualified pilot to set foot on the Antarctic Continent, although he had no opportunity to fly.

Immediately after Wilkins and Eielson made the first successful crossing of the Arctic from Alaska to Spitsbergen (1928) they began planning for a similar venture at the opposite end of the earth. Within the same year, the two men became the first in history to fly over both polar regions.

First Flight in Antarctica

John Grierson

THE PLAN was to set up their main base at Deception Island, whither *Hektoria*, through the storms and mountainous seas prevailing in that area, conveyed them, and then make an aerial survey to try and discover an advanced base about 600 miles to the south. Supplies would have to be brought forward by means of a number of ferry flights, for which one airplane would be used, whilst Sir Hubert prepared the other for a flight of some 2,000 miles across the unexplored region lying to the west, and ending up in the area of King Edward VII Land and the Bay of Whales. Such an arrangement presupposed that a favorable site could be found for operating his Lockheed Vega at full load, but the actual conditions they met that season were very disappointing.

In early November, when they landed from the ship, there was a notable lack of snow-covering on the land or firm ice in the bay, so much so that all ideas of using skis on the airplanes had to be abandoned for the time being. This really was bad luck because the records showed that for 14 years previously the bay had been covered in smooth ice about seven feet thick in November, remaining firm and solid until about Christmas. Now, when they went to examine the bay at close quarters, the ice was found to be less than two feet thick. Either the mildness and raininess of the season or the bay had melted the ice at its edges and honeycombed it in the center. This meant that the surface was uneven and the whole sheet would be liable to break up in a storm, thus sinking the airplane if it were left out.

Their two Lockheed Vegas were the first complete airplanes ever to reach Antarctica. Previously, an attempt to fly had been unsuccessful due to a certain lack of correlation in the stores supply organization; this had the unhappy consequence, in 1913, that when Sir Douglas Mawson landed an R.E.P. airplane in Adelie Island, it was found to be complete in all respects except for wings, which, in some unforeseen manner, had missed the boat. The Wilkins-Hearst Expedition now assembled their two airplanes, having found a spot on a hillside that seemed to offer limited possibilities for wheeled takeoffs. It was not very good, consisting of volcanic "tuff" which is a cokelike substance with a marked propensity for cutting into rubber tires, but they thought they could do a test flight from it, using this as an opportunity to look around and find a better place from the air.

On November 16 the first flight was made by Eielson, though it was not long on account of the cloudy weather, and the hope of searching for other landing areas had to be abandoned. Sir Hubert went with him on this auspicious occasion — the very first time that man had flown in Antarctica. Ten days later both airplanes took the air in better weather and searched for more expansive "airdrome." The results were disappointing since, although the machines were up several hours and flew in opposite directions, it was obvious that the lack of snow cover was general throughout the region, and there seemed to be nothing flatter than the scruffy bit of volcanic tuff they were already using. Either the terrain was high and mountainous, or the low-lying areas, where covered in snow to any depth, were badly crevassed.

A few days later Eielson was flying and thought it looked as though the ice for the big bay in Deception Island should be firm enough for landing. He went down to prove his point, only to find unhappily that he was wrong and, at the end of his run, went slap through the ice into the chilly water. Luckily Ben climbed out unhurt, but it was only thanks to the help of 20 whalers that they were able to pull the poor wooden airplane out of the hole in the ice, and manhandle it to a safe position where repairs could be carried out. Floats were fitted and, with these on, Crosson flew off the ice and landed the seaplane in the water alongside the ship. There was too much ice in the sea to make this sort of activity enjoyable; also when Crosson brought the machine in, he killed a number of seabirds as he landed, which was quite dangerous for him. There was therefore no alternative but to try and make the best of their patch of tuff, by smoothing a track down between the mounds of lava, a process not easily done without proper machinery. To get any kind of a strip, they had to labor for days with wheelbarrows, buckets, rakes, and shovels — almost with bare hands in fact — to achieve any semblance of leveling. Their "site" included two small hills and three ditches to be crossed, and on either side they threw up a wall of great stones removed from the track. The Vega needed a run of 900 yards to be really safe, but the greatest length they could get was a fraction over 800, and even that included two 20-degree bends. The eventual track was 40 feet wide and a soft gravelly sort of surface over the volcanic cinders, but it was the best they could do from such a squiggly runway. Wilkins would be lucky to get into the air with not much more than half his full load of petrol.

A ski-landing-ground over hard snow would have been much better. With wheels they knew that it would be most improbable that a landing could be made anywhere away from this one base, because the chance of finding another spot of levelish ground was so remote, whereas with skis there would surely have been some spots of ice or snow to allow a safe forced landing along the coast. Restricted as they were by weight considerations, they could only carry enough emergency rations for two weeks at the rate of 24 ounces per man, per day; these consisted of biscuits, pemmican, chocolate, nuts, raisins, and malted milk. In the cabins of the airplanes lay packs handy to swing into position on the backs of the aircrew, so that they could grab them the moment a forced landing was imminent. Each one was arranged to be independent of the other's supply, whereby if one man was lost through the ice, the other could carry on. In addition to his pack, each man carried block and tackle for pulling himself out of crevasses — an eventuality which could easily happen here.

Although in Antarctica the summer generally lasts from Novemвeι to the end of February, in Graham Land the good weather ends about the end of the calendar year. There was thus little time left for Wilkins to do his work this season, so when December 20 turned out to be a perfect day, he immediately jumped into his airplane with Eielson and took off from their rather curious airdrome at 8:20 A M. They climbed to 6,000 feet on a southerly heading, intending to cross the main Graham Land plateau to the east, but in the vicinity of Trinity Land, about 30 miles from Deception, the top of the plateau was still above them. It was supposed to be only 5,000 feet (rather like the mountains of Alaska) so once more it was evident that the existing maps were wrong. The top, from their present viewpoint, looked as if it could not be less than 8,000 feet, which made them hold off to the west and continue to climb to over 8,000 feet until they had enough height to head east across the precipitous escarpment of the tableland from Salveson Bay. Sir Hubert wrote: "Far to the south we could see a 'water sky' and to the west of our heading were long ice-free fjords, almost severing Graham Land." (A water sky consists of dark patches in the sky caused by the reflection of open water on the clouds.) As their machine flew above the barrier ice, on the east coast of Graham Land and along the edge of the Weddell Sea, Wilkins noted, "We could see beneath us huge crevasses into which our machine could have fallen and left no trace." Such were the sights to meet the eyes of these first men ever to look down from the air upon Antarctica, the vast continent of windswept ice and mountains which has a particular eeriness of its own because, unlike the Arctic, it seems that man has never inhabited this land, within the range of existing knowledge. The nearest approach to the climate having been formerly favorable to sustaining life was evidenced by the fossil of a semitropical plant brought back by John Rymill's Expedition in 1936. But the scientists who examined the fossil could not believe that the plant had been growing more recently, from its appearance, than 150 million years ago, when Antarctica must have been a warmer place, and might have been able to support man, had he then existed. It is even possible that this subcontinent was located nearer the main landmasses in those days.

At ten o'clock there appeared to be large or very low cloud ahead, "or perhaps," wrote Sir Hubert, "it is wind which over the Arctic

Eielson and Wilkins at Spitsbergen in 1928. Within the same year, they also conquered the Antarctic by air.

Wide World Photos

pack ice I know from experience, is indicated by a milk-white sky upon the horizon." Evidently his diagnosis was right, because some two hours later they struck a region of violent bumps, being the turbulence caused by strong winds. Now the plane was crossing the Antarctic Circle, and what appeared to be an ice-filled fjord on their starboard, cutting across the land, was allotted the name of Crane Channel. Nearby in the cliffs were black seams which looked to Wilkins as though they might be coal.

After they had been airborne for nearly five hours and it was about time to go home, they had become convinced that Graham Land was not a peninsula but a series of islands. Near their turning point Wilkins spotted two more glaciated openings, seemingly cutting the land from east to west. The northerly one, which was the lesser, he called Casey Channel. This was seen to "narrow in its center but appeared to hold only level ice, widening again in the distance, and we felt sure that the ice in the channel rests on land below sea level. We named it Casey Channel and the island south of it Scripps Island." Along the south coast of this island, there appeared to be another channel, which they named Lurabee, followed by a group of islands they called the Finley Islands.

To get a better view of their discoveries, the airmen had now descended to 2,000 feet and they saw what appeared to be yet another and wider channel of ice running across just south of the Finley Islands. This they called Stefansson Strait, as a gracious compliment to the man whom young George had served so well in Alaska some 14 years ago: he estimated its width as being over 20 miles. The "mainland" to the south was christened Hearst Land after the famous newspaper magnate who had lent his support to the expedition.

The actual turning point was estimated to be at 71° 20′ S. and 64° 15′ W. Several photographs had been taken of the discoveries mentioned and a number of lesser inlets and apparent islands were also named. Now, as they headed north, a storm could be seen gathering, and anxiety was felt lest the conditions of the weather at Deception Island would not be good enough for landing. Luckily they found themselves favored by a tail wind, and as they recrossed Graham Land it could be seen that Deception was already covered by the edge of the storm. The clouds were to low to go under, making them stay on top at 5,000 feet, unaware of their exact position until suddenly, through a chance opening, Eielson spotted the encampment immediately beneath and managed to nose his way down without striking any mountains.

From this flight of nearly 1,300 miles, repercussions stemmed which shook the world of geography. J. M. Wordie, the noted Arctic and Antarctic scientist and explorer, declared: "This discovery (that Graham Land consists of islands and is not a continuous peninsula as previously thought) is the most important in Antarctica since Shackleton discovered the Beardmore Glacier and Polar Plateau in 1908."

Sir Hubert Wilkins was not the only successful Arctic pioneer who had his eyes on the Antarctic. Richard E. Byrd had also been planning to be the first man to fly over the South Pole. When he learned of Wilkins' plan to use an airplane to survey the Antarctic, he went to Wilkins with a document he wanted him to sign which was a promise not to make the attempt on the South Pole before he (Byrd) had a chance. Wilkins did not sign but assured Byrd that he was only interested in survey work.

As Wilkins and Eielson were carrying out their pioneer flights, Byrd was carefully equipping the largest expedition ever planned, to make his assault. He arrived on the continent in December, 1928, with three ski-equipped planes — a Ford trimotor, a Fokker, and a Fairchild. The planes were fitted out with new aerial navigation instruments, many of which were designed by Byrd himself.

By the end of November, 1929, after firmly establishing "Little America," as a base and making many observation flights, the time seemed right for the Pole attempt. On November 28, Bernt Balchen, famed Norwegian polar flyer, warmed up the engines of the Ford trimotor, named the Floyd Bennett *in honor of the pilot who had taken Byrd over the top of the world. Harold June, copilot, Capt. Ashley C. McKinley, aerial mapping specialist, and Byrd climbed aboard. It was the beginning of another epic flight for Byrd that would open up a new era in the history of Antarctic exploration.*

My Flight to the South Pole

Richard E. Byrd

No THOROUGHBRED went into a race more carefully, scrupulously groomed than was the *Floyd Bennett* before the polar flight. Responsibility for its performance rested with no single man. It lay on the shoulders of the whole camp. It was a sobering responsibility, and I think that every man felt it in his heart.

We were done with these details shortly after three o'clock. At the last moment we decided to take aboard an additional 100 gallons of gasoline. There was no telling what kind of winds we would meet. If head winds, then the extra quantity of fuel would be invaluable. If not, we could dump it overboard before we reached the "Hump."

The total weight was approximately 15,000 pounds.

Haines came up with a final report on the weather. "A 20-mile wind from the south at 2,000 feet." It meant clear skies to the south. I went into my office and picked up a flag weighted with a stone from Floyd Bennett's grave. It seemed fitting that something connected with the spirit of this noble friend who stood with me over the North Pole, on May 9, 1926, should rest as long as stone endures at the bottom of the world.

There were handshakes all around, and at 3:29 we were off. The skis were in the air after a run of 30 seconds — an excellent takeoff. I was greatly relieved. A calm expectation took hold of my mind. Having started, we were certainly going to get somewhere.

There was a flashing glimpse of the men clustered near the runway — those splendid fellows whose willing help and indestructible spirit have never faltered, no, not once — and we faced the south.

The moment the Ford leveled off, the impalpable haze with which we had contended so often confused the vision, and we lost several precious minutes before we found the trail. But if Haines' predictions were correct, this would not last for long.

Our course was laid along the meridian of the trail, which at that point was 143° 45′ W. Although the trail did not always follow that meridian, it would bring us finally to Axel Heiberg Glacier.

The sky began to clear, under the sweeping movements of a southeasterly wind, and presently blue sky showed ahead. Haines was right, as always. Slowly gaining altitude, we passed 20 Mile Depot, then 44 Mile Depot.

From time to time we lost the trail, as our altitude changed or our distance from it varied slightly. But invariably by steering a straight course with the Bumstead sun compass we picked it up again.

Presently the northern edge of the crevasses was underneath. The trail then followed meridian 163° 42′ W. The wind was still from the east and it was necessary to nose the plane 10° to the left of the course, to make good a straight course to the south. Had there been anyone below to see, he must have been surprised at the sight of a plane headed well to the east but flying steadily to the south. With this diagonal push tending to press us from our course it was necessary to check the course frequently with the drift indicator.

Had you been there to glance over the cabin of this modern machine which has so revolutionized polar travel, I think you would have been impressed most of all — perhaps first of all — with the pro-

Shown here are the four aircraft taken to Antarctica by the second Byrd Antarctic expedition. Left to right are the Kellett Autogyro, the Fairchild Pilgrim Monoplane, Curtiss-Wright Condor, and Fokker.

National Archives Photo

Snow can be a friend as well as an enemy in the polar regions. Here men of Byrd's second expedition are shown making a plane hangar of snow blocks for the Curtiss-Wright Condor to protect it during the long winter night.

National Archives Photo

fusion of gear in the cabin. There was a small sledge, rolled masses of sleeping bags, bulky food sacks, two pressure gasoline stoves, rows of cans of gasoline packed about the main tank forward, funnels for draining gasoline and oil from the engine, mounds of clothing, tents and so on, ad infinitum. There was scarcely room in which to move.

June had his radio in the after bulkhead on the port side. From time to time he flashed reports on our progress to the base. From the earphones strapped to his helmet ran long cords, so that he might move freely about the cabin without being obliged to take them off. His duties were varied and important. He had to attend to the motion picture camera, the radio and the complicated valves of the six gasoline tanks. Every now and then he relieved Balchen at the wheel, or helped him to follow the elusive trail.

McKinley had his mapping camera ready to go into action either on port or starboard side. It was for him and the camera he so sedulously served that the flight was made. The mapping of the corridor between Little America and the South Pole was one of the major objectives of the expedition.

Balchen was forward, bulking large in the narrow compartment, his massive hands on the wheel, now appraising the engines with a critical eye, now the dozen flickering fingers on the dials on the instrument board. Balchen was in his element. His calm, fine face bespoke his confidence and sureness. He was anticipating the struggle at the "Hump" almost with eagerness.

It was quite warm forward, behind the engines. But a cold wind swept aft through the cabin, causing one to be thankful for the protection of heavy clothes. When the skies cleared, the cabin was flooded with a golden light. The sound of the engines and propellers filled it. One had to shout to make oneself heard. From the navigation table aft, where my charts were spread out, a trolley ran to the control cabin. Over it I shot to Balchen the necessary messages and courses. On receiving them, he turned and smiled his understanding.

That, briefly, is the picture, and a startling one it makes in contrast with that of Amundsen's party which had pressed along this same course 18 years before. A wing, pistons, and flashing propellers had taken the place of runners, dogs, and legs. Amundsen was delighted to make 25 miles per day. We had to average 90 mph to accomplish our mission. We had the advantages of swiftness and comfort, but we had as well an enlarged fallibility. A flaw in a piece of steel, a bit of dirt in the fuel lines or carburetor jets, a few hours of strong head winds, fog, or storm — these things, remotely beyond our control, could destroy our carefully laid plans and nullify our most determined efforts.

Still, it was not these things that entered our minds. Rather it was the thought of the "Hump," and how we should fare with it.

Soon after passing the crevasses we picked up again the vast escarpment to the right. More clearly than before we saw the white-blue streams of many glaciers discharging into the Barrier, and several of the inner and higher snow-clad peaks glistened so brightly in the sun as to seem like volcanoes in eruption.

Our altitude was then about 1,500 feet.

Now the Queen Maud Range loomed ahead. I searched again for the "appearance of land" to the east. Still the rolling Barrier — nothing else.

The quartering wind from the southeast blew with fluctuating direction and velocity, imparting an angle of drift as high as 20° at times.

At 8:15 we had the Geological Party in sight — a cluster of little beetles about two dark topped tents. Balchen dropped to an altitude of about 750 feet, and McKinley put overboard the photographs of the Queen Maud Range and the other things we had promised to bring. The parachute canopy to which they were attached fluttered open and fell in gentle oscillations, and we saw two or three figures rush out to catch it. We waved to them, and then prepared for a settlement of the issue at the "Hump."

Up to this time the engines had operated continuously at cruising revolutions — 1,580 rpm's for the big center engine, 1,600 for the smaller engines outboard. Now Balchen opened them full throttle — 1,750 rpm's for the center engine, 1,700 for the two outboard — and the Ford girded its loins for the long, hard, fighting pull over the "Hump." We rose steadily. We were than about 60 miles north of the western portal of Axel Heiberg, and holding our course steadily on meridian 163° 45' W. with the sun compass.

I watched the altimeters, of which there were two in the navigation compartment. The fingers marched with little jumps across the face of the dial — 3,000 feet, 3,500, 4,000, 4,500. The Ford had her toes in, and was climbing fast.

Drawing nearer, we had edged 30° to the west of South, to bring not only Axel Heiberg but also Liv's into view. This was a critical period. I was by no means certain which I should choose. I went for-

The first flight over the South Pole was made in this three-engine Ford monoplane piloted by Bernt Balchen in November, 1929. Named the *Floyd Bennett* in honor of Byrd's pilot on the North Pole crossing, it was capable of lifting 15,000 pounds, and cruising at just over 100 mph. A Fokker and a Fairchild, both single-engine monoplanes, were also taken along on the expedition for short-range survey flights.
National Archives Photo

ward and took a position behind Balchen. We would figure this thing out together.

The schemes and hopes of the next few minutes were beset by many probabilities. Which would it be — Axel Heiberg or Liv's Glacier?

There was this significant difference between flying and sledging: we could not pause long for decision or investigation. Minutes stood for gasoline, and gasoline was precious. The waste of so little as half an hour of fuel in a fruitless experiment might well overturn the mathematical balance on which the success of the flight depended. The execution of the plan hung on the proper judgment of the route over the "Hump."

True, we had a 40 per cent safety factor over fuel needs to the

Pole and back. This, of course, was a theoretical margin. It was a precaution against depletion resulting from head winds, and its value could not be weakened by a mistake in judgment. In fact, head winds had already exhausted some of this reserve.

Yet how well, after all, could judgment forecast the ultimate result? There were few facts on which we might base a wise decision. We knew, for example, that the highest point of the pass of Axel Heiberg Glacier, which Amundsen reported, was 10,500 feet. We would know, in a very few minutes, after June had calculated the gasoline consumption, the weight of the plane. From that we could determine, according to the tables which we had worked out and were then before me, the approximate ceiling we would have. We would know, too, whether or not we should be able to complete the flight, other conditions being favorable.

These were the known elements. The unknown were burdened with equally important consequences. The structural nature of the head of the pass was wide or narrow; whether it would allow us room to maneuver in case we could not rise above it; whether it would be narrow and running with a torrent of down-pressing wind which would dash a plane, already hovering at its peak of maximum efficiency, to the glacier floor — these were things, naturally, we could not possibly know until the issue was directly at hand.

I stood beside Balchen, carefully studying the looming fortress, still wondering by what means we should attempt to carry it. With a gesture of the hand Balchen pointed to fog vapor rising from the black rock of the foothills which were Nansen's high priests — caused no doubt by the condensation of warm currents of air radiated from the sun-heated rocks. A thin layer of cloud seemed to cap Axel Heiberg's pass, and extended almost to Liv's Glacier. But of this we were not certain. Perhaps it was the surface of the snow. If cloud, then our difficulties were at hand. Even high clouds were resting on the floor of the uplifted plateau.

There was, then, a gamble in the decision. Doubtless a flip of the coin would have served as well. In the end, we decided to choose Liv's Glacier, the unknown pass to the right, which Amundsen had seen far in the distance and named after Dr. Nansen's daughter. It seemed to be wider than Axel Heiberg, and the pass not quite as high.

A few minutes after nine o'clock we passed near the intermediate base, which of course we could not see. Our altitude was then about 9,000 feet. At 9:15 we had the eastern portal on our left, and were ready to tackle the "Hump." We had discussed the "Hump" so often, had anticipated and maligned it so much, that now that it was in front of us and waiting in the flesh — in rock-ribbed glaciated reality — we felt that we were meeting an old acquaintance. But we approached it warily, respectfully, climbing steadily all the while with our maximum power, to get a better view of its none too friendly visage.

June, wholly unaffected by the immediate perplexities, went about his job of getting the plane in fighting trim. He ripped open the last of the fuel cans, and poured the contents into the main tank. The empty tins he dropped overboard, through the trapdoor. Every tin weighed two pounds; and every pound dropped was to our advantage. The fumes filled the cabin, offending one's stomach and eyes. June examined the gauges of the five wing tanks, then measured with a graduated stick the amount of fuel in the main tank. He jotted the figures on a pad, made a few calculations and handed me the results. Consumption had thus far averaged between 55 and 60 gallons per hour. It had taken us longer to reach the mountains than we had expected, owing to head winds. However, the extra fuel taken aboard just before we left had absorbed this loss and we actually had a credit balance. We had, then, enough gasoline to take us to the Pole and back.

With that doubt disposed of, we went at the "Hump" confidently.

We were still rising, and the engines were pulling wonderfully well. The wind was about abeam, and, according to my calculations, not materially affecting the speed.

Liv's Glacier was before us almost in its full sweeping entirety — a Niagric torrent doomed to rigidity, with frozen whirlpools and waterfalls. Far ahead it bent in a wide curve to the west of south. About 35 miles away it disappeared into a vague white surface — could it be the plateau? We then had nearly the whole of Nansen's foothills on the left. One of these formed the eastern portal of Liv's Glacier. When we first saw them on the base-laying flight, they had seemed to be high and imposing mountains; but now they were obscure and small. Nansen was on the left, to the southeast, and filled the horizon. The marbled walls of Fisher Mountain, with its company of stalwart foothills, was on the right, crowding into the horizon on the southwest. The ice line of the glacier, where it met the Barrier, was quite distinct; but the immense crevasses which we had seen before were softened and subdued by the difference in altitude, and now resembled the fluted surface of a washing board.

The floor of the glacier rose sharply, in a series of icefalls and terraces, some of which were well above the (then) altitude of the plane. These glacial waterfalls, some of which were from 200 to 400 feet high, seemed more beautiful than any precipitous stream I have ever seen. Beautiful yes, but how rudely and with what finality they would deal with steel and duralumin that was fated to collide with them at 100 mph.

About ten miles up, the glacier was given over to terrific crevasses, where the weight of the flow carried it against solid rock.

At this point the stream of air pouring down the pass roughened perceptibly. The great wing shivered and teetered as it balanced itself against the changing pressures. The wind from the left flowed against Fisher's steep flanks, and the constant, hammering bumps made footing uncertain. But McKinley steadily trained his 50-pound camera on the mountains to the left. The uncertainties of load and ceiling were not his concern. His only concern was photographs — photographs over which students and geographers might pore in the calm quiet of their studies. Had we gone down in a tailspin, I am sure that McKinley would have operated his camera all the way down.

The altimeters showed a height of 9,600 feet, but the figure was not necessarily exact. More likely than not, the barometric principle on which it operated was influenced by local changes in pressure. Nevertheless there were indications we were near the service ceiling of the plane.

The roughness of the air increased and became so violent that we were forced to swing slightly to the left, in search of calmer air. This brought us over a frightfully crevassed slope which ran up and toward Mount Nansen. We thus escaped the turbulent swirl about Fisher, but the down-surging currents here damped our climb. To the left we had the "blind" mountain glacier of Nansen in full view; and when we looked ahead we saw the plateau — a smooth, level plain of snow between Nansen and Fisher. The pass rose up to meet it.

In the center of the pass was a massive outcropping of snow-covered rock, resembling an island, which protruded above and separated the descending stream of ice. Perhaps it was a peak or the highest eminence of a ridge connecting Fisher and Nansen which had managed through the ages to hold its head above the glacial torrent pouring down from the plateau. But its particular structure or relationship was of small moment then. I watched it only with reference to the climb of the plane; and realized, with some disgust and more consternation, that the nose of the plane, in spite of the fact that Balchen had steepened the angle of attack, did not rise materially above the outcropping. We were still climbing, but at a rapidly diminishing rate of speed. In the rarefied air the heavy plane responded to the controls with marked sluggishness.

It was an awesome thing, creeping (so it seemed) through the narrow pass, with the black walls of Nansen and Fisher on either side, higher than the level of the wings, watching the nose of the ship bob up and down across the face of that lone chunk of rock. It would move up, then slide down. Then move up, and fall again. For perhaps a minute or two we deferred the decision; but there was no escaping it. If we were to risk a passage through the pass, we needed greater maneuverability than we had at that moment. The pass was uncomfortably narrow. Once we entered it there would be no retreat. It offered no room for turn. If power was lost momentarily or if the air became excessively rough, we could only go ahead, or down. We needed power, and there was only one way in which to get it.

June, anticipating the command, left the radio and put his hands on the dump valve of the main tank. A pressure of the fingers — that was all that was necessary — and in two minutes 600 gallons of gasoline would gush out. I signaled to wait.

Balchen held to the climb to the last degree of safety. But it was clear to both of us that he could not hold it long enough. Balchen began to yell and gesticulate, and it was hard to catch the words in the roar of the engines echoing from the cliffs on either side. But the meaning was manifest. "Overboard — overboard — 200 pounds!"

Which would it be — gasoline or food?

If gasoline, I thought, we might as well stop there and turn back. We could never get back to the base from the Pole. If food, the lives of all of us would be jeopardized in the event of a forced landing. Was that fair to McKinley, Balchen, and June? It really took only a moment to reach the decision. The Pole, after all, was our objective. I knew the character of the three men. They were not so lightly to be turned aside. McKinley, in fact, had already hauled one of the food bags to the trapdoor. It weighed 125 pounds.

"Harold, a bag of food overboard," I said to June. He signaled to McKinley. The brown bag was pushed out and fell, spinning to the glacier. The improvement in the flying qualities of the plane was noticeable. The Floyd Bennett took another breath and renewed the climb.

Now the down-currents over Nansen became stronger. The plane trembled and rose and fell, as if struck bodily. We veered a trifle to the right, searching for helpful rising eddies. The issue was still in doubt and Balchen's irritation with the inexorable laws which limited our altitude waxed and grew profane. The head of the pass was still on a level with the plane's line of flight. Balchen was flying shrewdly. He maintained flight at a sufficient distance below the absolute ceiling of the plane to retain at all times enough maneuverability to make him master of the ship. But he was hard pressed by circumstances; and I realized that unless the plane was further lightened, the final thrust might bring us perilously close to the end of our reserve.

"More," Bernt shouted. "Another bag."

McKinley shoved a second bag through the trapdoor, and this time we saw it hit the glacier, and scatter in a soundless explosion. Two hundred and fifty pounds of food — enough to feed four men for a month — lay on that lifeless waste.

The sacrifice was the saving factor. The plane, literally, rose with a jump; the engines dug in and we soon showed a gain in altitude of from 300 to 400 feet. It was what we wanted. We would clear the pass with about 500 feet to spare. Balchen gave a shout of joy. It was just as well. We could dump no more food. There was nothing left to dump except McKinley's camera. I am sure that had he been asked to put it overboard, he would have done so instantly; and I am equally sure he would have followed the precious instrument with his own body.

The next few minutes dragged. We moved at a speed of 77 nautical miles per hour through the pass, with the black walls of Nansen on our left. The wing gradually lifted above them. The floor of the plateau stretched in a white immensity to the south. We were over the dreaded "Hump" at last. The Pole lay dead ahead over the horizon, less than 300 miles away. It was then about 9:45 (I did not note the exact time. There were other things to think about).

Gaining the plateau, we studied the situation a moment and then shifted course to the southward. Nansen's enormous towering ridge, lipped by the plateau, shoved its heavily broken sides into the sky. To the right of it Ruth Gade's tented arch gradually became, as we

129

watched, a white inverted porcelain bowl. A whole chain of mountains began to parade across the eastern horizon. How high they are I cannot say, but surely many of them must be in excess of 15,000 feet, to stand so boldly above the rim of the 10,000-foot plateau. Peak on peak, ridge on ridge, draped in snow garments which brilliantly reflected the sun, they extended in a solid array to the southeast. But can one really say they run in that direction? The lines of direction are so bent in this region that 150 miles farther on, even were they to continue in the same general straight line, they must run north of east. This is what happens near the Pole.

We laid our line of flight on the 171st meridian.

On the right was a range, which appeared to trend to the south nearly to 87° and more or less parallel to and perhaps a little beyond the 180th meridian — a line of low-hung peaks standing above the swelling folds of the plateau. Now, with the full panorama before us, in all its appalling ruggedness and gothic massiveness, we had a conception of the ice age in its flood tide. Here was the core, the center point of the Antarctic ice sheet. How deep it lay under us, whether 1,000 feet or 8,000 feet, we could not tell. But deep it must be, thus to dominate nearly all but the highest peaks which rimmed it, like the walls of a dam. Seeking an outlet to relieve its incalculable pressures, it presses through the passes which become glacial spillways, and makes for the sea. The parade of the mountains, the contrast of black and white, the upreaching peaks and the trisulcated troughs of the glaciers, the plateau spreading to an illusory horizon — it was something never to be forgotten.

The plateau seemed to be falling in a slope to the south. Our altitude was then between 10,500 and 11,000 feet. We were "riding" the engines, conscious of the fact that if one should fail we must come down. Once the starboard engine did sputter a bit, and Balchen nosed down while June rushed to the fuel valves. But it was nothing; to conserve fuel, Balchen had "leaned" the mixture too much. A quick adjustment corrected the fault, and in a moment the engine took up its steady rhythm. Moments like this one make a pioneering flight anything but dull; one moment everything is lovely, and the next is full of forebodings.

The drift indicator showed a variable wind from the east. To compensate for it, we had to point the nose of the plane an average of about 12° to the east, in order to steer a straight course for the Pole. The influence of the drift on the course was always a bothersome element. It had to be watched carefully, and any change in the angle of drift detected at once, so as to make good a straight course south. Fitted in the floor of the plane was a drift indicator which McKinley used in connection with his photographic work, and during the flight he constantly checked the drift with me. Whenever I noted any change in the direction or strength of the wind, I would steady Balchen on his course with the sun compass, first shaking the trolley line to attract his attention, then waving him on to the new course.

The basis of these calculations was the ground speed; and owing to the impossibility of determining the height of the plane above the snow, this value was not easily accessible. The altimeters register altitudes, only in reference to sea level. There is a way, however. By timing with a stopwatch how long it takes a crevasse, sastrugi, or smoke bomb to run the length of the drift indicator wire in the floor of the plane, and then turning north and passing over the object again, timing it a second time, it is possible by mathematics to get the speed.

Consequently, I spent a great deal of time kneeling on the floor of the plane, sighting sastrugi whenever I detected any change in drift. It was by no means a comfortable position. The temperature had dropped steadily since we reached the plateau, and when I opened the trapdoor a torrent of sub-zero atmosphere swirled in, numbing my face and hands.

These readings showed that while the engines were cruising at about 100 mph, the plane was actually moving over the snow at the rate of 90 statute mph.

From time to time June "spelled" Balchen at the controls; and Balchen would walk back to the cabin, flexing his cramped muscles. There was little thought of food in any of us — a beef sandwich, stiff as a board, and tea and coffee from a thermos bottle. It was difficult to believe that in recent history the most resolute men who had ever attempted to carry a remote objective, Scott and Shackleton, had plodded over this same plateau, a few miles each day, with hunger — fierce, unrelenting hunger — stalking them every step of the way.

Between 11:30 and 12:30 the mountains to the eastward began to disappear, gradually of course, dropping imperceptibly out of view, one after another. Not long after 12:30 the whole range had retreated from vision, and the plateau met the horizon in an indefinite line. The mountains to the right had long since disappeared.

At 12:38 I finally shot the sun. It hung, a ball of fire, just beyond south to the east, 21° above the horizon. So it was quite low, and we stared it in the eye. The sight gave me an approximate line of latitude, which placed us very near our position as calculated by dead reckoning. That dead reckoning and astronomy should check so closely was very encouraging. The position line placed us at Lat. 89° 4½′ S., or 55½ miles from the Pole. A short time later we reached an altitude of 11,000 feet. According to Amundsen's records, the plateau, which had risen to 10,300 feet, descended here to 9,600 feet. We were, therefore, about 1,400 feet above the plateau.

So the Pole, the mysterious objective, was actually in sight. But I could not yet spare it so much as a glance. Chronometers, drift indicators, and compasses are hard taskmasters.

Relieved by June, Balchen came aft and reported that visibility was not as good as it had been. Clouds were gathering on the horizon off the port bow and a storm, Balchen thought, was in the air. A storm was the last thing we wanted to meet on the plateau on the way back. It would be difficult enough to pass the Queen Maud Range in bright sunlight; in thick weather it would be suicidal. Conditions, however, were merely unpromising; not really bad, simply not good. If worse came to worse, we decided we could outrace the clouds to the mountains.

At six minutes after one o'clock, a sight of the sun put us a few miles ahead of our dead reckoning position. We were very close now. The sight was a check, but I depended more on the previous sight. At 1:14 Greenwich Civil Time, our calculations showed that we were at the Pole.

It is a confusing place, this imaginary point, the South Pole. All time meridians converge there. A person unfortunate enough to be living in the vicinity would have difficulty in telling just what time to keep. Time is reckoned by the interval between two successive crossings of the sun over the meridian at the place at which time is reckoned. As all meridians intersect at the South Pole, there is no particular meridian. The sun circles the sky at the same height above the snow horizon, and this height changes only an imperceptible amount every 24 hours. Directions, as we reckon them, would likewise mean nothing to this unfortunate creature. For unless he were traveling either north or south it would be impossible for him to walk in a straight line and still retain the same direction. His direction would change noticeably every few minutes; and to keep his

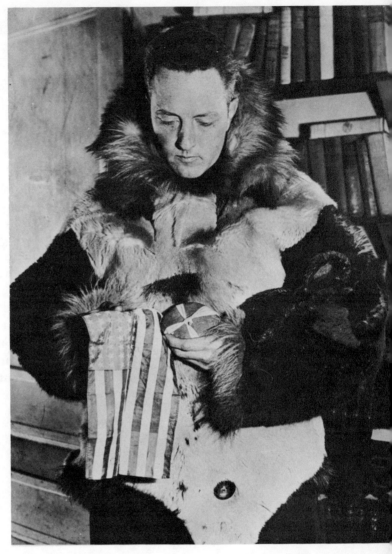

Richard E. Byrd was the first man to fly over both poles. He is shown here before the takeoff from Little America in 1929 for the South Pole flight. The U.S. flag he holds was weighted with a stone from the grave of Floyd Bennett, his pilot on the North Pole flight, and dropped at the geographical bottom of the earth.
National Archives Photo

original direction he would be forced to follow a spiral course.

A few minutes after the turn I opened the trapdoor and dropped over the calculated position of the Pole the small flag which was weighted with the stone from Bennett's grave. Stone and flag plunged down together. The flag had been advanced 1,500 miles farther south than it had ever been before our expedition reached the Antarctic. June radioed the following message to Little America: "My calculations indicate that we have reached the vicinity of the South Pole. Flying high for a survey. Byrd."

The altimeters indicated our altitude was 11,000 feet.

For a few seconds we stood over the spot where Amundsen had stood, December 14, 1911; and where Scott had also stood, 34 days later, reading the note which Amundsen had left for him. In their honor, the flags of their countries were again carried over the Pole. There was nothing now to mark that scene; only a white desolation and solitude disturbed by the sound of our engines. The Pole lay in the center of a limitless plain. No mountains were visible. In the direction of Little America visibility was good, and so it was on the left. But to the right, which is to say to the eastward, the horizon was covered with clouds. If mountains lay there, as some geologists believe, they were concealed and we had no hint of them.

And that, in brief, is all there is to tell about the South Pole. One gets there, and that is about all there is for the telling. It is the effort to get there that counts.

Ever since Byrd's successful flight to the South Pole, the airplane has remained the single most important tool of the explorer in the Antarctic. Lessons were learned by the flying crews on each flight; maintenance personnel on the ground acquired valuable experience between flights. The airplane, as a result, became even more reliable — and indispensable.

In the fall of 1929, Sir Hubert Wilkins returned to the Antarctic. Unable to use Deception Island as a base this time, he equipped his plane, a Lockheed Vega, with floats, and placed it aboard the William Scoresby operated by the British Discovery Committee to carry out oceanographic and biological surveys. Taking off from the edge of the ice pack, Wilkins' pilots were able to cross the ice belt that frequently surrounds much of the continent and make important discoveries. Ship-based operations by seaplanes became one of the most important means for exploring the large coastal areas for the next 20 years. It was this method that Norwegian whalers used from 1930 on to plot the coastlines of Enderby and Queen Maud Lands. This technique reached its greatest prewar success with the German Schwabenland Expedition of 1938-39 under Capt. Alfred Ritscher.

Prior to World War II, three basic methods of flying had been tried in the Antarctic — from land, from the snow, and from the sea. The first had been used by Wilkins but never from the continent itself. Byrd and Ellsworth used ski-equipped planes and achieved greater penetrations of the continent than anyone else. Ship-based operations were the most frequently used because they reduced the logistics problems considerably. No base construction was required, fuel was carried aboard ship, and all maintenance could be performed under relatively favorable conditions.

The Byrd Expedition of 1939-40 was the last major exploration effort for the duration of World War II. The forced technological improvements in aircraft and other means of transportation caused by the war were put to immediate use in the Antarctic as soon as the war was over. But there was a new kind of urgency injected into the exploration effort of the seventh continent. American military planners began to view with alarm the other great military power that had emerged from the war and was beginning to assert itself. The United States had to be prepared for polar warfare.

There were some military analysts who feared that full-scale military exercises in the northern polar regions would provoke the accusation that Uncle Sam was already planning to launch World War III. Operation Highjump was thus born in 1946; its mission was to train men and test equipment under polar conditions in the Ant-

135

arctic. In addition, it was to determine whether an air base could be established on the ice "with particular attention to later application of such techniques to operations in interior Greenland." A political task was also assigned: consolidate and extend United States sovereignty over the largest practicable area of the Antarctic Continent.

The Highjump expedition was divided into three groups: Eastern, Central, and Western. The Central Group was to push through the pack ice and establish an air base near the Little America site. Douglas R4D transports would take off from the carrier Philippine Sea and land at the new base. Exploration by air would proceed from there. The Eastern and Western Groups, using a seaplane tender as the main operations center, would sail around the continent in opposite directions using their seaplanes to explore the coastal regions as far as their range would permit. It was a huge undertaking, with 13 ships and 4,700 men taking part. Many "firsts" were established. Most interesting from the standpoint of polar aviation was the first launching of a heavily loaded land-based transport from the narrow deck of an aircraft carrier.

The First Air Base in Antarctica

Walter Sullivan

ON JANUARY 25, 1947, just one week after cargo was first lowered from the *Yancey*, the base was virtually ready to receive planes from the aircraft carrier *Philippine Sea*, which had arrived that day north of the pack and begun readying for her flight operations.

Seven hundred miles to the north an operation unique in aviation history was in the making — the launching of heavy, ski-equipped planes from an aircraft carrier. In planning the expedition many ingenious schemes had been discussed. One was to have the skis run down the flight deck in grease-filled troughs. Another was to sprinkle water on the deck so that it would freeze like a skating rink. Finally a broad ski was designed with a slot in the middle through which a wheel protruded.

The planes were twin-engined Douglas transports of the type designated DC-3 on the airlines. It was one of the most successful aircraft ever developed, for even in 1955, twenty years after its debut, there were four times as many planes of this type on the scheduled airlines of the world as any of the larger, more modern Douglas models. Six of them were assigned to the *Philippine Sea.*

Never had such large planes taken off from an aircraft carrier. Their wingspread was too wide for a normal takeoff down the length of the flight deck. Instead a shortened run had to be made diagonally across the forward part of the deck. Once the aircraft were in the air they could not return, since the flight deck was too short and narrow.

The carrier moved into a big bay in the edge of the pack at 68° 50′ South, 174° 40′ West, and in the evening of January 29, with the weather good both there and at Little America, the ship's bugler sounded "flight quarters." The plane crews threw waterproof bags containing a complete change of clothing into the planes in case they made a wet forced landing in the pack. Dry clothes, under such circumstances, would make the difference between life and death.

Admiral Byrd climbed into the first plane on the line as the ship headed into the wind and built up her speed to 30 knots. At the controls was Comdr. William M. Hawkes, who was to be in charge of the air unit at Little America. A line of tense faces down either side of the flight deck watched as he tested his controls and revved up the engines until the plane was straining at the leash. When he let go the brakes, the plane seemed at first to crawl, until abeam of the carrier's superstructure. Then Hawkes opened the jato bottles, letting loose jet blasts that gave the plane a tremendous boost. It leaped forward like a greyhound and climbed steeply into the air with 50 feet of flight deck to spare. The second plane got off with equal ease and the pair set forth together.

Hardly had they left the carrier and headed in over the pack, when the copilot saw the needle on the radio compass snap around and point toward Little America. It had picked up impulses of the powerful beacon on the Mount Olympus coming to them across almost 700 miles of floating white wasteland. Since this type of plane normally did not make long overwater hops, the aircrews were not used to being on their own navigationally. At home they normally flew from beacon to beacon. They therefore felt happy to have a guiding hand to lead them across the desolate regions below.

They sighted the ice shelf front from 60 miles away and, just six hours after taking off from the carrier, Hawkes set his plane down on the snow.

The landing gear worked beautifully. The wheels spun idly, leaving a shallow trough in the snow, while the skis carried the load. The second plane came in seven minutes later and both taxied over to where Admiral Cruzen and a small crowd were waiting to greet them.

As soon as word was received on the *Philippine Sea* that the first flights had arrived, the next two pairs were launched. All reached Little America safely, although the last plane had difficulty with both its radio and magnetic compass and was lost for several hours.

Not long after the planes arrived, the barometer began falling rapidly. The horizon almost vanished and a rising wind blew drift snow across the camp, obscuring landmarks. Preparations were rushed for the exploratory flights, the biggest job being to remove the heavy landing wheels on the six planes, but all work was soon brought to a standstill by the expedition's first blizzard. The 1,500 men of the Central Group had been lectured at length on the perils and problems of Antarctic blizzards. After two weeks in Little America they had begun to regard the descriptions as somewhat exaggerated. Then came their baptism of snow.

Operation Highjump *was an unqualified success. An impressive 70,000 aerial photographs were taken which enabled cartographers to map 700,000 square miles of territory accurately for the first time. But the United States was not the only nation vying for claims in Antarctica or seeking knowledge. Great Britain, Australia, New Zealand, Argentina, Chile, the Soviet Union, Norway, and France planned expeditions to the continent each season. As a result, the age of geographical discovery in the Antarctic is almost over. The basic reasons for going now are much more scientific and more for the testing of aircraft, vehicles, and ships.*

In July, 1955, scientists from many nations met in Paris to coordinate and plan the Antarctic activities of the International Geophysical Year (IGY). One purpose was to study the South Geomagnetic Pole and the earth's magnetic field at the southernmost latitudes. Of interest also was the interrelationship of sunspots, cosmic rays, the aurora, and magnetic storms. By December of 1955, seven major expeditions were making the greatest coordinated scientific effort in history at the bottom of the world. The largest group was that of the United States which was using the code name Operation Deep Freeze I. *Its mission: establish and maintain two scientific stations, one at the geographic South Pole and the other at approximately 80° S 120° W in Marie Byrd Land.*

The first and most immediate problem to be solved when establishing the station was that of transporting the thousands of pounds of supplies and equipment from the ships to the Pole. Only two parties had ever been to the Pole over land before, one under Amundsen and the other under Scott in 1911-12. The difficulties they encountered were extremely discouraging even in view of the possible use of tractor trains. Airplanes had advanced to the point where the materials for building the station and the bulk supplies for its support could be air-dropped. Ski-equipped planes could then fly in the men and delicate instruments.

There were several unknown factors to be considered before operations could begin. Could large-wheeled planes suitable for heavy cargo operations land and take off from a prepared airstrip in the Antarctic? Could ski-equipped planes land and take off on the polar plateau? There was only one way to find out.

The U.S. Navy, with the help of the U.S. Air Force, was assigned the task of logistic support of the program. The first year's task (1955-56) was to set up a base on the east side of McMurdo Sound near Cape Armitage.

On December 20, 1955, after the main base was established, two large P2V Neptune patrol planes and one R5D four-engine cargo plane flew from Christchurch, New Zealand. It was the first time that wheeled aircraft had flown from a land mass in the southern hemisphere and landed on the Antarctic Continent. A number of smaller aircraft capable of operating with either wheels or skis and helicopters were carried to the area by ship. In the subsequent weeks, all aircraft operated successfully and the base was established as planned. During the long Antarctic winter, a 5,000-foot runway was completed and ready for the next year's operation, Deep Freeze II.

By October, 1956, the next phase of the IGY operation was ready to begin. On October 16, the first aircraft, an R5D, arrived, followed by R4D's and a P2V. (The P2V crashed on landing with the loss of four lives.) On October 20, eight Air Force C-124 Globemasters began the logistic support of the operation. All elements were now in place for the airdrop of materials at the Pole — provided it could be shown that an R4D could first land and take off there. Admiral George J. Dufek, USN (Ret) set the day for the attempt as October 31. Patrick Trese, a professional photographer who went along on Deep Freeze II *to prepare a documentary film, wrote an unusual account of that historic flight.*

Que Será Será

Patrick Trese

IN BOYSTOWN, conversation among the pilots diminished as the day of the awful attempt approached. What little talk there was centered on the Pole, and it was speculative. How rugged was the surface of the plateau? How cold would it be? What was the minimum operating temperature for an R4D anyway? Could you expect a substantial loss of engine power attempting a takeoff at 10,000 feet above sea level? What about those wavelike snow formations called sastrugi? Would they crumble or stand firmly blocking the skis? Would the skis glide freely on the snow at the Pole or would they freeze solid? And, if worst came to worst, what were the chances of a rescue?

There were no answers; nobody knew for sure.

The unstated fear that pervaded Boystown was not at once apparent; there was too much work to be done, initially, getting the skis attached to the landing gear of the small transports. The R4D's had flown into the Antarctic and had made wheeled landings on the ice. They could not have carried all that weight on the long flights from New Zealand. But now, the skis were being attached slowly in the cruel October wind and the pilots spent most of their time down on the runway with the ground crews.

Bill and I tried to make films of this work and had a chance to observe the agony of the men laboring in the wind and blowing snow. There was no cover, but they kept at it, some of them, out of doors for 18 hours at a stretch. Often, when faced by a difficult mechanical chore, they would have to strip off their gloves and work bare-handed. At the warmest part of the day, it was eight degrees below zero. Five-minute mechanical chores took half an hour in the cold, and routine accidents became catastrophes.

Joe Long, the big plane captain who maintained Roy Curtis' R4D, was hit with a small spurt of gasoline. The fuel squirted inside his ear and froze instantly. They took him to the base infirmary for treatment, but he was back on the line the next morning. I asked him if his ear hurt and he said it did.

The first R4D was airborne October 25 and the push to the Pole began.

Gus Shinn and Douglas Cordiner left McMurdo on a reconnaissance flight. Capt. William "Trigger" Hawkes, a veteran polar aviator and the air officer of the task force, went along as an observer. This mission was to find a suitable place for the establishment of a small landing strip roughly halfway between McMurdo and the Pole, so they flew to the base of the Beardmore Glacier and looked around, returning much later in the day to report that landing conditions there were impossible.

The following day, they went fishing again and this time they scouted the area near the Duncan Mountains where Admiral Byrd and his crew had set up a fuel cache for his flight over the South Pole in 1929. Shinn, Cordiner, and Hawkes decided on a likely spot near the mouth of the Liv Glacier. This site, for reasons best known to the U.S. Navy, became known as the Beardmore base. I suppose it saved a lot of paper work if not confusion.

There was heavy, blowing snow on the runway the next day, so it was not until the 28th that the squadron tried to put all four of its planes into the air; one bound for Little America, and the other three for the Beardmore campsite. Harvey Speed made the Little

America flight; Frankie and Gus went to Beardmore. Roy Curtis also started off for Beardmore, but had to return to the strip when his skis failed to retract. It was probably just as well, for while the ground crew was working on the plane's hydraulic system, the aircraft somehow leaked 400 gallons of gasoline.

"Better on the deck than in the air," said Curtis, who was rapidly becoming a philosopher.

The auxiliary fuel tanks, which had increased the R4D's range, had been taken out of the cabins to make way for cargo and bodies, which explains Roy Curtis' shudders and the necessity for the half-way station on the polar route.

Frankie and Gus made the flight to Beardmore without incident and dropped off four men who had to construct the runway on the compacted snow and organize refueling operations in the wilderness, just 300 miles from the South Pole. The leader of this group was a Chief Petty Officer from Brooklyn named Mike Baronick, who had wintered-over at McMurdo.

It had taken almost seven hours to fly to the base site, and on landing the planes did not stop their engines; it was too cold. Mike and his men climbed out through the slipstreams and immediately started putting up the tent that would be their only shelter for several weeks. The two planes took off again immediately, but it was hard going on the eroded snow. Gus banged up a wing tip on his aircraft, but managed to get into the air and keep going. Frankie made it handily and circled the base site once before heading back to McMurdo. From the warmth of his cockpit he could see the four men waving to him from the depths of a cold, white world.

"They looked awful small," said Frankie, when he got home. "I sure felt bad leaving them there all alone."

By and by, the Beardmore men got their radio working and the Air Force Globemasters began dropping aviation gasoline by parachute. Mike and his boys had the whole thing set up and ready to go in what passes in the Antarctic for nothing flat. Before the month was out, Mike Baronick radioed to McMurdo that the weather was hot and dusty at Beardmore and he couldn't understand what everyone was waiting for.

In Boystown, conversation dwindled.

Captain Cordiner decided that Gus Shinn would fly the first mission to the Pole but, since his airplane was banged up, Harvey Speed's aircraft was taken away from him and given to Gus. The

plane was nicknamed the *Que Será Será* — whatever will be, will be —
and Harvey was fairly fond of it. Conversation in Boystown picked
up a bit, at least whenever Harvey was around. He was not profane
exactly, but he was mighty eloquent. He considered the transaction
as something just this side of grand theft.

Admiral Dufek decided that he would make the flight to the Pole
and nobody objected to this because it was, after all, his money that
was paying for it. But he also decided that Trigger Hawkes would
fly copilot to Gus. This, of course, bumped Doug Cordiner out of the
right-hand seat and put him back in the cabin with the admiral. It
became apparent that there would be no room for any reporters or
photographers on the first flight to the South Pole.

The engines of the R4D were turning over. The plane captain, a
tall southern boy named J. P. Strider, was holding the hatch open
from inside the cabin. "Come on," Dufek said to him, "let's get out
of here." Strider grinned and slammed the hatch shut.

Inside, Strider guided the admiral to his bucket seat. "Beg pardon,
Admiral," he said, "but I've been working since they got me up this
morning and nobody's gotten around to telling me where it is we're
going."

Dufek told him that they were on their way to the South Pole.

"Well, I'll be dipped," said J. P. Strider. "Don't that beat all!"

Gus Shinn had 15 jato bottles hooked onto the belly of the *Que
Será Será*, but he was saving them all for the takeoff from the South
Pole; so, in taking off from McMurdo, he used up all of the 6,000-foot
runway. Barely airborne with all the weight aboard, Gus had to fly
straight ahead for ten miles before he gained enough altitude to dare
to make the shallowest turn.

Bill and I stood together as the snow, kicked up from the plane's
propellers, settled on the runway. The little R4D diminished in the
distance as it flew low over the ice.

"Well," I said, "I hope the camera works OK."

"I just hope we get it back," said Bill.

About an hour later, Hank Jorda and his crew took off in their
four-engined R5D to fly aerial cover for the twin-engined *Que Será
Será*; but before Jorda could overtake Shinn — who was by that time
flying low over the Ross Ice Shelf — his plane lost power in its number one engine and was forced to return to McMurdo. The Air Force
Globemaster, piloted by Maj. Cicero J. Ellen, left on schedule, caught
up with Shinn, and stuck with him all the way. Bill was aboard it in

143

The first type of aircraft to make a landing at both poles is the military version of the Douglas DC-3 transport, known affectionately as the "Gooney Bird." A U.S. Air Force C-47 landed at the North Pole on May 3, 1952. A Navy R4D, the *Que Será Será,* shown here, made the first landing at the South Pole on October 31, 1956.
U.S. Navy Photo

hopes of shooting the landing from the air. With luck, we would have something on film before the day was out.

I took up my position in the Air Operations Building, where I could monitor the radio messages transmitted by the two planes on their way to the Pole. I could also follow the progress of the flight by keeping an eye on the chart table where a large map of the Antarctic Continent was covered by a plastic overlay. The planes called in once every half hour to give their positions to the Search-and-Rescue officer and to report on the operations of their aircraft. After each call, the pilots in Air Ops extended the red lines on the chart with a crayon.

Gus reported in at the foot of the Beardmore Glacier. He had flown 400 miles so far and had stayed low, not wishing to burn up fuel with an early climb. Even so, he had used up 3,000 pounds of gasoline.

144

The thin red line on the chart now changed direction, turning 90 degrees to the right as Shinn began his ascent up the Beardmore. It would be a climb from sea level to 10,000 feet in a little more than 100 miles, a laborious climb up the 12-mile-wide, silent river of ice. Those of us who had seen the Beardmore and its crevasses from the air knew that there was no place on it to land. From the sparse radio reports, we knew that Shinn and Hawkes were straining at the yoke to get up the glacier. The *Que Será Será* was making only 98 knots. One of the pilots remarked that this was barely 20 knots above stalling speed. After that no one said much of anything. The pilots stood around the table, staring at the chart.

Aboard the *Que Será Será*, J. P. Strider looked out the porthole to find that Shinn had reached the head of the glacier. The plane was flying now at about 12,000 feet and J. P. was shaking as hard as the aircraft. He was upset. The R4D, he said later, was moaning and groaning and the coffee wouldn't percolate. George Dufek apparently noticed the look on Strider's face. He waved him to his seat and said, "Make me a toasted cheese sandwich." J. P. felt better after that for some reason.

The radio in Air Ops crackled as C. J. Ellen reported that his Globemaster had made contact with the *Que Será Será* at the head of the glacier and would proceed directly to the Pole. They had waved wings at each other and everything seemed to be OK.

The radio messages from the R4D were growing fainter. But inside their cockpit, Shinn and Hawkes were a little more confident, now that they had a big brother in the air with them. The Globemaster, of course, could not land on the polar plateau, but it was comforting to know that the big plane was keeping them under observation, especially since Hawkes had just noticed through the windscreen that the breather lines in the starboard engine seemed to be frozen: the engine was pumping oil from the topside overflow and he did not like that much.

The navigator of the *Que Será Será*, Lt. Dick Swadener, was deep in his figures as the plane drove on across the polar plateau. Apparently his calculations dovetailed with those of the navigator in the Globemaster for, 40 minutes later, the *Que Será Será* homed toward a spot on the white expanse in the center of the contrails made by Ellen's C-124, swinging well above the surface in a lazy box.

Gus slid underneath the Globemaster's pattern and began descending slowly in a triangular course. For the better part of an hour, Gus and Trigger peered down at the terrain below. Because of a polar phenomenon called inversion, the temperature dropped as the plane lost altitude.

They made a decision to land with the sun at their backs so that they could use the shadows to increase their depth perception, even though this meant coming down crosswind. As Gus lined up for his final approach, Trigger lightened the plane's load by jettisoning 100 gallons of gasoline. They waited until the last possible moment to lower the skis: the heavy landing gear created so much drag at that speed and altitude that when they fell into position you had to land. With skis down, the plane did not have enough power to stay airborne.

But as Hawkes lowered the gear, a red warning light flashed on the instrument panel. It could mean that a ski had malfunctioned or that an electrical switch had frozen. Hawkes hoped it was the latter. The starboard engine was vomiting clods of congealed oil, which were thumping loudly against the control surfaces of the tail section; but this racket was nothing compared to the shudder as the *Que Será Será* touched down on the polar plateau. Gus had landed with his skis parallel to the sastrugi, but between these 20-inch-high waves of flint-hard snow the surface was gritty as sand. The *Que Será Será* ground to a sudden stop in a few hundred yards. For the first time in history, an airplane had managed to land on the South Pole. Gus, who was no romantic, kept his engines turning over to make sure that he would also make the first takeoff.

The large clock on the wall of the Air Operations Building at McMurdo Sound read 0834 Greenwich Mean Time.

On the Pole itself, the men of the *Que Será Será* were working out in the wind, raising a radar reflector screen, an ungainly piece of navigational gear that looked like a sick television antenna.

The first man out the hatch, and the first American ever to set foot on the South Pole, had been Rear Admiral George Dufek and he found that it was like stepping out into another world. The temperature was 58 degrees below zero, which is 90 degrees below freezing. Doug Cordiner followed him out of the plane and the two of them raised the American flag. This, in itself, was a chore because the snow was so hard. They had to use an alpine ax to dig a hole for the flagstaff. They had been at it for about three minutes when Dufek noticed that Cordiner's face, cheeks, and part of his nose had turned white from frostbite. The admiral told Cordiner to cover up and get warm.

Trigger Hawkes and radioman Bill Cumbie hauled a radar reflector from the aircraft and tried to set it up. Cumbie found that his hands were so cold that, after a few minutes of digging, he was unable to let go of the ax handle. He put his foot on the blade for leverage and freed himself. Then he went inside the plane, out of the wind, and stayed there until his fingers started working again.

Dufek, Hawkes, and Cordiner hauled the NBC camera from the cabin. They attached the wires which fed the machine with power and warmth, picked up the microphone and faced the lens to give their impressions of what it was like to stand at the very bottom of the world.

J. P. Strider, however, was more concerned with the R4D's starboard engine than he was with making history. The engine had been spitting oil so vigorously that there was now a streak of frozen lubricant all the way along the fuselage, three inches wide and five inches deep. Also, the skis had frozen to the gritty snow the way an ice-cube tray does to a refrigerator shelf. J. P. got out a length of nylon rope and called for some help in sawing away at the snow beneath the skis. Dick Swadener, the navigator who had a small still camera, had time for one quick shot of Dufek and Hawkes. Then he put his camera away and went to help Strider free the skis.

Above the Pole, Ellen's contrails were forming a thick cloud.

Gus Shinn finally got everybody back into the airplane and, with a good deal of anxiety, prepared to take off. Even the blasé Trigger Hawkes began to be concerned when Gus gave the engines full power, fired three jato rockets, and nothing happened. The *Que Será Será* stood stock-still in its tracks. Gus throttled down for a moment, then revved up his engines again and, at the same time, Trigger ignited the jato bottles he had left — 13 of them. The R4D leaped into the air, dragging its tail through the blackened blasthole. This damaged the trailing edges of both elevators as well as the leading edge of the port elevator.

From above, C. J. Ellen saw the little plane disappear in a cloud of snow and smoke and contrails. He was pretty sure that the *Que Será Será* had had it and he kept hollering at Gus over his radio.

But Gus and Trigger had no chance to reply. In front of them, everything was white. There were contrails hanging on the surface of the plateau and, to top it all, their breath, in the cold cockpit, had frosted over the windscreen. Hawkes was trying to clear it with one hand and retract the skis with the other. Warning lights were flashing on the instrument panel and J. P. Strider, hanging on for dear life behind the pilots' seats, noticed with alarm that the oil-pressure gauge was dropping like a stone — from normal, past minimum, down to critical. Hawkes was having trouble getting the skis retracted. The airspeed indicator registered 60 knots — well below stalling speed — so Hawkes stopped worrying about Gus's vision and went after the skis with two hands. Somehow, the *Que Será Será* stayed in the air.

It was not until 0940 that we received at McMurdo any communication from the R4D, and that was a brief operation message to the effect that the *Que Será Será* had taken off from the Pole at 0923 GMT and was now proceeding to the Beardmore camp for refueling. There were some statistics passed and the pilots got out their slide rules.

"Well," said one of the men finally, "if he has as much gasoline as he says he has, he should just about make Beardmore. That is, if he doesn't go sight-seeing. He can stay up for about three hours, according to my figures."

Two hours and 27 minutes later, the *Que Será Será* landed at Beardmore.

The Deep Freeze *operations have continued each year since the South Pole station was established. Each year the U.S. Navy and the Air Force have used both wheeled and ski-equipped planes and helicopters to complete their work and the yearly operations have become routine — almost. Commercial airlines have been operating over the Great Circle Antarctic route since December 22, 1956, when the Chilean national airline made the first flight, carrying paying passengers. Less than a year later, on October 15, 1957, a Pan American Airways plane, complete with two stewardesses, was the first commercial airliner to land in the Antarctic.*

The success of the United States in establishing the South Pole and Byrd stations has clearly demonstrated the value of using large cargo aircraft in the Antarctic. The limitation placed on operations is now one of time, since flying in and out of the continent is impossible during the long winter night because no navigational aids are yet installed. In the summer, the ice breaks up and flying of heavy aircraft on and off the runways is dangerous due to deterioration. Consequently, the major operating season has been only from October 1 to early December of each year. In spite of this, operations have continued.

VX-6: Deep Freeze Airline

Leverett G. Richards

McMurdo Sound, Antarctica. It took Capt. Robert Falcon Scott nearly three months to reach the South Pole from here in 1912.

It took VX-6 three hours in November, 1962. In fact, some of the crew were complaining of the heat as we soared in airline comfort over the spot where Scott and his four gallant companions froze to death 50 years before. We were sipping Navy "joe" in the cabin of the Lockheed C-130B Hercules, and the ski landing on the snow runway at the Pole was strictly routine. So was the takeoff at 40 below, despite the 9,200-foot altitude. We used no jato, although we had eight bottles available if needed. The "Puckered Penguin Airline" was right on schedule.

Yet in the next week VX-6, the Navy's Air Development Squadron Six, wiped out three aircraft in four days. Two more "strikes" were recorded in the next two months. All craft were damaged beyond economical repair on remote glaciers or snowfields literally at the end of the world.

This is the home of the "Puckered Penguins," the world's most unorthodox "airline." VX-6 was commissioned "to conduct operations in connection with the U.S. Antarctic program," the understatement of all time.

Actually VX-6 was handed the job of conquering the bottom of the world. The job could only be done by air, backed, of course, by a fleet of seven ships, escorted by four icebreakers. No other nation could begin to do the job. Most of the ten other nations that have scientific or political stations in the Antarctic use light aircraft for reconnaissance and small supply drops, but none has heavy aircraft capable of operating from the high Antarctic ice cap.

VX-6 not only conquered the White Continent, the last great unknown territory on earth, but remained to explore and develop it. This is one of the toughest jobs ever tackled by aviation. The Antarctic is not only the most remote spot on earth, but one of the coldest, highest, and roughest. Locked away behind a triple curtain of ice, hurricane winds, and mean, wild seas, it has repelled all efforts to unveil its mysteries from the beginning of time.

Conquest of this continent by air might be called a labor of Hercules. The C-130 Hercules did, indeed, build the new City Under the Snow at Byrdland, flying in all the prefabricated buildings and heavy equipment. But the Amundsen-Scott scientific station at the South Pole is the only installation of its kind in the world built and supplied entirely by air. Not a drop of oil or a pound of supplies has reached it over the surface of the hostile ice, which piles up higher on the Antarctic than anywhere else in the world. All other scientific stations in the Antarctic have been built and partly supplied by sea, or by tractor trains crawling over the treacherous crevasses towing 100-ton sleds. But not the South Pole Station. It is still locked away behind high mountains, too far from the coast for present means of surface transportation to reach it.

VX-6 called on the Air Force to parachute the prefabricated buildings, the diesel generators, and the bulldozers required to build the pole station in 1956. At that time the 18th Air Force's C-124 Globemasters were the only aircraft in the world that could climb to 12,000 feet, fly the 950 miles from the main supply base at McMurdo, and drop the 12-ton loads required.

The workhorse plane in modern-day Antarctica is the C-130 Hercules, which is flown by both the Air Force and Navy. The best flying months are from October through December. Little flying is done in the darkness of the long Antarctic night.

U.S. Navy Photo

A huge propjet C-130 Hercules lifts from the ice runway at McMurdo Station, Antarctica, to begin a long flight to inland stations on the continent. The 61-ton plane, equipped with skis on its tricycle landing gear, is able to land at Byrd and South Pole stations with supplies, and thus has revolutionized resupply techniques on the white continent.

U.S. Navy Photo

But it was the Puckered Penguins who were the first to land at the Pole and a hundred other impossible areas of this world's best deep freeze. Rear Admiral George J. Dufek, called out of retirement to head the first Naval Support Force, Antarctica, had to use any and all aircraft he could lay his hands on at the time.

Some, like the twin-engined Albatross amphibians, never got there. Twice they took off from Christchurch, New Zealand, on the 2,400-mile flight across the wild waters of the Antarctic Ocean. Twice they had to turn back.

The first flight of four ski-equipped C-47's also encountered head winds and had to turn back. They finally reached the lost continent, only to find a blizzard had blotted out the single runway on the floating sea ice of McMurdo Sound after they passed the point of no return. While the C-47's helped one another along the route, each with its own brand of trouble, a lone C-54, short of fuel, prepared to ditch. At the last moment the pilot, Comdr. Ed Ward, got down on the deck and groped his way in for a landing. He didn't even have time to "un-alert" his passengers, who were strapped at their stations, life rafts in hand, alerted for ditching.

The last of the C-47's flown by Lt. Roy Curtis, dived through a break in the blowing snow just in time to skid to a stop as both engines failed for lack of fuel. He had to be towed off the runway.

The lead P2 Neptune arrived before the blizzard started to blow, found the runway under low clouds, but didn't make the landing. One wing caught the ice during the turn to the runway, and the airplane was destroyed.

It was in the shadow of this ominous opening to *Operation Deep Freeze II,* the first year of the IGY (International Geophysical Year), that VX-6 contemplated the first landing at the Pole. Landings there are strictly routine now. But in 1956 no one was sure it was possible to land on the eternal snows of the polar plateau. VX-6 pilots who circled the Pole the previous year reported the snow was like feathers. There were those who feared a plane would sink out of sight as soon as it touched down. No one had been there since Scott, and he reported he could sink a tent pole full length in the soft snow with little effort.

On the other hand, Maj. Gen. Chester E. McCarty, commander of the 18th Air Force, had dropped five tons of diesel oil at the Pole from a Globemaster, October 26, 1956, and reported the sastrugi as hard as concrete, hard enough to wipe out a landing gear.

A landing had to be tried. Lt. Comdr. Gus Shinn nursed his staggering C-47 off the 6,000-foot ice runway at McMurdo, five tons overweight, climbed over the Beardmore Glacier and struggled on to the Pole. His *Que Será Será* was the oldest and weariest bird in the VX-6 roost, but she made it bleeding oil and hydraulic fluid all the way.

The old bird, now in the National Air Museum at Washington, D.C., was never the same again. She was battered and bent from nose to tail. A hole had been burned in her belly and the main spar of the left horizontal stabilizer was broken in two.

At that, Gus and his *Que Será Será*, still overloaded by 7,000 pounds at takeoff from the Pole, did better than the bigger, more powerful P2's. Comdr. Vernon J. Coley, VX-6 commander, the next year again tried to operate in temperatures below minus 50, only to freeze the oil in both engines and rupture the oil coolers. It was 26 days before the weather warmed up enough to fly out the stranded crew and passengers. The plane was in deep freeze for 40 days.

In January, 1958, Admiral Dufek and a party of reporters flew to the Pole to greet Sir Vivien Fuchs on his crossing of the continent, but were unable to take off, even with the aid of 16 jato bottles. The piston engines just didn't have the power at high altitude.

The answer to the VX-6 pilot's prayer came in the 1959-60 season when the Air Force sent a task force of four C-130's, commanded by Lt. Col. Frank Turk, to the Antarctic to test the project transports on the polar plateau and to check out Navy pilots in the big ski planes. Col. Turk's squadron had been using them to build and supply radar stations of the DEW Line on the Greenland Ice Cap.

The Hercules performed just as spectacularly in the Antarctic, despite the greater altitudes and lower temperatures. In the fall of 1960, VX-6 received its own fleet of four Ski-130's. The Antarctic has never been the same since.

"Each Hercules does the work of five C-47's," said Comdr. William H. Everett, current skipper of VX-6 in Operation Deep Freeze 63.

"We were lucky to stagger up the Beardmore with 5,000 pounds pay load in the old Gooney Bird. We could never get off the Pole without burning jato, which is like burning money.

"The Hercules hauls a 23,000-pound pay load to the Pole, grossing 135,000 pounds. On a long haul, like the run to Eights station, she carries 14,000 pounds pay load. Operating weight is 80,000, leaving 55,000 pounds useful load. We can carry up to 44,000 pounds of fuel

October, 1961, Lt. Philip K. Swartz, MC, USN (right), accepts the first mail seen in eight months at Scott-Amundsen South Pole Station. This and other sacks of letters arrived with Rear Adm. David M. Tyree, USN (center), Commander of Naval Support Forces, Antarctica, aboard the opening C-130 Pole flight of the *Operation Deep Freeze 62* Summer Support Season.

U.S. Navy Photo

with the pylon tanks, which gives us a 10-hour range for long rescue and recon flights."

The Air Force continues to fly about 700 tons of high priority cargo and hundreds of personnel each season from Christchurch to the ice, and remains to drop from 800 to 1,300 tons of supplies for the Pole and Byrd Station. The Navy Ski-130's do the rest. They have taken over almost the whole job of supplying the Amundsen-Scott Station at the Pole, at a considerable saving in costs of rigging and parachutes, not to mention an estimated 2 per cent loss due to breakage from airdrops.

The C-130's, worth more than 2 million dollars each, are too precious to be risked on unknown terrain where any snowfield could hide crevasses big enough to swallow the Empire State Building. The dauntless Gooney Bird is expendable. It is sent in first as a pathfinder to find a landing site, feel it out for crevasses and hidden sastrugi. Then Big Brother is called in with the heavy cargo while the Gooney acts as control tower and navigation aid.

Those skis have saved many a VX-6 plane — like the Ski-130 which calmly landed eight miles from McMurdo's airport when a sudden blizzard blotted out the base in November, 1962, and taxied into camp by GCA. A C-47, caught out during the same storm, landed a mile away and taxied under radar to McMurdo — the only "airport" in the Antarctic for wheeled aircraft.

The C-47's are the bush planes of the Antarctic. They do the "mountaineering," landing parties of scientists on remote, unmapped, unexplored snowcaps to conduct their scientific explorations. Four UH-34 helicopters share the "bush-hopping" with the four C-47's, aided by helicopters from the icebreakers. The choppers handle the shorter hauls and the mountaintop landings. Two Army UH-1 jet helicopters were added to the fleet in Deep Freeze 62 and 63, surveying mountain ranges, then landing at the South Pole to be dismantled and flown out. Never have so few scientists accomplished so much in so short a time, thanks to wings supplied by VX-6.

Commander Everett puts it more succinctly.

"Be it beans, bacon, beer, or bedrolls, you call; we haul."

Some say that flying at the ends of the earth in the polar zones has become routine. Perhaps it has. Airplanes fly thousands of accident-free miles yearly in both the Arctic and Antarctic regions. If you ask the pilots they may agree but with reservations. As one pilot put it, "Flying is 'routine' all right for hours and hours but it's those occasional moments of sheer terror that remind us that we can't relax completely."

While the giant C-130 Hercules transport has brought a kind of routineness to Antarctic operations, there are still those nightmarish moments that seem to come inevitably to all pilots — sometimes with fatal consequences. Martin Caidin, in his book The Long Arm of America, *describes one of those times when the hazards of the Antarctic — the savage cold, the terrible winds, the remoteness — almost added up to disaster.*

Trouble in the Middle of Nowhere

Martin Caidin

SOMETHING that pilots and crews fear in the Antarctic is mechanical breakdown or failure, or even minor trouble, when they are anywhere but at a camp. An accident in the middle of nowhere, on the great expanse of the frozen plateau, can quickly mushroom into imminent death. There just aren't the rescue facilities, the people, or the navigational aids for help to arrive. And the storms explode so quickly that many times there isn't any warning at all before dead-calm air turns into the fury of a wind exceeding hurricane force — and at 50 to 60 degrees below zero.

The unexpected snared a Hercules at 27,000 feet, while the airplane cruised en route from McMurdo to Byrd Station. In the space of five minutes the startled crew lost power on three of their four engines. The flight engineer went frantic trying to discover the cause and effect a remedy, but one by one the engines just quit turning out power. One engine meant no trouble. Then the second quit, and

156

things began to get sticky because of the fuel and cargo load and the altitude.

The pilot started an immediate descent to denser air to keep the Hercules flying. Then the third engine quit and that airplane was in *deep* trouble. . . .

The pilot knew he was getting into a mess well over his head. He ordered the engineer to open the cargo ramp and shouted at the crew to jettison the cargo — *everything* — and to get it the hell out of the airplane at once. Fighting the sluggish controls — with almost full weight on one engine — the pilot kept the Hercules in a steady descent, broken only by a pull-up to help roll out the cargo.

With only one engine remaining — and with no assurance that the last Allison wouldn't quit at any moment — the pilot bored in for a landing in the midst of nowhere, while the copilot and navigator were frantically sending out distress signals and position reports. Everyone hung on grimly as the big airplane screamed in low over the ice . . . and slid to a perfect landing.

Lockheed engineer Bill Smith picks up the story here:

"We sent out a field party in a Gooney Bird with special equipment and engine preheaters to find out what had caused three engines to quit just like that. I'd known of an Air Force bird that had to shut down three engines when hail beat up the air scoops, but we modified those years ago and it never happened again. I couldn't figure out what might have caused this trouble, and my hunch was that the engines were fine — but the fuel wasn't.

"Sure enough, the culprit turned out to be a very high concentration of water in the fuel. We had a problem on our hands; the airplane actually had a contaminated fuel system. The filter screens were solid *ice*. The water must have been pumped into the aircraft with the supply from McMurdo, through the single-point system of the Hercules. That's the only possible way we could have gotten such a great slug of seawater in an airplane. All fuel is brought in by Navy tanker and in those rough seas you can't help but to ship water into the tanks."

Lockheed technician Doug Chambley went along in the Navy's Gooney Bird to troubleshoot the problem; Chambley says he would prefer to forget the five days that followed. The trouble wasn't to be solved by demanding technical work; it had to be solved by muscle-bending, backbreaking physical labor.

"We had to open the fuel tanks in the wings," Chambley recalls with a trace of a shudder. "Then we had to climb into the tanks. Next in the job was to heat the water — the ice — in the wings and then sponge out the water by *hand* before we dared to send the airplane back into the air.

"You see, we had to sponge out the tanks, but we didn't have any sponges. Where do you find sponges in the middle of Antarctica? We were 500 miles from McMurdo and 300 miles from Byrd Station — almost right smack in the middle. All they had there was ice and snow, no *sponges*.

"It's amazing what that airplane will endure. . . . We tore apart every seat cushion we could find in the Hercules. We tore them up and cut the sponge rubber out of the seats, and *those* were our sponges.

"It took more than three days in the middle of the Antarctic to open all the tanks, and physically crawl in and clean the water out of every damn one of them by hand.

"Well, it was interesting, anyway. We finally had the opportunity to put our survival-school training — which was worse than the Antarctic — to good use. We dug underground quarters, set up tents and shelters, and we ate hardtack. We rigged up some old cans, made some fires with the jet fuel to melt water, and even managed to make something that passed for coffee. We lived strictly off our survival rations and equipment.

"We worked for four and a half days on that airplane until we had it ready to fly. On the fifth day we considered things safe enough for a takeoff, and the crew boomed out of there like there was no tomorrow.

"Apparently we hadn't cleaned out *all* the water, though . . ."

On the flight back to McMurdo, the crew lost two engines. With the airplane light in weight, the crew said to hell with it, and went wide-open all the way back to the main station. The pilot said he would have kept on with only one engine and if he'd lost that one, too, he was determined to glide all the way back to McMurdo.

Safely on the ground again, the crew, with the help of mechanics, flushed the tanks and purged the systems of fuel and any seawater that remained. They pumped the tanks full again, ran a thorough check of the engines, and the next morning the Hercules was in the air with 20,000 pounds of cargo, headed for the South Pole.

What is the Antarctic really like? Is it different from the Arctic? Why is it important? Why do so many scientists insist on going to the bottom of the world every year? What is the airplane doing to contribute to Antarctic activities besides supporting the IGY program?

These questions are frequently asked but seldom answered. In the following chapter from his book, David Alman answers them briefly but well. It is a fitting summary to the pioneering of Scott, Amundsen, Wilkins, Byrd, and the many others who have journeyed to this immense wilderness of rock and ice.

At the Bottom of the Planet

David Alman

IN THE HIGH northern and deep southern latitudes of the earth, solid water — in the form of ice and snow — is at least as common as the liquid kind. Across the snow-covered Antarctic landmass the winds create ripples in the snow, just as they do across the water, and as they do across the sand masses in the desert. In the Arctic, where the frozen packs are afloat rather than bound to earth, the winds drive the snow masses in slow, wide circles around the northernmost sea. All in all, the ice of the Arctic and Antarctic covers one-tenth of the world.

In the past million years four ice ages have come and gone, and man has survived them all. The peak of the last ice age came somewhat less than 20,000 years ago, almost at the brink of the known history of man. It is possible that we are still in the last stages of that ice age. One-third of the landmass of the earth was, at that time, covered by ice, but less than 5 per cent of the earth's water was needed to produce it. The seas were several hundred feet higher than they are today, and consequently the sites of the great coastal cities of today's world, many of the inland cities, and the island masses, were either under water — or under ice. It is assumed that over 10,000 years ago, our hardy, curious ancestors crossed a bridge of land — or ice — from Siberia to Alaska.

The great ice mass of the world is not, however, in the north. It is in the Antarctic, at the bottom of the planet, that we will find 85 per cent of the earth's ice. If this ice were to melt, we would easily be able to swim in and out of movie balconies in New York, San Francisco, and other metropolitan centers near the seas. But even a little bit of melting would cause great climatic changes over the entire world. For that reason, the ice of the Antarctic is of considerable interest to glaciologists, oceanographers, meteorologists, and other scientists concerned with the origins of the weather.

At the present time it is likely that the Antarctic ice is melting, although very slowly. One reason scientists think so is that between the time of Captain Cook's expedition to the Antarctic in the eighteenth century, and Admiral Byrd's expedition in the twentieth, the level of the world's seas has risen about five inches.

Today, the Antarctic is covered by 5 million square miles of ice — an area considerably larger than that of the United States. The depth of the ice ranges from several feet to two miles (by contrast, the depth of Arctic ice is generally less than 15 feet). Soundings beneath the ice indicate that the Antarctic may have mountains that are thousands of feet high, and valleys that are thousands of feet deep. Much of this land may be below sea level because of the crushing weight of the ice. Soundings also indicate that the Antarctic at one time probably had great rivers pouring into the surrounding seas.

Was the Antarctic ever warmer? Possibly, but the evidence seems to indicate that snow and ice have layered the continent uninterruptedly for all the known centuries. Under the pressure of changes in density, temperature, and weight, the ice undergoes slow change, yielding here, cracking there, bending elsewhere. It is not stationary, but moves thousands of miles, often into the sea itself, under pressure of the snow above. Great pieces of it break away from the main mass as a result of strains created by tidal movements.

Sometimes, there is literally *nothing* to see in the Antarctic: the intense, blinding whiteness of the snow is often so perfectly reflected into the air that a "whiteout" occurs in which one cannot distinguish between the snow and the sky, nor between the foreground and the horizon. At such times, airplane pilots cannot tell where they are, whether they are a foot off the ice — or a thousand feet high. In this unbroken whiteness a man is as blind and lost as he would be in absolute blackness.

Sometimes, as in the desert, one sees what does not exist. The angle at which the sun strikes at different layers of air in the Antarctic often causes a multiplicity of images to form. The images may be exquisitely detailed, and will remain for long periods of time, thus reinforcing the illusion that they are real.

And sometimes, because warm layers of air close to the ice may form "sound tunnels," a man can carry on an easy conversation with a colleague a mile or more away. Or he may hear the chirping of far distant birds or the barking of seals in the cold sea. He may also hear someone slapping against the Antarctic mosquito, and wonder: *On what — or on whom — does this insect feed when there are no people about?* At the other end of the earth — the Arctic — the mosquito has thousands of animal and plant species to live on; at the Antarctic the mosquito — who is not winged as his northern cousins are — has only a few primitive plants to share with him the distinction of being alive.

The Antarctic's biggest city is McMurdo. Like all tourist towns, its population fluctuates with the seasons, being smallest during the winter months (about 90 persons), and largest during the summer (about 300 persons). McMurdo is the gateway to Little America, Byrd Station, and — of course — the South Pole itself, which is 730 miles away.

Through McMurdo pass the glaciologists and other stubborn students of the Antarctic. The University of Michigan has a little classroom and laboratory at Camp Michigan, about 50 miles from Little America, headed by Dr. James H. Zumberge. His special interest is the Ross Ice Shelf, a huge projection of ice over the Antarctic Sea. Through this "classroom" winds of 60 miles an hour are not uncommon, nor are temperatures of *minus* 95° F.

Students at the Antarctic are provisioned with food and clothing, and kept comfortable and amused, with the help of the continent's only reliable means of transport — the airplane. Food, gasoline, oil, clothing, medical supplies, prefabricated buildings, scientific instruments, tractors, books, and games are regularly flown to the outposts. Frequently, the transport plane doesn't land, but simply drops its cargo by parachute, as is almost always the case at the South Pole itself, where Dr. Paul Siple and his colleagues have set up their laboratory.

What are these men doing on the silent, cold continent?

For one thing, they send up — and track — hydrogen-filled balloons that are instrumented to take weather data.

They exchange this data with other stations, and all of it is constantly being analyzed at weather laboratories throughout the world.

161

They send radio signals into the upper atmosphere, and analyze the echoes to determine what changes are occurring in the electrified layers of the atmosphere.

They take the temperature of the ice down to a depth of 2,000 feet.

They "map" the land beneath the ice by listening to the echoes of man-made explosions.

They take core samples of the ice, the land, and the sea bottom, to study the history of the Antarctic region. The unanswered questions about it are endless. For example, a simple, basic question: Why is the Antarctic so cold? Many weather scientists believe that much of the heat of the sun is absorbed before it reaches the Antarctic, and that the remainder is reflected away. But not all scientists are satisfied with this explanation, nor should they be.

Another question: What causes the ice ages? According to various theories, they occur as the result of irregularities in the earth's orbit, or the growth of sunspots, or periodic changes in the sun's heat. Some theories center on the earth itself: the scattering or absorption of the sun's heat by great clouds or by the dust of heavy volcanic eruptions, or alterations in the direction of wind currents due to the rise and fall of landmasses, or changes in ocean currents because of undersea topographical changes.

These are two of the many general questions that will have to be answered if one of the prime purposes for Antarctic research — accurate weather prediction — is to be realized. On the other hand, for those human icebreakers who are down there simply because they will go anywhere and do anything for the sake of knowledge alone, their purpose is fulfilled every day.

PART THREE

WAR BELOW ZERO

On a strong Arctic depends peace in the air age.

—BERNT BALCHEN

Introduction

WHEN WORLD WAR II BEGAN, it was inevitable that some of it would be fought in the Arctic. Both the Japanese and Germans realized the value of closing the distance between themselves and the United States via the Great Circle Routes if they hoped to win. The shortest distances between the continents lay via the Aleutian-Alaska route on the one hand and the Greenland-Iceland line on the other.

It was in the Aleutians that the most combat flying took place as compared with the Greenland-Iceland area. This was an area of jagged little islands surrounded by subzero seas, high winds, blinding snows, and dense fogs. It was here that the Eleventh U.S. Air Force fought the Japanese and kept them from approaching any nearer to the southern 48 states.

The campaign waged by the Eleventh fell into three phases: the first ended with the Japanese defeat at Pearl Harbor in June, 1942; the second ended with the evacuation of Kiska in July, 1943; the third started with the Kuriles offensive in the summer of 1943 and ended in August, 1945. Although the total number of missions flown, enemy planes destroyed, and targets bombed was unimpressive when compared to the other combat areas, the results were significant because the Japanese were never able to gain a foothold or threaten the mainland.

The war in Greenland was different and the situation there was much more potentially dangerous for the Allies. There were no large armies stationed there, no major campaigns or epic battles. It was, in the words of one writer, "a war of long distances and longer silences: a war of waiting."

The Nazis had recognized the importance of Greenland for many years. Luftwaffe weather planes had patrolled its coast since the beginning of the war. Indeed, for over 25 years German scientific expeditions had studied the Arctic weather; their "good will" flights across the Atlantic in the thirties were made with an ulterior military motive in mind.

The U.S. Air Force was also well aware of the strategic value of both Greenland and Iceland. Both were logical stopover points for

165

any airplane ferrying route that might be opened up. In the summer of 1941, Bernt Balchen headed an expedition to Greenland under secret orders from Gen. Henry H. ("Hap") Arnold to establish an air base on the west coast of Greenland above the Arctic Circle. It was to be the northernmost American air base in the world. By the time war was declared, the base was ready.

And so the war in the Arctic regions was not a big war. There are no monuments commemorating battles fought there and no fields of crosses. There are only broken fuselages buried beneath the drifting snow, an occasional stone cairn to mark a grave, or a broken dogsled beside the trail. Nevertheless, the war fought below zero was important because without the ferrying stops on both the western route to Russia and the eastern route to Europe, large numbers of planes would have to be transported by ship to the war front with consequent losses due to enemy submarine action, not to mention the penalty of time. Furthermore, the information gained from the knowledge of the weather over the Arctic routes enabled war planners to accurately predict the weather for operations in the battle zones.

The selections in the following pages are representative of the experiences of the relatively few who flew and fought amid the darkness, silence, and cold to help win the war for the Allies.

After the bombing of Tokyo by Jimmy Doolittle in April, 1942, the Japanese shifted their strategy of striking toward the south and southwest to one of attempting to capture the island of Midway and establishing bases in the Aleutians and Alaska. In June, the Japanese raided Dutch Harbor and occupied two major islands in the western Aleutians — Attu and Kiska. American reaction was as quick as the war situation would permit. On August 30, 1942, American troops landed on Adak Island, 250 miles from Kiska; within two weeks, airfields were hastily constructed and the first coordinated, fighter-supported bombing mission took off to attack Kiska on September 14.

Throughout the winter of 1942-43, planes of the newly designated Eleventh Air Force attacked the two Japanese positions whenever the weather permitted and sometimes when it didn't.

Alaskan Offensive

Maj. Ben H. Pearse

IN HIS HEADQUARTERS hut on one of the Andreanof Islands in the Aleutian chain, Maj. Wilbur Miller, fighter squadron commander, sat at the end of his cot and leaned against his desk, an empty ammunition packing box, while he called the roll from a pocket notebook on his knee. Squadron pilots answered quickly as their names were read off. Stuffing his notebook back in his pocket, Major Miller tore off a piece of wrapping paper from a package under the cot and sketched a rough semicircle representing Kiska Harbor.

"You all know that harbor well enough by this time," he began in a tone as conversational as though he were outlining a training flight instead of the plan for the next day's mission, "so I won't need a map. Here's the dope for tomorrow."

"We'll follow the photographic ship over and rendezvous five miles southeast of Little Kiska." He outlined a circle route east of the harbor and drew a line. "We'll come in on the south side of Little Kiska," he said.

"Now, our objectives are antiaircraft guns alone this time. The bombers have been getting it pretty heavy, and we've got to knock off every gun we can before they come over. We'll have two minutes to get in and out before the bombers are due, so we'll have to get out of the way fast."

He looked up to impress his audience and pushed back his fedora hat, with its major's leaf pinned on the front of the round, uncreased crown; it was the only relic of civilian life on the island.

"I don't want anyone wandering around chasing Japs tomorrow," he warned, "so leave the camp areas alone." He joined in the grin that spread around the circle of faces. He referred to an incident which had given the Air Force its biggest laugh to date. The incident occurred during a strafing raid not unlike the one they were now preparing for. One of the fighter pilots had caught a Jap with his pants down — literally. Winging in low over the camp area on Kiska, he found himself bearing down directly in the path of a Jap dashing half dressed from a tent and running for more solid cover. The pilot got to laughing so hard at the little figure with the huge strides that he almost forgot to pull the trigger.

"Now for those who weren't over this morning," the major continued, "the antiaircraft guns haven't been firing when we come to them. The Japs have been keeping their heads below the revetments until we get past 'em and then popping up to shoot as we're going away. The wingmen have got to watch that. When they pop up to fire at the lead plane, the wingman has got to knock 'em down again.

"Joe, you follow me in. We'll go in over the south side of the harbor, circle around, and duck out over that ridge just before we get to head on the north side. We'll circle offshore until the bombers have dropped everything, but don't get away.

"Chuck, your flight will go in over the north head and swing around to come out toward the southwest. Tom and Bill, I want you to be top cover and stick pretty close to the photographic plane. One of those Zeroes might get too close. Red, your flight goes straight in for those ships in the harbor. The bombers say the most accurate antiaircraft fire is coming from that destroyer and that other ship you'll find near it. Come in low, deck level or lower if you can. The Japs can't get those guns of theirs down very well.

"Mac, you're to spend all your time looking for submarine nets. I don't care if you don't fire a shot. Don't, unless someone shoots at you. You fellows with the P-40's will go with a bomber that's to look over Gertrude Cove on the south side of Kiska. Somebody thought they saw a couple of subs in there this morning. If you don't find anything, you can come over and join us. There's a little valley that

Making life as miserable as possible for the Japanese invaders of the Aleutians at their Kiska and Attu Island bases was the continuing task of the Eleventh United States Air Force. Working under weather conditions literally the worst in the world, hazardous missions over arctic seas and desolate and inhospitable islands were the routine of these flyers.

U.S. Air Force Photo

runs from Gertrude Cove almost over to the harbor, but be careful you don't get tangled up with us. You'd better wait until the bombers have finished and you'll only have Joe and me to watch out for in case we have to come back for another shot at those float planes just north of the dummies. Any questions now?"

"What time do we take off?"

"Who's going?"

The major pulled out his notebook again and read off a list of names.

"The rest of you will get to go in the afternoon if the weather holds out," he said. "Takeoff will be at seven-fifteen. Be there at a quarter of seven. You can get chow starting at a quarter of six. Any of you that haven't got alarm clocks be sure to tell the sergeant so he can wake you in plenty of time. Now get a good night's sleep."

Next morning, back in the headquarters hut of Brig. Gen. William O. Butler, commanding general of the Air Force, a little group of officers and enlisted men sat huddled around the radio. On schedule to the minute, they could hear the rasping voices of their fighter pilots, punctured with static, as the peashooters dove down over their targets at Kiska.

"Look out, Bill, there's one above you."

"Take that one, Ed; I'll cover."

They drew closer to the radio to try to make out the voices. It didn't take much imagination to picture the hurricane of fire being loosed by the .30's, the .50's, and the 37-mm. cannon from the peashooters. Then came sharp commands over the radio as the bombers swung into action. A few minutes of breathless, unseen action, and then out of a welter of calls, answers, and hurried warnings a strange voice was heard clearly.

"Where you going now, Eddie?"

The Jap radio operator on Kiska even had the name right as he tried to draw out the raider's next move.

There was a fraction of a second of relative silence; then came the answer in an unmistakable Texas clenched-teeth drawl that not even a throat mike could hide.

"None of your goddam business, Jap! I'll blow your radio shack off that island."

A torrent of profanity drowned out the static and fairly made the little table radio at headquarters writhe. The general pushed back his chair and threw up his hands. "I thought I knew some cusswords," he muttered.

Then came the Jap voice again, a little less well disguised this time in the heat of the excitement.

"Come back here, American. You die."

"We'll come back, don't you worry. With more bombs, Jap."

Then a sharp call for the PBY rescue ship. The call brought the little group to the edge of their chairs.

"P-39 down just west of Little Kiska," it said.

The group around the radio exchanged glances. That would be almost in the mouth of the harbor.

"Drop a life raft, somebody," they heard next. Then:

"Where is it? Where is it? Can't see it from here."

The group around the radio at headquarters discussed the chances of the fallen fighter pilot as the planes returned from the raid.

All the B-24's returned; all the peashooters but one came back. In little knots along the runway the crews talked excitedly.

"I saw him get out of his ship," said a pilot. "He was floating on his back, waving me on, but I don't know whether the PBY found him or not. It was pretty close to those guns on Little Kiska."

"Maybe the Japs picked him up," added another. "He came down just outside the harbor."

Lt. A. T. Rice, who got two of the five Jap float planes bagged that day, swore softly to himself. "I'd trade the two I got in a minute for the one that knocked him down," he said.

The ground crews were swarming over the peashooters, removing empty ammunition belts, checking motors, and surveying the bullet holes in wings and fuselage.

"Hey, Sarge, I need a new aileron." A tall, rangy pilot, who looked as though he never would be able to fold himself into the cockpit of a P-39, wiggled the left aileron, half shot away by an enemy anti-aircraft shell. "Here's something for the scrap-metal collection, Sarge, but the controls worked OK all the way home."

Another pursuit pilot turned over in his fingers a bullet he had fished out of the ammunition compartment in front of the cockpit and whistled softly to himself. "I wonder where the hell that one came from?" he said.

As the weeks of trying to dislodge the Japanese from Attu and Kiska went by, aircrews of the Eleventh Air Force gained much valuable experience. Unlike the other battle zones around the world, however, the worst enemy, which had to be fought continually from the time the engines were started until they were shut down, was the weather.

Up Where the Soup Begins

Herbert Ringold

ALEUTIAN FOG has been described as the kind of weather you can cut with a knife. Don't believe it. There isn't a knife made that can go through the stuff. We were only ten miles from a man-sized mountain for three months before we ever saw the damn thing. We got used to not seeing the sky. When you returned from a mission, your report would invariably begin: "Well, I was flying along in the soup —"

You could see the wind blowing from two different directions at the same time. That's the truth. One day the weather report read: "110-mile-an-hour winds — and strong gusts!" We had to tie down the B-17's and B-24's most of the time. Either we would attach a 55-gallon water tank to each wing, or sink a steel bar or wooden plank into the snow, tie a rope around it, and attach it to both ends of the ship. Even with that we had trouble.

At Umnak it rains up. When the wind decides to blow upward, everything goes with it, including the falling rain. But plenty of it came down. For days our airfield looked like a lake, with the ball turrets of the 17's all the way underwater.

It gets sort of cold up that way, too. In some parts of inland Alaska it gets down to 80 degrees below zero. So at Umnak we were practically sweating with our 35 below. And at times it really got up to decent temperatures. For a while, it was warm enough to play baseball and volleyball on Umnak.

To top it off, we had williwaws. A williwaw is the result of strong winds building up on one side of an island, passing over the island,

and pushing all its strength downward on the other side. You just don't fly through a williwaw.

After a while you get used to the weather. But it's harder to get used to the waiting. You spend half your life waiting for the weather to open so you can do some flying. Fighting the Japs wasn't bad at all — it was the sitting around, waiting for the chance to fight. Sometimes we'd be only 20 minutes from our target and wait for weeks to get to it. We used to stay in bed so long we had a tournament to select the "sack champion." A fellow named Hanson copped the honors with 26 hours in bed at one stretch.

When the weather became clear enough for us to see our hands in front of our eyes, we knew there was some flying to be done. Then we'd go out on the milk run. These were the weather flights we made to send meteorological reports back to the base every 30 minutes. We called them milk runs because they were so damned monotonous. It wasn't uncommon to be flying through the soup on such runs and report back "weather unflyable." That's how crazy it all was.

One of the "better" flying days. Consolidated B-24's move to takeoff position for a raid against Japanese-held targets in the Aleutians.

U.S. Air Force Photo

Six million pounds of bombs were dropped by Eleventh Air Force planes in the months following the first bombing raid on Kiska until the Japanese were finally dislodged. The continual harassment by the medium and heavy bombers had prevented the enemy from building an airfield and bringing in reinforcements by air. In the interim, however, the going had been rough. Japanese ack-ack was good and they were using the latest float-equipped Zeroes as interceptors. Men died fighting this "forgotten" war. Here is the story of one of the many bombing raids carried out against Kiska.

Air Guerrillas Over Kiska

William Gilman

OUR RAIDS ON KISKA had been going on for over nine months. It was attrition and was undoubtedly having its wearing effects — upon the Japs and upon those war-weary flyers who later went back to Anchorage for hospitalization. But the Japs still held on. Our heavy bombers covered the island with craters. Sometimes these coincided with targets, sometimes not. The targets were small and most of them were well buried within their revetments. This wasn't European-style bombing where, if you missed the center of a block-long factory or railroad yard, you probably demolished at least one corner. Here you had to hit bull's-eyes.

It was being learned that deck-level bombing provided the best way of knowing that the target was really demolished. Such attacks call for young, reckless men. Higher-altitude attacks by heavy bombers are perhaps as dangerous. They are fat, comparatively slow targets for the antiaircraft gunner to shoot at again and again. The low-leveler comes in like a meteor, too fast and low for bigger AA guns to touch, but of course through the splattering hail of machine-gun batteries and lower caliber but faster-fired shells. The deck-level attack may not be more' dangerous if it comes without warning, but it seems so. And if the surprise element is lacking, then the story is different.

In the Bomber Command's quonset, I pointed out to Colonel DeFord that I was simply explaining, not complaining. Going over

Kiska at great height was interesting enough while it lasted, but in retrospect it was raiding at a respectable distance from the enemy. Seeking the Jap fleet had been just eight more hours of air travel. DeFord sat at his desk quizzically looking at me over his cigarette-holder. This stocky Air Force veteran's tiny office with its four desks was crowded as usual. In addition to staff officers sweating out a mission due back, there were two young lieutenants present.

DeFord called them over and introduced them. The short burly one with Jack Dempsey's face was George Barber, of Lubbock, Texas. The other, a tall blond sapling with a silken mustache, was William Candy, of Braintree, Massachusetts. Typical young Americans both, "Stump" Barber, twenty-four, was a graduate of Texas Tech and a newlywed. Bill Candy was the son of a well-known Boston engineer and had spent two years at the Massachusetts School of Art. His mustache didn't hide the fact that he was still a bubbling, picture-painting kid of twenty-three.

As pilot and copilot respectively, they had been raiding together since December. On tomorrow's mission, March 30, Candy was flying his own Mitchell on Barber's wing.

The colonel said, "You can go on their special mission if you care to. I guarantee it won't be anything tame."

Details? DeFord grinned. "It's secret. If you want to go, wait for a call. Barber and Candy are each taking a B-25 from here. You can fly with Barber who will command. At Amchitka they'll stop to pick up four mediums. Barber will brief the pilots there — if you want to drop out then, that's OK."

Out at the "Hotel DeGunk," quonset for visiting officers, the orderly called me to the phone at eight the next morning. It was to hurry over to Bomber Command and bring along my sleeping bag because we'd probably lay over at Amchitka after the mission. I dressed hastily in several layers, topped by the parka. Once again I borrowed a bunkmate lieutenant's GI shoes — they were too big and could be kicked off in a hurry if there had to be swimming. At Bomber Command, Capt. Eddie Bendere loaned me his flying mitts and DeFord turned over his flying boots with a proviso: "I want them back."

A jeep took me in my borrowed finery to the revetments where Stump and Bill were already supervising the loading of bombs into their planes. These were the famed Mitchell mediums, decidedly different from the heavy Liberators I was weaned on, although with

175

Aleutians, 1943. A B-25 of the Eleventh Air Force takes off against a background of snow-covered mountains for Kiska.

the same twin rudders. Here was a smaller, faster ship with a five-man crew instead of nine, and two motors rather than four.

Barber outfitted me with chute, preserver, and tin hat, and proudly displayed the patches covering holes shot into his ship, the *Texie Doodle*. As we waited around I got the first inklings of what sort of joyride this would be. A crew member said all were volunteers. Another said it was to be a deck-level attack at twilight.

The how and why of this mission began shaping up. Its ingredients were bluff and bravado. It was a sequel to past events. Earlier in March, Barber with Candy copiloting roared over Kiska, had a wing flap shot off but got back teetering on one wing. Other raids followed. On the 26th, they went out with the squadrons seeking the Jap fleet beyond Attu. Homeward bound, the flight of mediums peeled off from the heavies to get rid of their bombs on Kiska.

The island's Japs apparently thought our airmen were interested only in a sea-air battle that day and were asleep on the job. Also, the Mitchells approached from an unorthodox direction, sweeping in over low cliffs at the western end of Kiska's waist. By accident, Barber's plane came in just right, giving astonished Japs no time to man their guns. It hurled over installations at 50 feet, heading down upon the camp area with Stump snarling and yelling, "You rats, I've come back for my wing flap!"

The radar shacks were so enticingly near. The Japs running for foxholes were so easy to mow down with machine guns. But Candy toggled his bombs away in vain; they hung up and wouldn't drop. In the nose, the bombardier, Lt. John LaRock, fought his machine gun in vain — it was jammed.

Barber and Candy returned to Adak boiling with resentment at the Japs and at themselves, talking themselves into a fury. It came then — why not get permission to repeat the raid, surprise and all? An all-volunteer affair, with no rank higher than lieutenant allowed.

Barber figured out the angles and Candy drew the sketches. There would be six mediums with no bothersome escort. They would fly to the west past Kiska as if they were heading for a twilight raid on Attu. Kiska's Japs would detect them and conclude that the silly Americans were going out to pound Attu's runway again. Between the two islands, they'd turn back, sneaking low over the water. They'd swoop over the same cliffs and rush down the plateau, tearing in with guns blazing, depositing their 300- and 500-pounders upon the targets. In their racks the bombs would be assigned — so many for this target, so many left for the others.

They'd burst in on Kiska in three flights of two planes apiece, each assaulting its assigned targets. Although Kiska meanders about 30 miles from north to south tip, the Japs found it practical to avoid crag dwelling and concentrate their installations in the narrow-waisted center by Kiska Harbor. Here were the camp area, sub base, and plane hangars. The harbor lay between North Head and South Head, with the nearly completed runway running into the former. But the main target was about in the center of the four-mile-wide waist. It was the pair of almost buried buildings which housed Kiska's main radar installations.

This station, the sub base, the runway and a newly discovered 90-mm. gun protecting the airfield were the primary targets. The rest of the job was to bomb and strafe the hangars, barracks, radio stations, and ack-ack nests.

How our flyers could know what to find on Kiska and where to find it was mainly a tribute to the wonders of aerial photography and to experts trained to recognize what the picture enlargements reveal.

We took off, Candy's plane behind Barber's. After a while LaRock and I went on hands and knees through the crawlway to his station in the "greenhouse." This mild young fellow wasn't exactly ferocious. It was just that he was deadly serious about his business and apologizing for what happened the last time.

"There were the Nips, running all over, and this same gun here jammed! But it won't this time. Gosh, it would've been like shooting rabbits back home in Louisiana. Oh well, I'm pretty lucky, though. Here I am, only two weeks in the Aleutians — and already on my fourth mission."

And so this bombardier, an ex-clerk, checked and rechecked the ammunition and twirled the gun in its pivot. It was his job to drop bombs. But on low altitude attacks, it was the copilot who dumped out bombs without bombsighting, and the bombardier operated the nose machine gun.

We soon dove at a barren little island, bombing it mightily and swinging around to strafe the smoking tundra. Everything worked fine. New bombs would be waiting at Amchitka.

At that base there was a reunion, our crews and those of the four waiting Mitchells. Candy's copilot, Lt. John T. Rodger, stood up under vociferous kidding. He was from Kalamazoo.

Barber made an announcement. "We've got a few hours yet this afternoon, and lots to do in them. But first we'd better get chow. Our takeoff is six o'clock sharp. That means we can't take time for evening chow at 5:30. We'll have to get supper when we come back."

Some stayed to supervise the ground crew. The rest of us piled into a jeep, overflowing upon its running board and hood. To those remaining, Barber called back, "Don't forget to eat soon. We meet at the ships at 5:30. After that, nobody eats. I won't — honest."

The shout came, "Don't forget to wire the Japs we're coming."

The jeep took us to the runway's far end, to a nest of poised fighters. Clutching our sleeping-bag bundles and kits, we began scrambling and sliding over hills of melting ice and slushy tundra, weaving through gulches, and hopping over streams. It helped one understand these war flyers down the Aleutians. Their boots were mud-caked, trousers mud-lined, faces mud-streaked. Far back, at Anchorage and Fairbanks, where they went if lucky enough to get leave, they slept in fine quarters, dressed in pinks, saw and danced with a few real women. At intermediate Aleutian bases, they lived in rounded metal huts, had hot water and cots, plenty of actress photos and detective magazines, and laundry service. Here at the end of the line they passed along one frayed copy of a nudist magazine, nuzzled their way into sleeping bags in mud-floored tents, stood up to eat chow that was rather rugged too. You smelled like a goat, felt like a dog, and, boy, how swell it was to hurl the hell inside you upon the heads of the Japs.

We slid down a revetment into the tent of Capt. Kenneth Spears, Intelligence officer for the airdrome's Bomber Command. The latest news?

Well, two regular missions had gone to Kiska today, and the Japs there were probably buzzing like disturbed hornets by now. A Zero had been seen in the air near Attu, and we pricked up our ears when we heard that it might be a land-based ship — that was bad news. Yes, Kiska now had at least that one 90-mm. battery and it would be swell, Spears said, if this mission could knock it over.

Somebody asked Barber: Suppose the engines on one of the six Mitchells didn't check out?

"My plan stands. Six ships go, or none go."

Takeoff time. One after another we raced down the runway and then circled the island, assembling in formation. Barber would lead the attack later, but right now another plane was in front because it alone had a navigator aboard. There was plenty of time yet. LaRock and I stayed in our ship's unoccupied navigator's cubbyhole. Through the crawlway to the rear we could see a sitting robot, only immobile legs and elbows protruding. It was the turret gunner, head and shoulders out of sight, scanning the horizon.

This was fine flying. It called for music and poetry. We were twin-tailed porpoises, lazily rising and falling with the air currents, no flashing telegraph poles to indicate that we were speeding westward.

LaRock and I explained in more detail where we were from in the States. Then he fiddled with the plane's heating system; it wouldn't work. He went to the relief tube, came back hitching his trousers, put on his tin hat, and dropped to his knees.

"I'll get everything ready in the greenhouse," he said, and crawled out of sight.

I was wishing time would leap forward, wanted to be racing in on Kiska and get it over with. Lt. Quentin Standford called back from the copilot's seat, "Is your mouth dry? Mine always is at a time like this."

We lit cigarettes again. I grew tense when I saw a vessel on the water. Then I saw it was a plane. I relaxed when it became one of our Mitchells skimming low, teasing the waves, practicing.

We had not seen Kiska through the congregating mists, but were past it by now. I could imagine Nipponese intelligence officers on Kiska receiving radar reports about us, wondering if our objective was really Attu, or was this some more Yankee trickery?

Barber was peering to the north. We were past Buldir Island, which is 60 miles beyond Kiska. I kept wishing, "Let's turn. It's time to turn."

A storm was on us. We were 200 feet above rearing waves, and Stump cursed the wind that was driving us off course. Would we postpone? We didn't want postponement.

Then the pilot's shoulders moved, one up and the other down. The ship banked off to the right and Stump yelled, "Here we go!"

Still another last cigarette. And after a few long minutes, it was there, the looming ghastliness of Kiska Volcano ahead, the storm behind us. Barber called, "Better get in the nose."

Our ship now led. I wormed down the crawlway. LaRock got off the seat and I buckled myself into it. He was on one knee sighting his machine gun, an elbow resting on my knee. LaRock looked up and grinned when I juggled my heavy feet so that the copilot's machine gun's barrel ran between my knees.

Above the twin-engined roar, LaRock was singing. He yelled an explanation, "Always sing and whistle at a time like this — keeps my mind off it."

We were skimming the water, coming in at an angle, and Kiska's midsection was here. Ahead was a sharp valley, hardly more than a big gully. From my recollection of Candy's charts, that's where we'd be going in. I was chewing my gum rapidly and wondered if that was a cavity in my tooth. But we didn't go in there. Stump was gunning the motors. We were charging over a cliff farther down the coast. It was confusing. LaRock's gun was chattering and he wrestled with it as the plane bucked in air currents. His red tracers were streaming toward something I couldn't see yet. I thought he was crazy. This couldn't be it yet — he was simply warning every Jap on the island and ruining our chance for surprise.

Then I saw he wasn't crazy. This was it. Stinging red flickers were coming at us, from our left and right and from straight ahead, off every ridge and out of every hillside. You couldn't see the lead itself; it didn't patter on our glass dome like hail. It was invisible and everywhere.

This was a barrage and our motors were screaming through it at 300 miles an hour. The plateau sloped down and so did we over the spinning brown tundra 25 feet below. A roof — nothing more. The rest of the building nestled within its earthen revetment walls. Just a mound with a lid. The lights in the panel at LaRock's shoulder went out. Standford had toggled bombs away, yelling, "This one's for Connie, and this one's for Mac — and these are for you, Tojo!" (Connie and Mac were other Mitchell pilots — they had failed to return from Kiska raids.) But we were past already, and in the nose I couldn't see the 1,600 pounds of havoc blow up.

It was up to us and our bombs, very definitely. The ruse had failed. We had flown into batteries as anxious to see us come as we had been to get there. From our ship we saw only five scurrying Japs. I don't know whether LaRock's bullets hit any of them. Or Standford's whose gun was coughing between my knees, covering the floor with ejected shells. What we saw in one flicker was behind us the next.

I was trying to look all around. Everything in me wanted to sit there transfixed, feeling very nude in the greenhouse, staring straight ahead. The red flashes at us from the hills were joined by a July 4th sprouting of fireworks from the camp area ahead. We curved down a ravine, which sprayed us from both sides. The Japs were throwing it at us blindly, trying to touch the winged meteor, confident that what missed us would catch Candy behind our left wing. There was no way of knowing whether Candy was with us anymore.

Now we were flashing past barracks, and our bombs fell again. Again they dropped as we skimmed the seaplane hangar. And now we were over Kiska Harbor. A small boat wallowed at our right without a soul on deck. LaRock was cursing, fighting his gun. He fell backward, returned to his knees and gripped the gun again. "It won't fire, damn it! It won't fire!" he yelled.

But the boat was behind us now. I didn't realize it till later, but we were then no more than 25 seconds older than we were when we first charged over the cliff. North Head was a few hundred feet to our left, with red bulbs of gunfire going on and off like an animated electric sign. For the first time I felt mortally afraid. This was the last gauntlet. Were we going to be blown up now, at the very end?

North Head was gone. We were hurtling past Little Kiska, guardian isle of Kiska Harbor, and saw the smoking tundra fires left by Lightnings on a raid early in the day.

There was a plane ahead and high above us. A long, flat wing. LaRock swung his gun to bear on it; it was working again.

The plane hovered. Then it banked and we saw the maternal lines of the Catalina.

I slipped on the headphones. Barber was calling in the other five pilots. Then the Japs jammed us with screeching noise, and I tore off the phones.

LaRock and I found ourselves doing the same thing, scanning each other for signs of blood. Not a sign. But something was wrong. It irritated me. Then we saw what it was. A freezing blast of air was blowing in. Dead ahead, a bit to the right of the tip of the plane's nose, was a jagged vacant space where there had been glass. We grinned.

I crawled back and lit a cigarette. Barber was still trying to contact the other pilots. He looked worried. I looked out through the top dome and could see nothing wrong. Five B-25's — and our own made six. As we reconstructed it later, here is what had been happening . . .

Our plane laid the bombs on the radar shack, and our tail gunner saw the building erupt. Candy saw it too, his plane rocking with our blasts as he dumped 1,500 pounds on a nearby powerhouse. We then bombed and strafed hangars and barracks nearer the beach before sailing out over the harbor. One of Candy's bombs, aimed for a barracks, sailed through the doorway of another. His plane had been hit a few times. Ours had only the broken nose glass.

At our right, Flight C's Lt. Ray Stoltzman dropped four bombs upon the sub base, and Flint confirmed an explosion which rose 250 feet. Then "Stoltz" streaked across the harbor, machine-gunning the ship and dropping his last two bombs on or near a radio station at North Head's tip. His plane hadn't been hit.

But Lt. Norman Henricksen, piloting the plane just behind, had it harder. One of Stoltzman's 500-pounders blew up in his face. Henricksen was leaning to the left at the time. That alone kept a five-inch-long bomb fragment, which sailed through the windshield, from decapitating him. The blast alone sent up fragments which shattered the copilot's windshield and battered one wing. In addition, the plane had bullet holes in each engine nacelle and a chunk torn out of one wing by a 20-mm. shell fragment. But the plane flew well

What American troops found on Kiska in August, 1943: wrecked Japanese planes, oil and gas drums are a mass of rubble as a result of USAAF bombings.

U.S. Air Force Photo

enough. Except that there was worry over bombs. Only one had fallen. The sub base was dug in at a corner where two hills met, forming natural revetments. To get in on the target, the pilot had to use a fighter plane's squirming, diving approach. This caused two live bombs to hang up, suspended from only one shackle and their other ends bumping against the open bomb-bay doors.

Lt. Albert Hahn, the bombardier, went back to see about them. From the rear came the radio operator, T/Sgt. Robert Irish. Neither was wearing a cumbersome parachute for so tight a squeeze. They met above the bomb-bay doors, open sea below, and Hahn able to hold on only to Irish. Hahn slipped pins back into the fuses, unscrewed the deadly detonators and kicked out the two bombs. Others which hadn't fallen remained snugly in their racks.

There were specks of glass in Henricksen's eye and below it. The flight surgeon, back at the base, later removed them without trouble.

The remaining two Mitchells were in A flight, at our left. They had troubles too, although they registered bomb hits upon a radio station, the big-gun battery, the runway, and also strafed some trucks. It was again a case of the lead plane getting through with less trouble. But behind Lt. Bill Jackson's bomber flew that of Lt. Bill Geyser, who was that Aleutian oddity, an actual Alaskan, from Anchorage.

His bombardier, Lt. H. R. Hodges, was wounded over the right eye but not seriously. There were five holes in the plane's right wing and four in the left. Bullets and shell fragments had slashed into each engine. Something had hit one propeller, and it was racing several hundred revolutions a minute faster than the other.

Geyser might handle that by juggling his controls, but that's where the grim rub came in. His entire hydraulic system was shot to pieces and its fluid was dripping through the plane. Consequently: he couldn't let down his retracted wheels for the coming landing; he couldn't operate his wing flaps; his bomb-bay doors were open and he couldn't shut them; worst of all, he couldn't operate his throttles. He faced a wheelless belly landing for which he couldn't reduce speed.

Enemy fire had done something to the plane's interphone circuit. Geyser started crawling to the rear to see if anybody was hurt. Half-way, he bumped into the radio operator crawling forward to ask the same question. They reassured each other, and Geyser returned to take over the teetering plane from his copilot, Lt. Bud Binning.

The latter now wanted to see why some of his bombs hadn't dropped. He found three live 300-pounders hanging down, bumping against the open doors.

He managed to kick them out . . .

It was now a matter of sweating homeward Geyser's crippled plane which was frozen to a speed he couldn't change. By radio, Amchitka knew of his plight. Firepots outlined the runway assigned to him. We saw an ambulance racing up. It was not yet completely dark; we could see swarms of infantrymen silhouetted upon the hills.

One after another, our planes sat down. But Barber was squadron leader and stayed with Geyser, flying at his wing. We saw him come low over the runway to look it over. Another circle around and lower this time for another anxious scrutiny. Again we circled and this time Geyser was landing. Somewhere in that descent he cut out his motors — no more engine control of the bomber now, no wing flaps either. His bomb-bay doors dragged the ground but he was hesitating a moment, then he took the plunge. He slid straight as an arrow for a thousand feet, then the plane swerved and left the runway in a burst of dirt.

Our own plane zoomed in a wild turn as Barber came around to get another look at the crash. We saw the wreck and soldiers swarming. The result was amazingly lucky. The plane was a total loss, but every man within hopped out through the top hatch like a rabbit to get away from fire or explosion. Had Binning not risked his life kicking out the live bombs, back along the line, the outcome would have been different.

Unable to land on its home base in the fogbound Aleutian Islands, this Eleventh Air Force B-24 Liberator returning from a bombing mission found a safe landing spot on one of the tiny islands in the Aleutians. Hardly damaged, the bomber was salvaged by ground crews of the Eleventh Air Force and flew again against the Japanese.

U.S. Air Force Photo

*The presence of the Japanese in the Aleutians was not the only rea-
son for American air units being in Alaska. Bases had to be built
from which bombers and fighters coming from American production
lines could be ferried to Russia under the lend-lease program. In September, 1942, the ALSIB (Alaska-Siberia) route was opened. In the
two and one-half years that it was in operation, over 6,000 planes of
various types were flown from the United States and turned over to
the Russians at Ladd Field near Fairbanks. From there they were
flown to Siberia via Nome. It was a different, but no less dangerous,
way to fight the war in the air.*

Lifeline to the U.S.S.R.

Herbert Ringold

WHEN THE ROUTE was first opened, deliveries were few and far
between. Men were killed, aircraft cracked up with alarming regularity. For a while it appeared that the promised delivery schedule
would not be met. Moreover, the winter of 1942-43 was the coldest
in all the recorded history of Fairbanks. The temperature dropped
to 67 degrees below zero. At some way stations, men lived in tents in
that kind of weather — and the latrines were outside. Engine oil
froze to solid ice. Weather changed from CAVU to zero-zero in seven
minutes. At Ladd Field, it was not physically possible to work outdoors for long periods in temperatures that turned breath into icicles,
froze eyelids together, and caused severe cases of frostbite, sometimes
necessitating amputation. Mechanics took turns running in and out
of heated hangars to service the planes. If any part of the body
touched a piece of metal, flesh and metal could not be separated
without cutting. If a single drop of 100-octane gas fell on the skin, it
would raise a blister about an inch high. The fingers of some mechanics were eaten away like the hands of lepers.

Capt. Thomas Hardy was B-26 Project Officer at Fairbanks, and
he had two brand-new Marauders, in tip-top shape, serviced by some
of the best mechanics in the business. Only four hours of flying time
a month are necessary to qualify for flying pay. During January, 1943,
the weather was so bad that Captain Hardy did not get flying pay.

Gradually, with the help of the untiring work carried on by Brig. Gen. Dale V. Gaffney's Cold Weather Testing Unit at Ladd Field and the pioneering of Col. Ponton De Arce, first commanding officer at Great Falls, the principal difficulties were licked.

Flying the route in the early days presented the kind of hazards that grandchildren will never believe. Along the 1900-mile run, there were only four radio ranges. They were on the air only half the time — and then they were completely unreliable. Pilots said that the best way to run into a mountainside was to stay on the beam. Landing conditions were dangerous because most fields had only soft-dirt runways.

There was no weather information of any kind in an area where the only thing that could be forecast was that the weather would be unpredictable. Pilots took off under perfect flying conditions and ran into a snowstorm five minutes out. They just stuck their ships into the weather and flew until it got too tough. Then the trick was to find out where they were and how to get back.

There is a valley between Watson Lake and Whitehorse which became known as Million Dollar Valley because we lost more than a million dollars' worth of airplanes up there in a short time. It was easy for experienced pilots to guess what had happened. The planes ran into weather — blizzards, thunderstorms, fog, severe icing, and ceiling zero in the mountains. In that area, there were absolutely no navigational methods to determine approximate position. Every hundred miles of frozen terrain looked just like every other hundred miles. Every mountain range presented the same ugly picture. Radios were useless — distances were too great to establish contact. The pilots just flew around blindly until they found this likely-looking valley, which seemed to offer an avenue of escape. Then they crashed.

Despite all the hazards of the trip, one man made it in a Piper Cub. In December, 1942, Capt. Malcolm Pruitt looked over his insurance records and took off from Great Falls in a Cub that had a range of only three hours. He knew that he could not make the 242-mile jump from Edmonton to the flight strip at Grand Prairie without adding extra hours to his flying time. So he went into a hardware store and purchased a funnel. Then he scraped up 22 one-gallon gasoline cans and cut a hole in the gas tank which extends into the Piper cockpit. He kept one eye on his course and one eye on the gas. Every time the gas supply dropped, he heaved another gallon into the tank.

After flying out of Edmonton for four hours and fifteen minutes,

Soviet airmen take over a Lend-Lease Douglas A-20 at Ladd Field, Fairbanks, Alaska.

U.S. Air Force Photo

This one didn't make the Air Transport Command field at Nome, but it was repaired and eventually got to the Russo-German front.

U.S. Air Force Photo

he was still nowhere near his first stop. The outside temperature was a smart 20 degrees below zero, and Pruitt had no heater. He finally went down into nine inches of snow in the middle of a farmer's field. He figured that he could telephone for help — but the farmer had no phone.

When he got out to his plane, he found that the motor had frozen. Pruitt had already had too many troubles to let that bother him. He found a washtub, built a fire in it, and shoved the tub under the motor, heating it up sufficiently for the takeoff. After an hour of night flying without instruments, he landed again at a little railroad town in the Peace River country. Finally, he got into Grand Prairie and eventually delivered his plane to Fort St. John, 796 miles from Great Falls.

Getting through in those days was often a matter of luck. Some of the most experienced pilots in the Air Forces went down — and they and their planes haven't been found yet. Because of the lack of radio ranges, it was impossible to notify the base as to the approximate position. A wrecked plane was nothing more than a flyspeck against a background of snow and ice that extended for thousands of miles.

There were no roads, no people, no shelter, and very little chance of finding food. It was the kind of territory that even Renfrew of the Royal Canadian Mounted has never visited. Many crewmen who crashed were found frozen to death. There have been exceptions; Lt. Leon Crane got back after 84 days in the wilderness. On the other hand, a crew bailed out within sight of an airfield — and their plane is still undiscovered.

Capt. Thomas Dichiara was coming back from Fairbanks as a passenger in a C-60. The plane went into a spin, and Dichiara bailed out. While he was floating down into that frozen barren country, the pilot righted the ship and flew on. Dichiara was very much alone. He had no idea where he was, so he just picked a direction and headed off. In 30 minutes, he came across the only railroad track in that part of the world. Fifteen minutes later, a train which runs only once a week came along and picked him up.

Today, conditions in that area have been changed. Where there were only four radio ranges, now there is a range station every 150 to 200 miles. With one exception, all legs are interlocking. Instead of hundreds of miles without a possible landing site, there are now 13 regular landing fields and 8 flight strips, 100 miles apart. The Alcan Highway provides a perfect checkpoint with a station every 40 miles.

An Arctic Rescue System has been organized which has effectively combated one of the most serious of all problems faced along the Northwest Route — the question of the mental hazard faced by airmen who knew that in case of trouble their chances of survival and rescue would be exceedingly slim. A radio network is maintained, and five stations have aircraft assigned for the specific purpose of helping in the search and dropping supplies. A survival kit has been perfected, complete down to frying pans. There is a standing reward of $100.00 awaiting any trapper who furnishes information resulting in the rescue of grounded airmen.

But the men who were given the job of setting up a rescue system were faced with a problem that ordinary rescue methods could not overcome. Crews were forced down in locations inaccessible even to a man dropped by parachute. Planes cracked up in the middle of heavily wooded forests or on the top of mountain peaks. It was often necessary to land a rescue party miles away from the stricken airmen. But the rescuers could not carry the heavy sleds and equipment needed for the evacuation work. The problem had no answer until Lt. David Irwin came up with the idea of using parapups.

Lieutenant Irwin lived in the north country for years before the war. He said that he could train his dogs so that they could be parachuted out of an airplane. Then the sleds could be dropped to the rescue party and the dogs hitched up. A test flight was made, and Lieutenant Irwin merely pushed the dogs out of a C-47. The chutes opened automatically and the dogs landed without injury. Now the use of parapups is a routine method of operation. Everything has worked without difficulty except that Lieutenant Irwin has been unable to teach his dogs to yell "Geronimo" as they jump.

Every time one problem was solved, another arose which demanded immediate attention. The toughest of all was the problem of winterizing the airplanes. Hydraulic fluid wouldn't flow at minus 30 and 40. Even at less cold temperatures, the fluid became so stiff that airmen had to sit with their feet braced against the landing-gear operating valve in order to lower and raise the gear. A lighter fluid was developed that would pour in zero temperatures.

The spark plugs wouldn't heat. As one pilot put it, "By the time I got out to the end of the runway, my engine sounded like an asthmatic outboard-motor boat." A new spark plug was invented with a longer electrode protruding into the combustion chambers of the cylinders.

The oil supply to the engines was cut off because moisture ran down into the oil-tank sump and promptly froze. Hundreds of feet of control cable were useless because the grease in the system froze as solid as concrete. A mechanic who helped lick the problem said, "For a while there, we were going crazy. We'd put the correct tension on the control cables to allow for a temperature of minus 15 degrees, and a drop to minus 40 caused the cables to tighten and pull something loose. Then when we fixed them for minus 40, the thermometer went up to minus 10 and expansion set in. We finally arranged a complicated system that solved the problem.

One of the problems that still hasn't been completely licked is the undramatic question of making allowances for the differential in the expansion and contraction ratio of the various metals. Aluminum does not expand at the same rate as copper. Copper has a different contraction ratio from steel. When one metal contracted, the connecting rods had to be tightened to allow for the change. Then the other metal would contract, and the work had to be done all over again. When the temperature changed, one metal would expand, requiring a loosening-up process all around. But the second metal had not yet expanded and the proper allowance had to be made. After this was worked out for minus 20, the temperature went to minus 40, then zero, then plus 5 — and that's the way it went all winter.

The fact that we are delivering aircraft to an ally who does not speak our language presented yet another problem. The Red Air Force pilots had never before seen the planes which they were to fly, and the language difficulties were enormous.

Captain Wolfson reported his experience with the problem of checking out the Russians. "A young Soviet pilot with a girl interpreter came over to my P-40 for a check. The Russian climbed into the cockpit, the girl got on one wing, and I got on the other. He asked me only four questions, and then took off.

"First thing he wanted to know was, 'How do you start it?' I told the girl, she told him, and he said, 'Da' — Russian for yes. Then he asked for the maximum pressure and the rpm for the takeoff. His next question was, 'How do you keep the oil temperature and the coolant temperature up?' Finally, he wanted to know how to operate the radio. Then he took the plane up for its test run. And he knew how to fly it, too."

Captain Wolfson's experience took place before a regular system for checking out the Russians was adopted. Maj. Frederick Kane, operations officer at Ladd Field, was in charge of that problem, and

Note the Red Star of Russia on these Douglas A-20 planes at Ladd Field. The Red Star was painted on before American airmen flew them north to Fairbanks from Montana.

U.S. Air Force Photo

A P-39 covered with snow just after a snowstorm at Ladd Field, Alaska, 1944.
U.S. Air Force Photo

he solved it handily.

"For a while," said Major Kane, "we used interpreters in our bigger ships, but that didn't work out too well because there were too many technical terms which the interpreters could not be expected to understand.

"So we fell back on the universal language of all airmen — signs. In A-20's, a Russian would lie prone in the passageway directly in back of the pilot. We would point to the instrument recording the manifold pressure used for the takeoff, and the Red Air Force flyer would memorize it. If we reduced the power at a certain time, we would point to the proper instrument. They knew exactly what we were doing, and we got along very well.

"For fighter planes, we used the cockpit check and lectures. Some of our men spoke Russian and they bore the brunt of this work. All Tech Orders were translated into Russian and mimeographed.

"One of our most unusual situations occurred with the tower operations. The Soviets had never used radio control before. They said that if everything was clear, they just came in. We explained that our regulations demanded the use of radio control, and they learned it our way.

"That gave us a problem in the tower. Our few Russian-speaking men had more important things to do than to become tower operators. We found a civilian who could speak both languages, but he didn't know anything about aircraft procedure. When an airborne Russian called in for a landing clearance, the civilian explained what was wanted to the tower chief, he outlined the necessary procedure, and back it went in Russian to the pilot. Now, of course, we have lots of people up there who talk both languages.

"Those Russians are good. Remember, they have a ferrying problem as complicated as ours, or worse. But they got those planes to the battlefront and made good use of them."

Today, the Northwest Route is nothing more than a routine ferry hop. No one can say to what extent the planes ferried along the route helped turn the tide at Stalingrad and enabled the U.S.S.R. to throw back the enemy. The Russians know very well that in bridging the gap between Great Falls and Fairbanks, many Americans died for the same purpose as the defenders of Moscow. As one Soviet general said, "There are graves of those who died among the snows of this route which mean as much to us as those at Smolensk, Stalingrad, or Sevastopol. We feel they died fighting beside us."

193

On July 4, 1943, a group of long-range B-17 Flying Fortresses and P-38 Lightnings equipped with belly tanks left an Air Force base in Maine on a pioneering flight to England by way of Greenland. It was the first combined flight of bombers and fighters to try the Arctic airway to Europe's war front. Bad weather and enemy radio interference led some of them to disaster. Six planes — 25 men — were forced down in a mass crash landing on the Greenland Ice Cap.

One of the P-38 pilots on that flight wrote a firsthand report when he returned to the States. But it was more than an account of hazard and hardship under subzero conditions. It is a picture of what a World War II fighter pilot was like.

Flight East

Lt. Harry L. Smith, USAAF

OUR FLIGHT took off from an Army airfield in Maine, assembled fast, and headed north. Climbed through broken clouds and ran through a stray piece of fuzz now and then . . . up to 13,000 feet before we'd topped it all. The usual week's layoff had rusted my waste gate so that the old bucket didn't percolate like any sixty I've seen . . . Egghead (Lt. R. H. Wilson) whipped by me several times to give the intimation that everything wasn't exactly in show formation, so I finally managed to plow up into position.

The clouds cleared when we hit the Gulf of St. Lawrence and that puddle looked real pretty. We were over the overcast better than ever a few miles further on . . . holes in the cloud revealed a terrain that warn't good for man nor beast.

Time sped on and before long, zingo! Stape (Lieutenant Staples) kicked the old 17 over on a wing, and down we came — Labrador base on the nose, and so soon? 'Tain't possible when you're indicating 185 mph. There it is though, staring yuh in the face, so . . . I guess those blasted trucks move along, even though it is not so pretty good for us — damn Flying Fortress. Learned that Hub (Maj. E. G. Hubbard, Sqdn. CO) had been lost in the muck and turned back.

The Labrador base is a hellhole with slimy chuck and knotty beds, and an enemy squadron of 109's, disguised as mosquitoes, have so much of Hub's blood in them that they sent him a card on Father's Day. Allah, take me home! What the coke, though? Letcha beard grow, ya teeth turn yellow, and live today, 'cause we ain't made to last forever. Some of those lads on the other side would give more'n I've got to be right here where these old flying boots are now. . . . And so to the sack.

Labrador to Greenland. As the crow flies, 995 miles . . . as we flew, God only knows, but a good 1,200, I'll wager.

7/6/42 — Takeoff 11:00 G.M.T., on the ground at 18:00 G.M.T.

Egg and I were hanging around our crates giving 'em the last touch after running the engines on morning preflight when winddaing! . . . Spider (Capt. D. W. Webb, Commander of Tomcat Flight) hits his Bucket, winds her up and starts billowing forth — damme, looks as if we're taking off. Several hundred miles of cold drink ahead, and nothing but a blast of pop to say "Le's go" . . . I hit the seat, alert style, wind old Sugar up and blast out on the strip — the Egg crates are snafu'd as usual so we have plenty of time to get set for the gun. Two 17's, two peashooters, and now — me. Whoa, Josephine! Pulled 'er off at 95 and got a partial stall . . . that isn't happy with 2,000 pounds of gas below your belly.

We line 'em up, East North East, and for once that rugged country isn't hazed up today. As far as you can see, the field is the only place you could set a poker chip on. An hour out and the cold North Atlantic, here named that Davis Straits, smears into the horizon with a goodly smattering of icebergs to keep the frost content true. Sugar, this ain't trew love . . . P-138's just don't land on water! Half an hour we've passed the coast and we're over the top — damn nice. You can't see the puddle, and she looks like clear sailing from now on. Another 1,800 secs. tick by and we slam into the convergence of two layers . . . up through a hole and then another until — hell, the stuff goes up to infinity. We turn back northwest, skirting the front at 16,000 feet, and looking for the little hole that isn't there. For two hours we turn into it, bank to the northwest, up, down, through holes, through the soup; no horizon, no ground, no sky . . . clouds, stratus, cumulus, cirrus . . . the works! Can navigators operate in stuff like this! We've picked up no beams!

Stand by ypsiporrah! Spider just stalled out and dropped a wing down through the overcast. Disappeared. Damn this lumbering crate that's leading us. You almost stall every time they turn into you. The rest of the flight comes into the clear a moment later, on top. Every-

195

one looks back, praying like hell that old Spider will show up, 'cause a peashooter isn't made for sole ocean hops. There he is, way below and to the right, coming up through a hole. A minute and he's back in formation . . . Swee'Pea, that's enough of that. The two 17's and Spider start gabbing about the situation now. Come on lads, make up those blasted minds of yours . . . Bacha, one navigator, says it's closer to Labrador; Bill Bayless, the other, says it's closer to the auxiliary field in Greenland. I can hear Spider calling: "Hello, Yellow Leader, I don't give a damn what you do, but do it quick!" Hanna, pilot of No. 2 B-17, spots a supposed clear hole about the time Stape ascends through the soup after a trip down to take a look. Yellow section joins back on Stape, and the last we see of Hanna is five specks speeding off through the cirrus.

We take a gander at ourselves and after a spot of chitchat feel that Greenland is our only chance. So it's up to 20,000 for a last try-over, and if that isn't possible, stick 'em through it! Sugar, if you don't think it's cold over those Davis Straits at 20,000, just let the meter tell you that she's 30°C, and that's not so pretty good with no heater, gloves, or boots, and in a summer flying suit and jacket. Fact is, my fingers are so numb I can't feel 'em, and I forgot I had toes two hours ago. Cousin, it looks as if this is IT! We've two hours' gas to go, and still that front is as solid as a mountain. Here we go into the STUFF! Hang on, Egg . . . I almost take the wing off that 17 trying.

The overcast seems to be made up of ice crystals. It keeps flowing off the 17 like condensation trails. Leaves a wake like a baby snowstorm. Blast this 160 mph. Damn turbo keeps cutting in and out . . . makes you work like a pump to keep in formation. Chickadee, if these engines quit now there'll be no more Tomcat Yellow Flight. Minute after minute we hang in there. Sometimes it seems like the 17 is flying a vertical turn and you're looking straight up at it. If only those turbos would quit cutting out. Will this stuff never end? What will happen to us if this stuff extends to the coast and over? Well, what the hell, a guy can't live forever . . . eventually, why not now?

After a thousand years the clouds begin to thin; a few stray sunbeams slip in, and zingo! We're out in the clear, and there's the most beautiful sight I've seen in all my 23 years . . . the west coast of Greenland. Thank God for putting that place ahead of us! It would be just as pretty if it were the Sahara Desert. Boy, does that old ground look delicious!

The flight turns left and follows the coast northward. Sugar, you blasted beautiful bucket, you can quit running any time now, because I'll set your tin hide most any place along that shore and be a live cookie.

So 'tis, after another hour of flying up the coast, we take the right fjord, and the auxiliary field comes into sight. I've seen a more inviting-looking field. The flight comes over in ragged formation, we're *tired;* no one knew when his crate was going to run dry. Pull around in a Lufbery, buzz the runway, circle and set 'em down. Thank God for pushing us through that one. Here are 13 men that have used up every bit of luck anyone should rightfully have, and lived to tell the tale. A bouquet of orchids to Bill for bringing us through, and love'n kisses to Stape for keeping that boat from rocking and giving us a chance to hang on to him.

Our tails are so sore from bouncing in those peashooters that we all slept on our stomachs for the next two days.

Auxiliary Field, Greenland to Iceland. 7/15/42. Takeoff 3:45 A.M. G.M.T. . . . flew eight hours and forty-five minutes.

Caphoniz Cafranz! It's only 2 A.M. . . . we've had no sleep for the last 18 hours . . . but the weather is good. Green Flight finally joined us, so Hitler, here we come. Eight days is a long time in this monotony of eat and sleep, so le's give 'er the kiss-off. Poor Buck! some knucklehead let his ship roll off the strip, and the tail was torn up. More of this monotony, 'tis rough!

After the usual delay and snafu, we all wind 'em up and taxi down the strip . . . stop, start again and, after the two 17's, we hit the breeze, the last remnants of dawn still clinging in the sky. We mill around, form at last, then head east, climbing to 13,000 feet to top the cap and its usual layer of cloud. Baby, it sure starts freezing soon over the ice cube . . . and these winter flying suits come in plenty handy. Two hours out and the east coast goes under. The water is filled up with icebergs . . . ALLISON, keep 'em flying. Looks plenty good ahead, except for a helluva big front to the north. Half an hour off the coast and we're over the top again at 10,000. Still looks OK. We are climbing a little to stay above the stuff, up to 14,000 and level off. Fifteen minutes pass and now it ain't looking good. I'm colder than an Alp dog's nose, and we're up to 16,000. A hole up front sends Green Flight down to see the bergs below, but they report rain, snow, ice. They are back up with us, and my fingers are sure as hell frozen. Wonder how the other lads feel?

This ain't true love, Spider says, so back we turn. No more of

197

trying to make five crates into one and then sticking 'em in the soup. So it's a 180 turn (damn, it's cold), the good old coast turns up in an hour, and two more of the same will put us home with momma! The layer over the cap has built up a little and we are at 13,500 going home. Somehow it feels warmer. I might even manage a whistle but for the altitude. Sure didn't want to stick my nose in that soup again. An hour-fifteen back from the coast and some stuff looms up to about 18,000 . . . wouldn't it be funny if the field were closed in. Haw! Funny as hell!! "Haw" is right: the leader just called and said the field is closed but the other, 500 miles away, is open. Sugar, whatta we do now? Stape goes down to take a look at the cap. The visibility is not good, and that haze blends with the ice, obliterating the horizon. Come on, chum, let's get out of here. Some chatter about setting 'em on the cap here but the second field sounds better, so it's south we head. Rpm at 1,500, was 1,750, manifold pressure from 23 inches down to 19. Run every tank, and heave the drop-tanks over when they are empty. Sugar, I had a hunch this playing in weather would pop our tails! All the P-crates are stalling along at 140 indicated, full lean, altitude 13,000 feet.

Time seems endless now. The old Bucket got five hours on the nose from her belly tanks . . . three hours more to go and then she's all through. The rest of the ships are strung out all over the sky, every man striving to use the last drop of gas to his best advantage. Hanna in the No. 217 goes ahead to spot the course (what course?) but we are fast enough at our settings to keep him in sight. More reports have come in from the bombers that the second field is still OK. I've still an hour and a half so at least I may make it. Don't know about the other fellows. We're all running low.*

Thirty minutes more and the clouds open. Mountains ahead. Sugar, it looks like we're home! Sure hope it is not an hour's drag up that fjord to the field; Mac says his gas is mighty low. I still have plenty so I step 'er up a bit and pull into close formation. What the hell, only six 38's! Has one gone down? Nope, just had my head up, and didn't notice that Bugs had gone back hours ago with engine trouble. Hanna, leading Green Flight, seems to have turned inland,

---

* We later learned that all our radio reports had been rec'd OK at the bases BUT! The reports we got in code were just the opposite from conditions observed at the two fields on the fifteenth of July, 1942. Evidently the enemy had picked up our frantic calls for aid, and sensing our plight, endeavored to make sure of our end by misdirecting our leaders. OK, Jerry, we'll jot that down in the books.

and is soon lost from us. What gives? Stape pulls a 180 and heads back for them. We're all through now if the leaders start circling. I call and find that the second field is not ahead. In fact, we don't know where we are! In the meantime Mac has radioed and said his gas was too low to go on, so he's going to try a landing with his wheels down. . . . Luck, lad! There's a guy with guts, trying to set one of these flying bricks down on God-knows-what with gear extended — she squats at 100 mph, and when you flip, Bub, that ain't good!

Mac levels off in a low flat approach, his wheels touch, white spray kicks up behind him like dust. He's down and rolling; watch it, man! It's all over. The crate rolled about 200 yards and then flipped like a shot rabbit. A good try, but damned expensive for one man. Egg circles and sets his crate down wheels up. He's a long way from Mac but down in good shape. He radios and asks where Mac is . . . they tell him straight ahead . . . so he plows across the snow on the run. Hope he gets there quick; smoke is coming out of the turtled ship now. Spider orders all the ships down, and they come in one, two, three. Spider and Big A-Bird lose their props, but get out and head for Mac.

I've got an hour's gas left so fly low over Mac's crate . . . Susie-Q, it's happened! It's true! The lad is climbing out, he's waving at me. Old Mac! I pull 'er up in a roll over him, and circle to approach.

The two 17's are still loafing around putting out SOS's. With the sun at my back, using the shadow of the ship to judge the depth (landing on ice is just like landing on water), I come in, trying to get as close as possible to the other ships. Cut the gun at 200 feet, off mixture, switched props to "feather." Hold 'er off with the props just turning till she stalls . . . bump . . . snow flies, the old crate slides along, and that's all!! Another landing! Didn't even bend the props, but I guess she won't be taking off soon. Fill out the form, dump chute and crawl out. Damn, busted the oil coolers. Well, it could be worse.

Start running for two tiny figures off the left. Holy Joe, but the snow here wasn't made for running. Fifteen minutes of wading, and I'm pooped. The figures are just as far away as ever. Can see what Egg meant, calling for direction of Mac's ship . . . it isn't even in sight. The crates are all at least 300 yards apart, Egg's about three-quarters of a mile away and Mac's not at all. Look back just in time to see Hanna bring his crate in and set 'er down on the bottom. Good enough. Walk back and talk to 'em. They want to know about

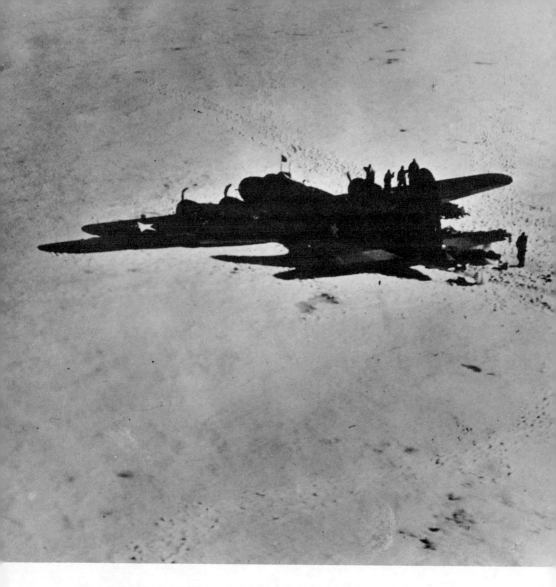

Forced to land, this was one Boeing B-17 that never reached England. The crew was eventually rescued from a Greenland icecap by a U.S. Navy plane.

..*U.S. Air Force Photo*

Mac, and I tell 'em he's OK. Stape circles another quarter hour, then starts his approach. Damn, he's dragging it in for miles away. Boy, don't sit her down there, we'll never get to you if anything happens. But up he comes, belly turret dragging the snow, and plumps the old lady down about 200 yards away. Good boy!

7/16 . . . We are on the east coast of Greenland! How we ever got there no one seems to know. Our SOS got through. Mac is OK except for shock and a nasty gash in his arm — got it on broken glass when he tried to climb out. Hope that cut doesn't get infected. Yellow Flight is to live in one 17, and Green in the other. The Hotel Dodo and the Hotel Big Stoop.

7/17 . . . Don't know how rescue will ever find us if this fog keeps hanging in. Makes it about twice as cold. Thermometers all read below zero. Seems to be a bit of confusion as to whether our SOS was received or not. Hope someone gets on the ball. These blasted bombers were not built to house 13 men. Every time you try to sleep, you get a fur-lined flying boot in your puss. Mac's arm doesn't look good.

7/18 . . . Praise Allah! A C-47 came over today and dropped us a chute with some rations. Did you every try chewing up the edge of a desk for entertainment? You get the same feeling eating some of this concentrated chow. Make damn good dog food, though, if we only had some dogs.

7/23 . . . A Navy "Cat" came over today and said a dogsled was on its way to bring us out. This place is like La Guardia Field now. Airplanes overhead all the time. Only difference is that none of them ever land. The "Cat" flyer, Atteberry (sic), sure is a hot bomber, drops stuff right at your feet. Maybe learned it from the Japs at Pearl Harbor. We took the radio-beam receiving set that runs on batteries, and set it up to get music from Reykjavik, Iceland. Hot jive! We all went out and had a regular jam session on the wing of the 17. Attebury (sic) said he was tempted to land and join the party!

7/24 . . . The dogs are coming. Just showed over the horizon . . . only one thing wrong, they've got five dogs and only one sled. What are the rest of you guys going to do?

9 P.M. . . . Fred Crockett, Lieutenant U.S.N. (he was with Byrd in the Antarctic) and two Army men are going to walk us off the cap. Their advice is to take nothing, but we've all got about 50 pounds on our backs or on improvised toboggans of cowling, etc. Hanna and R. H. Wilson have a load that looks like one engine of a B-17. I'm

betting they don't get it all off. Everybody is plenty gay.

Heigh-ho, heigh-ho! It's off to civilization we go, after eight days on the earth's best refrigerator. The lads with the big loads string along at the end. The first mile wasn't bad, but Fred sets a good pace . . . wearing skis. A rest of five minutes is sure welcome. Coats and other unessential gear are starting to come off now. This appears to be the start of the longest hike we ever took. After the first hour, the line of men is stretched out about a mile and a few pieces of gear could be seen back along the trail. Cast off! The third hour is really rough going. Gear is being dumped off wholesale . . . $75.00 trench coats; .45 automatic pistols, uniform blouses and pinks. Enough to set up a PX. The front of the line stops for a breather, and is off again before the tail can catch up. Baby, it's bloody rough walking on a half-inch crust of snow in flying boots and pulling a makeshift toboggan with 50 pounds of gear on it too. This ain't true love!

Fred seems to stop less often now that we're going downhill. The slope helps some, but after every ridge there is just another and another. Legs move mechanically, and there are plenty of sweet-looking blisters to amuse people with later. Half the gear has gone by the way now. We've been out eight hours. Fred said it was 17 miles to the ship but it must be more like 117. Over every rise, I expect to see the ocean, but there's only snow, snow, and more snow.

There she is! The bay where the ships will be. Fred won't hazard a guess as to how far yet . . . must be pretty far. It's all downhill now. The dogsled (which started two hours after us) has passed. Fred has gone on ahead to fix some coffee. Down to one slope, then another . . . seems endless. Men are strung out along the trail as far as you can see in either direction, laying down, walking, stumbling. You're on your own now, brother, there isn't anyone behind to pick you up. Wilson and Hanna lost their cargo miles back. Hanna carries nothing, Wilson a bag on his shoulders. Too bad, all that stuff. Everybody walks along as if in a trance, eyes glazed, plodding on like a wooden doll. Once I fell by the trail, but the men passed on. Think someone said, "That's all, brother!"

After an eternity we come to the last slope and see the beach . . . at the bottom of some 200-foot mountains. That last mile isn't going to be like the boardwalk at Atlantic City. We finally totter, baby, I mean totter, into the camp at the top and rest up for an hour or so, have some coffee, and then start down. Not a bad trail; at least, there's some dirt except for a small glacier. A near vertical drop the last 600 feet, down which you slide over rocks, gravel, snow, ice, and mud. How we got down there in our condition without breaking a neck . . . you tell me. Guess it wasn't in the books, that's all.

We finally got aboard the cutter after six hours of waiting for it to break its way to us through the ice. Once I said the coast of Greenland was the sweetest thing I ever saw. That's retracted. It was the steak those Navy boys gave us aboard the cutter. That was true love, Spider said. Brother, you can say that again.

Colonel Bernt Balchen, the man who flew Byrd over the South Pole and who had participated in many exploratory flights over both polar continents, is probably the most experienced subzero pilot in the world. In addition to his other Arctic "firsts" he was to add still another: he was the first Allied pilot to bomb a German installation on the western side of the Atlantic which was the northernmost bombing mission ever carried out by the U.S. Air Force.

Raid on Sabine

Col. Bernt Balchen

WAR IN THE ARCTIC is a silent war; and in the silence and the vast distances an enemy moves undetected. A man is only a dot in all that whiteness; huts and radio towers are invisible from the air amid the boulders and uneven patches of snow; the drifts cover an intruder's tracks as fast as they are made. Only the scouts of the Sledge Patrol, traveling by dogsled up and down the barren shore, may stumble on a secret hiding place.

Formerly the members of this unique patrol were Danish and Norwegian trappers, as well as a few Eskimos, who made their living running traplines during the winter along Greenland's east coast. Their tiny cabins were scattered at intervals along the trail, they owned equipment and teams of dogs, their knowledge of the country could not be duplicated. In the fall of 1941, Rear Admiral E. H. Smith, U.S.C.G., Commander of the Greenland Naval Patrol, organized these civilians, and they were hired by the United States Army to form a regular military patrol of the east coast of Greenland as far north as 77°, working out of various stations along the coast, visiting the unoccupied huts along the trails, and reporting any signs of enemy occupation.

On March 13, 1943, as three members of the patrol were approaching Sabine Island in northwestern Greenland, they observed a couple of tiny figures moving along the ridge of Tafelberg Mountain. Realizing that no human beings were supposed to be in that area, they made for a nearby trapper's cabin at Cape Wan, on the south side of Clavring Strait, planning to investigate further in the morning. In the hut they found two strange sleeping bags and a green uniform tunic with a swastika on the sleeve. As they were searching for further evidence, their alert ears detected someone approaching; they had no time to harness up their dogs, but set out on skis for the nearest patrol station at Eskimonaes, some 95 miles south.

Their precipitate flight had given the enemy two good dog teams. On March 24, a small party of Germans commanded by Lieutenant Ritter arrived at Eskimonaes in the sledges abandoned by the Danes. They attacked the base with rifles, automatics, and hand grenades, firing a machine gun into the air to give the semblance of being in force. The occupants, equipped only with hunting rifles, evacuated hurriedly. Fortunately they had a portable radio transmitter; less than 24 hours after the station was silenced, they were able to report what had happened. The Germans seized three additional dog teams and sledges, confiscated a number of soft-nosed cartridges which the trappers used for hunting game, and placed all personal effects of the Danes in one hut, together with the Danish flag and about a hundred fox skins; everything else they destroyed. Beside the flag they left a characteristic note:

> *March 24: The U.S.A. protects its defense interests here in Greenland. We do the same also. We are not at war with Denmark. But the administration on Greenland gave orders to capture or shoot us, and besides that you gave weather reports to the enemy. You are making Greenland into a place of war. We have stayed quietly at our posts without attacking you. Now you want war, so you shall have war. But remember that if you shoot with illegal weapons (dumdum bullets) which you have at hand here in the loft of the radio station, then you must take full responsibility for the consequences, because you are placing yourselves outside the rules of war. Note we have put all personal effects of the hunters and all pelts in this hut, while we have destroyed the radio apparatus operating for the U.S.A. (Signed) Commandant of the German Wehrmacht Detail in Eskimonaes.*

On his way back to Sabine Island, Lieutenant Ritter and his men encountered three more members of the Sledge Patrol, returning to Eskimonaes after a reconnaissance to the north. The driver of the lead sled, Eli Knudsen, did not hear the German command to halt; one of the Nazis killed him outright, and he was buried in a stone shelter beside the trail, with a cross and Danish flag on his grave. Ritter took the other two sled-drivers as prisoners to Sabine.

There he made a curious decision. One of the captured Danes was released and told to his amazement that he could go home. With the other prisoner as his guide, Ritter set out alone to investigate a reported weather station at Mackenzie Bay. As soon as they were out of sight of the German base, the powerful Dane disarmed the German lieutenant and took him as prisoner in turn. Together they set off on a fabulous 350-mile trek southward to Scoresby Sound, headquarters of the Sledge Patrol. For a month they lived together on the trail, eating their meals side by side, sharing the same sleeping bag at night. They arrived at Scoresby Sound about the first of May, where the sled-driver turned over his German prisoner to the authorities.

Meantime, we were making rapid preparations to carry the attack to the enemy. The spring thaws were increasing daily, the mud was over two feet deep at our base in southern Greenland; it was decided that I should proceed to Iceland and undertake the bombing of Eskimonaes and Sabine from there. In view of the distance involved — the round-trip flight from Iceland to Eskimonaes is as far as from London to Africa — we realized that the fuel supply of the Fortresses we were using would give us a very close margin for bombing and strafing. Consequently we used one bomb bay to carry 300-pound demolition bombs, and placed an emergency fuel tank in the other.

We took off from Iceland about eleven o'clock in the evening of May 13, in the strange silver twilight of an Arctic spring night. As we headed north, the midnight sun began to appear over the horizon. By the time we reached Eskimonaes, about three o'clock in the morning, it was shining as bright as noon. The sun was in the northeast; Eskimonaes, on the south slope of the island, lay in deep shadow, the small buildings and radio station almost lost amid the rocks and splotches of snow.

We made several preliminary passes at low altitude to orient the bombardiers with the target. We could see how completely the Germans had destroyed the stations; doors swung open, windows were broken and vacant, there was no sign of life around the half-burned and wrecked buildings. Scratches made by sled runners were still discernible on the ice, leading both north and south, but in the Arctic it is difficult to tell how old a sled track may be. Although we assumed the station was deserted, we carried out our orders, dropped our bombs, strafed the buildings, and left them burning as we headed back to Iceland.

Our fuel supply was barely sufficient to get us home. I realized that for our mission to Sabine Island we would need Liberators with long-range tanks, using the Fortresses to cover us in case we were attacked en route by German aircraft from Norway which were still patrolling the east coast of Greenland and northern Iceland. While the Liberators were on their way from the States, we laid our plans for our coming raid on Sabine; the first bombing of German installations on this side of the Atlantic, the northernmost bombing ever attempted by the Army Air Forces.

On May 25 the weather broke favorably for the flight. The Liberators were loaded each with ten 100-pound demolition bombs; in view of the distance, the two Forts carried no bombs, but placed auxiliary fuel tanks in their bomb bays, giving them greater capacity for combat maneuvers in case we were attacked en route by patrolling German aircraft from Norway. The Forts started half an hour ahead of the faster Libs, at about four in the morning; the flight made its appointed rendezvous at nine over Bontekoe Island in eastern Greenland. There the B-24's and one of the B-17's waited for five minutes; with Captain Turner in the other Fort, I headed toward Sabine to reconnoiter the target and estimate the amount of antiaircraft fire to be expected. The other ships were instructed to assemble 50 miles southeast of Sabine, at 5,000 feet, and await our report.

The morning light was brilliant as we approached the target. The sun glinted on the icy hills, the white snow patches and black rocks made a striking checkerboard pattern beneath us. The elevation of Sabine is about 2,000 feet; the island is oval-shaped, some 12 miles in length, with a bight on the eastern side where the German base was located. As we flew over this area at 5,000 feet, we could make out two main buildings: one two-story affair which we judged to be the radio station, another one-story shack several hundred yards away which seemed to be a storehouse. In the middle of Hansa Bay a German supply ship was frozen in the ice; it was a 300-ton trawler, its masts and smokestack sawed off to make it as inconspicuous as possible. The sides of the ship were banked with snow to camouflage it further. There was a ledge of rock behind the camp area about 100 feet high, on which their antiaircraft emplacements were located; but, although we could see people running toward the guns, we encountered no ack-ack fire at the time.

Our Fort returned to the rendezvous point, and I ordered the

Liberators to attack at 4,000 feet. The supply ship and the two main buildings were to be their primary targets. They came out of the sun, right over the station; but owing to the confused pattern of dark boulders and white snow the bombardiers could not identify the target accurately. I ordered them to stand at one side; and Captain Turner and I circled in our Fort and came down from the north through a valley, diving onto the main building at about 50 feet. As we approached, we gave it everything we had with our forward machine guns; the tail gunner took over as we passed. Pulling up over the station, abreast of the ledge, we were met by a burst of machine guns and cannon fired horizontally at point-blank range, but no hits were scored. Looking back, we could see smoke from our incendiary bullets pouring out of both buildings, making them easy targets for the Libs.

Now the big 24's came around, and I saw the first bomber make a perfect run over the camp. Inexplicably no bombs were dropped, and he circled for a second try. The second Liberator made a pass, and got off his bombs. As he finished his run, the first Lib came over once more; this time he got his bombs away accurately, scoring several hits and causing considerable damage to the surrounding area. We followed the bombing with low-level strafing with both armor-piercing and incendiary ammunition, giving a thorough hosing of lead to any object we could see on the ground, and also firing over 1,300 rounds into the supply ship in Hansa Bay. After staying over the target as long as our limited fuel supply permitted, the bombers were pulled off and a direct course was set back to Iceland.

Our war in Greenland was not a big war, as wars go. There were no major battles, no epic encounters of planes or tanks, no headlines in the hometown papers. Loneliness doesn't rate a citation; they don't give medals for waiting. The casualties were not very glamorous: frozen lungs, a couple of missing fingers or toes, an amputated leg. There are no fields of crosses today to mark its battlefield: only a broken fuselage drifted deep with snow, a pair of crossed skis beside the trail, a forgotten dogsled lying forever at the bottom of a black crevasse.

But it was an important war, for the knowledge of the Arctic that we gained, at the cost of these men who gave their lives on the Ice Cap, will insure the safety of tomorrow's aerial travel in the north. The bases and weather stations they fought to maintain, amid the darkness and silence and cold, will be future stops along the new air route to Europe. Some day our whole conception of geography will be changed; the earth itself will be rolled over on its side, and the spindle of the globe will run, not from Pole to Pole, but from one side of the Equator to the other. Then the Arctic will be the very center of our new world; and across Greenland and northern Canada and Alaska will run the commercial airways from New York to London, from San Francisco to Moscow to India. Today's highway of war will be tomorrow's avenue of peace.

During World War II, every operation of any type from the simplest single-plane mission to the D-day invasion depended vitally on the accuracy of the weather information coming largely from the main region of frontogenesis — the Arctic. It is from the northern latitudes above the Arctic Circle that the severe weather outbreaks over Europe and North America originate. To control the flow of weather information coming from these areas is to know what tomorrow's weather will be like. In World War I, for the first time in history, weather reporting became an important consideration when planning military campaigns. During World War II, both the Germans and the Allies with territorial interests bordering on the Arctic exerted great efforts to gain this vital information. The ice and the weather information which both sides strove to radio in secret codes to their respective headquarters decided the time and place of future operations. German meteorological stations were set up in east Greenland, Spitsbergen, Bear Island, Jan Mayen, and Novaya Zemlya. German submarines reported the weather in the other water areas at regular intervals. Automatic "robot" weather stations were also used which broadcast air temperature, pressure, wind velocity, and wind direction several times a day.

The task of countering the weather-reporting activities of the Nazis was divided between five of the Allied nations. The Danish sledge patrols and the United States Coast Guard assumed responsibility for eastern Greenland; the British and Norwegians were concerned chiefly with the areas north of their countries, and the Russians patrolled the Franz Josef Land area and Novaya Zemlya. It was only a matter of time before the opposing sides would clash.

One of the most heroic of the British pilots who undertook to fly supply and reconnaissance missions in support of the Norwegians stationed at Barentsberg, a former Russian settlement on Spitsbergen, was Flight Lt. D. E. Healey of the R.A.F. Coastal Command. Flying a specially equipped Catalina amphibian, the P/210, he flew many long, arduous 2,700-mile flights from Iceland ferrying men and supplies and reporting on German activities. The Germans, also located on Spitsbergen, were aware of the Norwegian camp and had made several attacks by air. If ammunition and supplies did not come, it was only a matter of time before the Germans would land an invasion party and the source of much valuable weather information would be lost to the Allies. It was Healey's job to prevent that if he could. The following account tells of his last flights in "the secret war."

Move and Countermove

Douglas Liversidge

THE NORWEGIANS at Barentsberg were growing despondent. So far the only aircraft they had seen were those of the Luftwaffe. With monotonous regularity the German planes flew in at 07.00 and 18.00 sometimes strafing, on other occasions merely circling as if to frighten the Norwegians into submission.

It was with surprise and expectation, therefore, that during the afternoon of May 26, the drone of an aircraft disturbed the lonely vigil at Cape Heer. The observers excitedly searched the skies. "Look!" shouted one of the men, pointing to a black speck which rapidly grew bigger. Whatman insisted on caution; perhaps the Germans were changing tactics, he thought. Hiding from view, the party watched as the aircraft flew far into the fjord. Some 30 minutes went by before it altered course, circling over Green Harbor and losing height.

"It's one of ours," cried Whatman, seeing the telltale blisters of a Catalina. "Quick, the Aldis lamp."

Within seconds, the improvised contraption was flashing, the men anxiously wondering if they could catch the attention of the British crew. They waited breathlessly, and to their relief saw the responding flash.

Soon they had conveyed the story of the tragedy and the speedy need of help. Without further ado, the plane turned southward over the sea. Healey, who was at the controls, could not afford to waste time. He had been airborne since the previous day and ahead of him there was still a 14-hour journey, with the possible hazards of foul weather and enemy aircraft. But the Catalina arrived home unscathed, alighting on the protected waters of Sullom Voe.

The news which Healey took to the Shetlands sparked off intensive activity, and led to some of the greatest flights of the war. The emergency dictated the utmost speed. Within 48 hours Healey and P/210 were again heading northward, and on May 29 the men at Barentsberg shouted with joy at the sight of the Catalina approaching from the sea. Several times Healey flew low over the fjord searching in vain for an open channel, but each attempt was foiled by ice.

Finally, he had to parachute the food, medical stores, and weapons which were eagerly collected by the waiting men.

Being specially adapted for Arctic flights, with her long-range tanks and impressive array of compasses, P/210 was doubtless the speediest means of reinforcing Barentsberg. But the price was the inexorable demands of the fantastic endurance and skill of Healey and his crew. Two days later Healey embarked on the third of these incredible sorties within a week. For more than 17 hours this indomitable pilot pitted his skill until frightful elements forced him back to base.

But on June 7 the Catalina managed to alight. The bay ice had begun to break up. Even so, ice floes were scattered treacherously over the fjord. Healey was acutely conscious of the risk he was taking as he turned his plane seaward. To maneuver the heavily loaded flying boat among the jagged ice blocks was virtually out of the question. To strike one was to end in disaster. Yet he could not forget that men were seriously wounded and needed urgent treatment.

As the aircraft lost height, the floes grew larger, stressing the confused pattern of the sea and ice. Skillfully, Healey steadied the aircraft as the massive plane touched water, plowing a streaming furrow that took it perilously close to the heaving ice. P/210 alighted safely, but even after taxiing carefully between the floes, it could get no nearer than a mile from the shore.

"We will have to ferry in collapsible boats," Healey told his crew. He realized that this would not only be tedious, but dangerous too. For encumbered by ice, neither P/210 nor the boats could scarcely survive if the Luftwaffe attacked. And, of late, German aircraft had been more evident.

Happily on this occasion the elements came to the Allies' aid. Clouds gathered low over Spitsbergen like a thick wad of cotton wool. The clumsy boats, worming between the floes, operated without enemy notice, conveying vital supplies, arms, and reinforcements, and finally ferrying the wounded to the plane.

Safely back in the Shetlands, Healey completed an astonishing feat. Within nine days he had fulfilled four flights; each had been of more than a day's duration. Altogether in that period he had flown for more than 97 hours, at times fighting either vile weather or Luftwaffe patrols. By his courage he had restored the morale and offensive power of the garrison at Barentsberg. In so doing, he had ensured a meteorological service and the passage of the Arctic convoys.

To build up the Norwegians' supplies, Healey accomplished more flights in the next two months. Several times P/210 was lucky to survive. Once a Heinkel 177 chased the Catalina for more than two hours, the British plane only escaping in cloud. Though lightly armed, a number of engagements were fought with Junkers 88's, and on June 27, Healey marked his flight by destroying one of these aircraft at Spitsbergen. But there was little time to enthuse over this victory. Soon after takeoff, the Catalina entered a harassing bank of sea fog which stretched all the way back to the Shetlands.

For all this heroism Healey deservedly received the Distinguished Service Order, and to his navigator, Flt. Lt. E. Schofield, went the Distinguished Flying Cross. Yet, tragically, Healey's days were numbered. With the rest of 210 Squadron, he proceeded to north Russia to assist the convoy, P.Q. 18. These flights concluded, he was chosen for a final flight to Spitsbergen. His mission was to call there for a British officer and then return to Britain. At 07.17 on September 25, Healey left in excellent weather for the journey north. On nearing Bear Island the treacherous weather changed with scant warning. The Catalina tore into a head wind which by now was some 70 knots. The aircraft shook violently in the savage gusts. The crew felt the shocks — terrible shudders which made the whole plane rock. It seemed folly to go on and when the Norwegians radioed that it was madness to alight at Spitsbergen he abandoned the flight. He intended to try again next day, and therefore made for Murmansk.

Suddenly on leaving cloud, some 200 miles from the Russian coast, the rear gunner caught sight of the enemy. Astern, and approaching at speed, was a Junkers 88. The Catalina's hooter blared an alarm, and the crew scrambled to action stations, waiting tensely as the gap between the aircraft shortened.

The encounter was brisk but short. The initial burst from the Catalina's starboard gun found its target, promptly destroying the German desire to fight. As it rushed past it might have been the end of the German plane, but the Catalina's front gun jammed. Momentarily, Healey saw the vivid flashes of parting shots from the enemy's rear. Then shells crashed noisily through his windscreen causing chaos and death. In a flash he saw the Catalina's nose reduced to a tangled mass, then felt the searing, sickening pain of bursting shrapnel. With the assistance of Wing Commander Johnson, a passenger, the second pilot got the Catalina down safely off Kildin Island. Healey, the only casualty, was beyond aid; he died almost at once and was later buried by his comrades in the local cemetery at Grasnaya. His death ended a saga: in all conditions he had flown for more than 500 hours over the northern seas.

PART FOUR

FLYING THE ALASKAN BUSH COUNTRY

On every side of us are men who hunt perpetually for their personal Northwest Passage, too often sacrificing health, strength and life itself to the search; and who shall say they are not happier in their vain but hopeful quest than wiser, duller folks who sit at home, venturing nothing and, with sour laughs, deriding the seekers for that fabled thoroughfare?

—KENNETH ROBERTS
From foreword to *Northwest Passage*

Introduction

No ANTHOLOGY of polar aviation would be complete without mention of the Alaskan bush pilots who pushed back Alaska's frontier and brought civilization to "Seward's Folly." The development of Alaska has paralleled the development of aviation; in fact, the airplane was being used there as the principal means of transportation long before the rest of the United States took aviation seriously.

Shortly before his death, Lincoln's Secretary of State, William H. Seward, who had been widely ridiculed for negotiating the purchase of Alaska from Russia in 1867, was asked what he considered the most important achievement in his political career. He replied, "The purchase of Alaska — but it will take the people a generation to find out." In 1935, General William "Billy" Mitchell, martyred advocate of air power, told a committee of the House of Representatives that "Alaska is the most central place in the world for aircraft and that is true either of Europe, Asia, or North America . . . I believe in the future he who holds Alaska will hold the world, and I think it is the most strategic place in the world."

Billy Mitchell did not live to see anyone heed his advice to strengthen Alaska but, as with so many of his pleas for understanding the wonder of the airplane, he was ahead of his time. He was thinking as the airman thinks and it took a war to show how valid his thinking was.

In contrast to the progress of aviation elsewhere, it was not the military pilots who would lead the way in learning about flying in the Alaskan area. It was the free-lance bush pilots with their daring, initiative, and skill that helped win the battle against the elements and proved that flying was not only feasible but safe in what is today our forty-ninth state. Theirs is a never-ending saga of courage and determination matched in American history only by the pioneers who pushed their wagons westward and made a nation out of the wilderness.

It was only a few years ago that Alaska was completely ignored as far as commercial aviation was concerned. The bush pilots, without federal aid of any kind, without adequate navigational equipment, or official encouragement, pioneered the Alaskan skies and prepared the way for both commercial and military flying. They flew every conceivable kind of plane into every nook and cranny of Alaska where there was any reason to go. The men themselves were as different as men can be. But they had one common characteristic — guts.

Alaska has been called "the flyingest country in the world." It is probably no exaggeration. There are over 8,000 miles of federal airways in Alaska but only 3,600 miles of highways. The huge mountain ranges and spongy muskeg make road building a nightmare. Dogsleds and caterpillar tractors can be used in winter for overland transportation, but in summer only the roads, such as they are, are available. The airplane is the only means of modern transportation that can be used all year round.

The start of flying in Alaska was as primitive as the country. It tried to begin in 1912; it finally did two years later.

Alaska's Earliest Birdmen

Jean Potter

THE FIRST PLANE in Alaska was built in 1912 at the Gold Rush settlement of Nome.

The big stampede was over. The windswept tents were gone — and the violence — and the sickness — and the sudden wealth and poverty.

Nome was settling down to be a good town.

It had wooden houses with bay windows jutting out over narrow streets, fine clocks and barber poles and a handsome hotel, the Golden Gate, of gingerbread architecture. It had several churches, two newspapers, and a man to teach piano to the children.

He, Henry Peterson, gray-haired, proud-walking, loud-talking fellow, sort of an eccentric, had the first plane built.

For months Professor Peterson and his helper hammered and sawed at a funny-looking rig in a shed. School kids flocked around and stared. It had a rotary-type engine and the frame was strung with piano wires. Peterson told the children never to touch it. He said it was a flying machine.

Eskimos named it *Ting Mayuk* (Bird of the Tundra).

White men, before long, were calling it rougher names than that.

Peterson sent for an aviator from the States. One cold spring morning he said the plane was all set. Horses dragged it two miles out of town to Gold Hill. Hundreds of merchants and miners followed through the deep snow. Everybody paid a dollar and got a ribbon badge.

Peterson tied a long rope to the plane and asked for volunteers to get it flying. Everybody wanted to help.

They pushed and pulled it up the slope.

They pushed and pulled it down.

The engine growled, the wings shook, the aviator tried his best — but the airplane just plowed through the snow like an auto.

Some said they thought it needed a smooth piece of ground. Peterson said maybe it needed a stronger engine.

The next day people were laughing all over town.

The first plane to fly in Alaska took to the air at the log-cabin city of Fairbanks on the Fourth of July, 1914.

It was the biggest, rowdiest Fourth of July Fairbanks had ever known. There were foot, horse, and bicycle races, tugs-of-war, rock-drilling contests, baseball games, and — an AERIAL CIRCUS.

Arthur Williams, owner of the Arcade Restaurant, and two other merchants hired aviator James Martin* from the States and paid his boat fare all the way north; also his wife's; also the freight on his small tractor biplane. It cost them thousands of dollars.

The circus, they advertised, would be held at the ball park. It would be a big show with a high charge: five bucks a head. They slung a rope from the lower bleacher to the racetrack, so large a mob did they expect when Martin went through his terrifying maneuvers.

They took a bad loss, those sporting backers of Alaska's first airship. When the plane went up, the ball park with its bordering rope was almost empty. Roofs, woodpiles, and fences all over town were covered with people. Some even climbed to the belfry of the schoolhouse to watch the show "for free."

Never anything like it; Martin's machine, after one false try, lifted into the air. Round and round it went for nine whole minutes, 400 feet above the baseball diamond, before it settled down.

The birdman said he did not care to fly very far from the park. Chimneys of the woodburning town were puffing so much smoke he might lose his way.

* James Martin, one of the earliest pioneers of aviation in the United States, invented the first successful tractor biplane in 1911 and set a world speed record with it of 70 mph. He was an Army consulting engineer in World War I, and a close friend of General Billy Mitchell's. He subsequently invented numerous other aeronautical products and manufactured both planes and automobiles at a factory at Garden City, Long Island.

Still he sailed the sky.

People saw him do it — four different times.

The Fairbanks *News-Miner* printed a long article. "Regarding the possibility of flying through the atmosphere with heavier-than-air craft," the paper reported, "the minds of many of the sourdoughs of Alaska have been set at rest."

The Army Air Service, much reduced in size after World War I, retained many DeHavilland DH-4 biplanes for use as first-line aircraft in spite of their obsolescence. Under the leadership of General Billy Mitchell, the struggling stepchild of the Army was trying to prove itself and convince the American public of the value of air power in national defense.

To keep his pilots sharp and give them long-range navigational practice, the dynamic Mitchell ordered Capt. St. Clair Streett and three other pilots to blaze an aerial trail from the nation's capital to its furthermost possession at the northwest corner of the continent. Four aging DH-4's were to fly from Washington, D.C., to Mineola, New York. From there, they would fly to Nome, Alaska, via the northern states to Saskatchewan, Alberta, British Columbia, and Yukon provinces of Canada. It was a 4,500-mile flight over rough and uncharted wilderness one way.

On July 15, 1920, eight intrepid airmen — five pilots and three mechanics — departed Mineola and arrived at their destination in Alaska 53 hours, 30 minutes flying time later without a serious accident. It was an incredible flight considering the route, the type of aircraft, and the relative inexperience of the pilots in cross-country flying. They returned to their base on October 20, completing the 9,000-mile flight in 112 hours' flying time "with the same airplanes, same motors, and the same spark plugs." One of the pilots on that historic milestone flight into the wilds of Alaska wrote a "pen picture" report . . .

Blazing the Aerial Trail to Alaska

Lt. Clifford C. Nutt

THE DAY WE LEFT MINEOLA, July 15, 1920, was one of the very worst of the whole flight from the standpoint of visibility. We couldn't see the ground from 1,000 feet so three of the planes dropped to 500. Captain Streett, however, lifted to 8,000 feet to get out of the fog, so got lost from the squadron which proceeded to Erie, where Captain Streett joined us the next day. Meanwhile, it had rained, the field was wet and muddy; we couldn't get hold of a roller, so we tried to make use of a truck to put the field in shape. But the mud and water stuck by us, and when Crumrine took off he made a nose dive right into the marsh itself. Luckily, however, no one was hurt and no damage was done.

Leaving Erie, we cut directly across the lake for 85 miles bucking a strong head wind. For an hour and a quarter we were out of sight of land, and, owing to the haze, we hadn't even a horizon line to guide us. The mist met the water in indistinguishable gray haze into which we ourselves seemed to melt without anything to guide us. Lieutenant Nelson was driving at that time and I watched him from the cockpit tipping first one wing and then the other or going nose down under the impression that he was really driving a straight course.

Grand Rapids gave us a royal reception. At Winona, Minnesota, we received a request from the Twin Cities Aero Club to land at St. Paul and Minneapolis. This stop was the only one made not on our regular route. The hop to Fargo took us out of the forest and lake region into the flat grain country. The prairies were so level it seemed as if we might have taxied over them. The landing field at Portal was really across the international line in Canada or North Portal which is merely a railroad junction. From Portal to Saskatoon was the only leg of the journey in which we had the wind with us. We made the 310 miles in three hours, and at Saskatoon got our first taste of that Canadian hospitality which added so tremendously to the enjoyment of the long journey.

About 100 miles from Saskatoon we left the prairie country, and got into a region of forests and lakes, with low rolling hills, some of them 6,200 feet high. At Edmonton, Captain Streett's machine had a leak in the gas tank, and we were held up there for three days getting that patched up.

Our first attempt to leave Edmonton was unsuccessful because of low-hanging clouds. Taking off at 1,000 feet we had to drop to 300, and when about 100 miles out, Streett motioned for us to return. The next day, in spite of a stiff wind, we made the jump to Jasper Park. Here we found one of the best landing fields on the whole route, though it is located ten miles from Jasper. It is about 600 yards by 300 yards and in good condition. Tents were provided for our accommodation with a Chinese cook in the mess tent. Gas and oil were on the field, and after cleaning up our "buses" and getting everything in shape for the next day, we were ready for a bath. But it was

Lineup of the Alaskan flyers, Bolling Field, D.C. Left to right: Capt. Douglas, Lt. Nutt, Lt. Nelson, Lt. Crumrine, Lt. Kirkpatrick, Sgt. Long, J. E. English.

U.S. Air Force Photo

a choice of two evils. We either had to get in the water or be literally eaten up by mosquitoes. We chose the water. It is impossible to conceive of the multiplicity and ferocity of the mosquitoes in this region; and, indeed, to the very northernmost limit of our flight. They almost block traffic, they are so numerous, and they certainly block progress, preventing work at some seasons of the year. By building smudges around our tents and sitting up around a bonfire for a part of the night, we managed to get a little rest in spite of the mosquitoes, and by getting an early start next morning made two hops that day.

Soon after the hop-off at Jasper, Captain Streett's machine caught fire, caused by the oil tanks being too full and overflowing down the exhaust pipe; but Henriques, who was driving, put the plane into a side slip and was going to land in the river, but as they descended, the change of balance had stopped the flow of oil and the fire extinguished itself. We got into Prince George just ahead of a rainstorm and without Streett; but a wire from him explained his mishap. We lighted flares to aid him in finding the landing field. The outline of the field was indefinite; so when Streett alighted he came in with great speed and overshot, rolling out of the dimensions of the field itself into a cutover stretch beyond where he struck a stump that took off about four feet of the end of his left wing, breaking both main spars and tearing all the ribs out; also the left half of his horizontal stabilizer and the aileron. To get a wing sent to us in the quickest possible time would take eight days. So we got busy on the job ourselves, with the help of a big Swede carpenter who was a wonder and who had some wonderful spruce timber. He framed up the wing for us, built ribs and spars for the stabilizer and the aileron. Of course, each of us had a piece of linen for patching. We pooled our supply and covered the wing, but the dope Lieutenant Kirkpatrick, the only chemist we had in the party, was able to concoct from cellulose nitrate, unrefined banana oil, and several quarts of anil acetate, proved not very efficacious, as the linen was about as flabby when it dried as it had been before wetting. But, we took a chance on the new wing anyhow.

Our next stop was at Hazelton, at the head of the Skeena River. Hazelton is right in the mountains, and these are covered with high timber. Due to the frost, even when the timber is removed and the land plowed level and cultivated during the summer, when it thaws out again next spring, it is as rolling and rough as the waves of the sea. Knowing of these conditions, we went on by train to inspect the landing field before making the jump in our planes. Finding its dimensions inadequate, Captain Streett arranged to have the grain cut from a field adjoining to make room for us to alight with safety.

Our next jump was to land us in United States territory again, but to reach Wrangell, we had to jump over the Coast Range Mountains; at least, that is what we thought we had to do from our maps, which showed the trend of a river or of a mountain system, and depicted everything else as perfectly smooth, level country. In point of fact, the region has never been explored or surveyed. Fortunately, we had a clear day for takeoff. When we began to ascend for our hop over the mountain, we found that the mountains rose too, and higher than we had. Instead of being 5,000 and 7,000 feet as showed on our map, when we reached a height of 7,000 feet we found we needed 3,000 more to get over the top, and when we tried to skirt the range, we found it wasn't really a range at all with a valley on the other side,

Lt. Kirkpatrick, Lt. Nutt, and Lt. Nelson at Fairbanks, Alaska, on the return journey, Alaskan Flight, 1920.

but just close-packed mountain peaks filled with snow and ice between. These glaciers looked like level seas of dark-green water. At Wrangell, the only landing field available was on a little island in the Stikine River, which at high tide, wasn't an island at all. We landed in about six inches of water which had grown to a foot before we took off.

From Wrangell we went by way of Chilkoot Pass and Skagway to Whitehorse. Crumrine blew a tire at Whitehorse, but, filling his casing with rope packed tightly, he wrapped the outside with rope, taking off with us to Dawson, and landing safely despite the hard jolt from his mended tire.

The flight to Fairbanks, the northernmost point reached, was over the most desolate region of the entire course. For miles there was no sign of a trail, not even an Indian trail. Then, suddenly, we picked up a trail that appeared here and there along the route, quite clear and well-defined. We afterwards learned that General William Mitchell of the Air Service had led an expedition into this country and cut this trail 20 years ago in making a survey for the purpose of establishing a telegraph line to connect with a cable to Siberia, which project was later abandoned.

Fairbanks, with a population of 2,000, is the largest town west of Alberta, and the whole town, reinforced by the mining camps of the vicinity, was out to meet us. The route to Ruby was over low hills and swamps. There are no maps of the country, because there has been no survey. It has been impossible to make one. In winter the country is covered with snow and ice, and the only means of travel is on skis. In summer it is covered with tundra and travel is impossible.

At Ruby we landed on a sandbar which conveniently appeared in the river at the right time. We made the hop to Nome skirting the Bering Sea, with weather conditions changing every hour; keeping in touch by wire with the wireless at Nome, as soon as we got a flash reporting the weather clear, we jumped in our "boats" and hopped off. We flew at an altitude of 1,000 feet, zigzagging our way to avoid rainstorms. When we saw a fairly clear spot ahead we steered for it, but for the most part it was just steady pushing through black clouds.

Carl Ben Eielson is, without doubt, the most famous and beloved of those aerial pioneers who chose the Arctic skies for their flying. His name is synonymous with Alaskan development and his flying exploits have become a part of the legend of the Far North. It was he who led the way to help establish the airplane as the most reliable means of transportation in what is now our forty-ninth state.

Eielson was born in North Dakota in 1897, grew up there, and graduated from its state university. He went to Alaska in 1922 to teach school in Fairbanks but had to finally admit that what he really wanted to do was fly. He had joined the Army Air Service in 1917 and won his wings just before the armistice was signed. He returned to North Dakota, organized a flying club, and barnstormed briefly before he wrecked his Jenny taking off from a pasture. Although unscatched in the accident, he decided to quit flying and become a lawyer. Working as a congressional guard in Washington, D.C., to earn money for tuition at Georgetown University, he was persuaded to go to Alaska to teach mathematics and general science.

Once he had decided that the lure of the cockpit was stronger than the classroom, Eielson raised money from local Fairbanksans and the legend began. Beloved and respected, Eielson was to die in November, 1929. In 1948, the newly born United States Air Force named its huge installation at Fairbanks in his memory. As one writer has said, "he did more than any other one man to advance aviation in Alaska."

Typical of Eielson's many "firsts" is the pioneer flight he made on February 21, 1924 when he inaugurated airmail service in Alaska on a route between Fairbanks and McGrath. The 260-mile trail he blazed proved that the flying machine could replace the dogsled and that regular and frequent delivery of mail by air was possible in the Arctic. It was this success and the experience he gained flying the mail under all possible weather conditions that brought him to the attention of Sir Hubert Wilkins.

Following is the report Eielson made to his superiors in the Post Office Department after his historic flight. It deserves to be preserved in the literature of aviation.

First Airmail Service in Alaska

C. B. Eielson, Airmail Pilot

OUR LANDING FIELD, which is 1,200 feet long and 600 feet wide and surrounded by low scrubby trees, was covered with from two to three feet of snow. The snow up here is of a very light, dry, powdery variety. It does not pack well, as is the case in the States, because there is so little moisture in it. The skis on the airplane dug about a foot and a half into the snow, thus making it impossible to taxi except by using about 1,300 rpm. I find that the wide skis are more practical for this country.

The thermometer registered five below zero at the start of the first trip. There was no wind. The sky was about two-thirds overcast with clouds, which lay at an elevation of 4,500 feet.

I carried 164 pounds of mail, a full set of tools, a mountain sheep sleeping bag, ten days' provisions, five gallons oil, snowshoes, a gun, an ax, and some repairs. My clothing consisted of two pairs of heavy woolen hose, a pair of caribou socks, a pair of moccasins reaching over the knees, one suit heavy underwear, a pair of khaki breeches, a pair of heavy trousers of Hudson Bay duffle over that, a heavy shirt, a sweater, a marten skin cap, goggles, and over that a loose reindeer skin parka, which had a hood on it with wolverine skin around it.

Wolverine skin is fine around the face because it does not frost. On my hands I wore a pair of light woolen gloves and a heavy fur mit over that. I found I had too much clothing on even when I had the exhaust heater turned off. At five below zero I was too warm. I could fly in 40-below weather in perfect comfort with this outfit and the engine heater. On my second trip I cut out the caribou socks, the duffle trousers, and the heavy fur mittens and was entirely comfortable.

May I not suggest to the Department that all mail pilots be supplied with reindeer skin parkas and large size moccasins. I have worn the fur jumpers that are in use outside and it is my opinion that they are not to be compared with the parkas. This is the consensus of

228

opinion among the old-timers here, who have tried everything to ward off the cold. The parkas are knee length, they are very light, they pull over the neck so no wind can blow in through the flaps.

The following are the advantages of the parkas:

1. Cost only $40.00 for a good one.
2. Light and roomy. Do not bind.
3. Have a hood on them which can be pulled over the head and tied so that only the eyes are exposed. The fur around the hood is wolverine so it does not frost.
4. Can jump in and out of planes as well with one on as if you did not have it on.
5. In case of forced landing, pilot could walk as well with it on as off. It is impossible to wear the jumper as it is too heavy for walking.
6. Greatest warmth for its weight.

The moccasins are advantageous because they are light, warm, and comfortable. As many pairs of stockings as are necessary can be put on. The rudder can be felt all the time, thus giving better control.

I took off the field on February 21 at 8:45 A.M. The skis dug into the snow until I got up a little speed then gradually lifted out. I ran 800 feet before I left the snow. I turned the motor to 1,450 rpm until off the ground. I then cut it to 1,300. I turned the motor from 1,250 to 1,350 on the trip. The motor never missed coming or going. The tachometer did not work steadily, but the engine was perfect. My airspeed indicator did not work at all and my compass was off about 40 degrees in some direction on account of magnetism in the engine. Both of these I have since corrected. As I am well acquainted with the country over which I am flying I did not depend on my compass except to follow relative readings taken by pointing the plane at landmarks which I knew.

After testing the motor and balance, I hit my course. The first 50 miles I followed the Tanana River, which is a fair emergency field though the ice is a little rough in places. At Nenana, a town of about 100 inhabitants, I left the Tanana and steered across the country. I veered to the left of a straight course in order to follow the flat country and stay near the roadhouses, which are located on the mail trail at intervals of about 35 miles.

After about an hour and a half I spotted Lake Minchumina to my right. I was then halfway between the lake and Mt. McKinley, each of them probably 30 miles away. I passed to the left of the Munsatli

Carl Ben Eielson went to Alaska in 1922 to teach mathematics and general science at Fairbanks High School. He persuaded local businessmen to buy him an airplane and began the flying exploits which have become legendary. He flew the first air-mail in Alaska and piloted Wilkins from Alaska to Spitsbergen, Norway, in a single-engine plane, for which he won the Distinguished Flying Cross and the Harmon Trophy. That same year he became the first man to pilot a plane over the Antarctic Continent. He was killed in a crash in November, 1929. Eielson Air Force Base, Alaska, is named in his memory.

Library of Congress Photo

Mountains and a little later saw the main Kuskokwim River, which I followed in to McGrath, my destination. I landed on the Tacotna River at McGrath at 11:35. It took me 2 hours and 50 minutes to cover 260 miles, straight course, and I had a slight favorable breeze. The way I had come I had covered about 315 miles. There was about a foot of snow on the river; an excellent landing field. I came down smoothly, sliding about 500 feet after the skis first touched the snow. As I had plenty of room, I intentionally made a fast landing.

The mail was transferred to dog team, the gas tank was filled with the same kind of gasoline (Domestic Aviation Gasoline — about 62 B test), three gallons of Mobil B were added to what was left in the tank. (I cannot change oil over there as there is no Mobil B there.) The thrust bearing was filled with oil, clearances checked, and engine inspected. Then had lunch, loaded on 60 pounds of mail (which was

all they had), and started the motor. I had no experienced help what-
soever as no one over there had ever seen a plane. It was difficult to
start the Liberty all alone. I got a man to hold my hand while I
swung the propeller, no one being in the cockpit. It will be easier
from now on as I am instructing a helper at McGrath.

I left McGrath at 2:35 P.M. — that was the earliest I could get ready
on first trip. I knew this was pretty late as darkness descends early
here in February. I did not want to stay over as the day was good and
I thought it might be very difficult to start the motor after it stood
out all night in the cold and it would be hard on the motor. As there
was no wind I thought I could get back in better time by flying a
little faster and taking a straighter course. I expected to get home by
5:10 P.M. — that is, just at dusk.

I flew over Appel Mountain and one hour and fifteen minutes later
I reached Lake Minchumina, which is nearly the halfway point. This
was on schedule so I thought I was all right. Later I passed over a
stream which was not on my map and I thought it must be the
Kantishna River. Later I reached the Kantishna River and I thought
it was the Tanana River as it was time for me to be nearing Nenana.
To the left I saw a bluff that looked like the Nenana bluff; I checked
it further by noticing a river going around the bluff, but I was positive that it was Nenana when I saw a river entering the Tanana at
the point where the Nenana River enters the Tanana at the town of
Nenana.

I struck for the bluff, and everything was all right excepting that
the town of Nenana was not in its place. I knew I must have veered
to the left so I started up the Tanana to find Nenana. I followed it
for half an hour, that is, 50 miles.

By this time it was pitch-dark. I could not believe that I had got
50 miles off my course after the same compass course had brought me
to Lake Minchumina halfway, and this was exactly on the course.
I could not see the lights of Nenana so I left the river, going east. I
thought I must have got on the Kantishna River and that I was following it back to Mt. McKinley as the country looked flat in the
pitch-darkness. The sky was entirely overcast — not a star showed.

I wandered about completely lost for most of an hour, then I knew
that the river I had left was the Tanana. About this time I saw a
light, so I cut my altitude and went down to it. It must have been a
trapper's cabin near the Chatanika River. I was tempted to set the
ship down there and have a nice place to sleep, but I knew I would

wreck the ship if I did, so I decided to look around some more. I went back to the big river I had left, and when I was following it down I saw a flare in the distance. I hit for it and it turned out to be my home field. There was a light in front of the hangar. I guessed at the extremity of the field and went in. I hit a tree in gliding and broke off one ski. In landing, I nosed over and broke my propeller. The trouble was all fixed up in three days and the plane ready to go again.

The entire town had been waiting at the field for more than an hour. I had been in the air four hours and ten minutes on the return trip. I landed at 6:45 P.M. I had been in the air seven hours that day, covering a distance farther than from Fairbanks to Siberia, Fairbanks to Point Barrow, or Fairbanks to Juneau. This seems incredible in Alaska for it takes a month of hardship at this time of the year to go from here to Nome by the fastest route — dog team.

Another of Alaska's air pioneers was Noel Wien who, like Eielson, was also of Scandinavian descent. Learning to fly in Minnesota in 1921, he came to Alaska in 1924 and quickly achieved a reputation for cautious daring as a pilot for the Fairbanks Airplane Company owned by James Rodebaugh. His motto was "Take 'em out and bring 'em back" and he did.

It was Noel Wien and not Carl Ben Eielson who was the first pilot in Alaska to cross the Arctic Circle and land on the north side. In the spring of 1925, he flew two miners to the town of Wiseman, 80 miles above the line. On the return trip, however, he ran out of gas and landed on a sandbar in the dark with only a couple of dried buns for food. It took him three days to fight his way back to the nearest civilization.

The near mishaps, accidents, and hair-raising exploits did not deter Wien from continuing to fly. Each flying day provided experience which enabled him to accumulate over 8,000 hours of Alaskan flying before he decided to leave it to younger men. One of the earliest of the early pioneers, he is one of the very few to escape death in flight. Today there is an airline in Alaska which bears his name and the name of his brother who was also attracted to the Arctic.

Noel Wien: Conservative Pioneer

Jean Potter

EARLY IN 1927 Noel and Ralph Wien founded an airline of their own. They borrowed money to buy one of Rodebaugh's old Standards and based at Nome, giving the Bering Sea town its first steady plane service. In the first two months of operation they took in $4,000 and, with the aid of a local-bank loan, paid $10,000 for a second plane — the Wilkins expedition Stinson *Detroiter*. "A cordon of police may be necessary," said the Nome *Nugget*, "when Wien takes off in his Stinson. There are six persons anxious to fly to Fairbanks and the plane will not hold that many. There are two passengers for Candle and possibly a flight will be made to Kotzebue with diphtheria antitoxin." Business continued to boom.

Wien nearly lost his Stinson in a freakish accident the first winter. Landing at Lake Minchumina late in December, he left the plane on the snow beside the roadhouse and went to bed. He woke during the night to the wail of high wind. Hurrying outdoors to check his ship, he saw nothing where it had stood but whirling snowflakes. The Stinson was gone.

Storm and wind continued for three days, sweeping drifts from Minchumina till the surface was sheer ice. On the second day the plane's dim shape appeared briefly far out on the lake. The third day it was gone once more. When the weather cleared, Wien found his $10,000 craft two miles away on the opposite shore — its "flippers" and prop blades bent, its control rods and skis broken. He spent two days repairing it with a monkey wrench and a blowtorch, and continued his journey. The people of Nome suffered more than he from the mishap. It delayed his arrival till after Christmas, and he had all their Yuletide gifts and mail aboard.

The following year he made up for this, arriving at Nome on Christmas Eve with a full load of letters and presents. Children scampered around his plane and jumped up and down. Old women wept; in their memory, Nome had never received any packages at holidaytime. No town in Alaska appreciated air service more keenly than Nome appreciated the Wiens', especially in winter; from the ice-locked settlement it was a journey of several weeks to Fairbanks by dog team.

It was in March, 1929, half a year before Eielson's journey to death, that Wien successfully made the first round trip by air between America and Asia. Accompanied by mechanic Calvin Cripe, he used the all-metal Hamilton in which Eielson was later killed. The route, too, was the same, likewise the purpose. He had signed a contract to haul fur from a vessel which was caught in the ice off North Cape, Siberia.

"Sincere congratulations," William MacCracken, Assistant Secretary of Commerce, wired Wien from Washington on completion of the first round trip between the continents. "This is a most worthy pioneering effort." By Wien's account, the trip was uneventful. The spring sun was bright. "We just simply waited for clear and unlimited weather," he commented, "and if we'd run into a storm we would have turned back awfully fast."

They did have "a little trouble," he added, on the return trip. Cripe, he said, was the one who had a rugged journey and deserved credit. The oil tank of the Hamilton, built into the leading edge of the wing, received no heat from the engine, and as they soared above forbidding, rough drifts — higher than any Wien had ever seen in Alaska — the cap froze. Pressure rose dangerously. Although it was 50 below zero that day, Mechanic Cripe opened the window and stretched out into the ice blast. Just able to reach the vent, he punched it open with a knife, but it soon froze shut again. He repeated his almost insufferable task every 10 or 15 minutes during the six-hour flight.

Soon after his journey to Asia, Wien married Ada Bering Arthurs, daughter of the Nome postmaster. Later that year he sold his company to Alaskan Airways and he and his wife made an extended trip to the States, where they were at the time of the Eielson disaster. When Wien returned he organized another family outfit, operating out of Fairbanks. He has had many offers of work in the States and Canada, but has chosen to continue his work in Alaska.

Wien no longer flies actively. A few years ago he sold control of the family company to his brother Sig and today he is distributor for the Cessna Aircraft Company in northern Alaska. He plans to spend the rest of his life in the Far North.

"Alaska," he explains, "keeps a fellow guessing. . . . It tugs at you all the time. . . . The States are too tame."

When the roll is called in the Valhalla of all good pilots, it will surely include a long list of names of men who "flew the bush." Doubtless Carl Ben Eielson, who pioneered the airmail in Alaska and later flew Wilkins to Spitsbergen and over Antarctica, will top the list. Other names will be Noel Wien, Russ Merrill, Ed Young, Frank Dorbrandt, Joe Crosson, Harold Gillam, Matt Nieminen, Harvey Barnhill, S. E. Robbins, Alex Holden, Ray Petersen, Bob Reeve, and many others who made "impossible" flights to inaccessible areas to save lives, deliver mail and freight, and otherwise improve the lot of people who chose to live and work in the interior of Alaska.

One of these pioneers — Bob Reeve — also owns his own airline now. He has become a living legend because he flew where no one else wanted to fly, and did things with an airplane no one else wanted to try. He is a bush pilot's bush pilot.

Reeve first came to Alaska in 1932, after three years' flying freight and mail in South America. He arrived in Alaska as a stowaway with twenty cents in his pocket. To get a start in flying there, he offered to rebuild a wrecked plane for the privilege of flying it. It was the start of a charmed career of a man who survived countless mishaps, near misses, and crashes, and who represents the "good old days" of bush flying before regulations, navigational aids, and accurate maps. The following excerpts from his biography show the primitive stage through which cold-weather flying has come. . . .

Glacier Pilot

Beth Day

DURING THAT FIRST WINTER flying in Alaska, in the fall of 1932, Bob developed his own technique for maximum engine efficiency in cold weather. He soon discovered that no amount of heating by firepot could warm up the engine to really safe takeoff power. "The most you could get was from one-half to two-thirds normal horsepower." To increase the safety factor of the flight and lessen strain on the engine, Bob warmed up the engine as best he could, then took off empty, flew around the field for a few minutes, landed, put the engine cover back over the engine, and let the plane sit for a period, with the heat generated from the brief flight spreading and diffusing all over the parts, while he loaded the plane. This allowed all parts of the engine to acquire the normal metal expansion required for efficient operation. He was then able to take off on his trip with normal horsepower. This method was especially effective on the engines of that period, since they contained a mixed assortment of metals — aluminum, steel, and bronze — all of which had different coefficients of expansion.

An engine that had been thoroughly preheated, Bob found, was much less apt to develop dangerous carburetor ice during its operation. As air and fuel were metered through the carburetor jets of the float-type carburetor, a 40-degree temperature (Fahrenheit) drop occurred, that under certain atmospheric conditions and temperatures formed ice in the carburetor throat from the moisture content of the air. This ice restricted the flow of the mixture to the diffuser section and choked off the engine power. Since cold air was denser and gave more boost to the engine's power, Bob learned to start his takeoff with the carburetor heat partially applied to guard against internal engine icing (the heater was controlled in the cockpit by a push-pull control connected to the spill valve). Then, as the takeoff run progressed, he shut off the hot air and shoved it on full cold to obtain the added power boost. Clearing obstacles with this extra spurt of power, he once more applied the carburetor heat during level flight.

Although few pilots, Reeve found, paid quite as much attention to these problems of winter flying as he, a higher percentage of takeoff accidents was averted because of the "kindly qualities" of subzero air. Sixty-below-zero air was so dense, and had so much lift to it, that "it forgave many deficiencies in both engine and human performance." Yet its attendant frost was a constant enemy. Only a fraction of an inch of newly laid frost, the amount which could be gotten in a few minutes' unloading time on the ground, was sufficient to destroy the lift of the plane's airfoil. In the mornings, Bob found, a small layer of frost had almost always formed between the time he removed the wing covers and was ready to take off. "The last thing you did before takeoff was to take a rope and slide it back and forth along the wing and remove the last coating of frost." The "tail feathers" (stabilizer) as well had to be cleared.

To cut down fire hazard, Bob made sure that the carburetor was thoroughly drained of gasoline at night, and dry when the torch was put under it the next morning. After the engine was properly thawed, he added the gas and preheated oil. In pouring oil from the can back into the engine, some always spilled outside the tank — which became to Bob a sign of good luck. If he didn't accidentally spill some oil as he poured it in, he deliberately splashed a little over the engine cowling.

That first winter, fresh from a warm country and having active circulation, Bob wore lightweight underwear and clothes, then heavy wool, and a fur parka over that. By the next winter, however, he was into traditional Alaskan long johns and wool clothes under the inevitable "parky." Flying into Chisana one day, his goggles fogged over just as he was coming in for a landing. Blinded, he slipped the goggles back and stuck his head out to see what he was doing. In the open air, at 60 below zero, his eyes promptly "frosted." He barely made it to the ground, then cradled his head in his warm hands till the pain died down and he could see again. "There was no more flying that day!"

A year later, flying a cabin plane into Chisana, Bob ran into another serious round of eye trouble. He had laid his fire extinguisher, loaded with pyrene, on top of some freight behind his seat. Flying through a narrow canyon, he felt something spray his cheek, and turned around to receive the full spray of pyrene directly in his eyes, which blinded him. The fire extinguisher had shaken down, landed on the handle, and set itself off. "I'll never know," sighed Bob, "how I made it through that canyon. I was completely blinded. But there was nowhere to sit down, and I couldn't do anything but keep flying." Eventually the natural fluid in his eyes washed out the pyrene to the extent that he could see a little, and he flew on to his Chisana landing.

"During my first year of flying in Alaska," Bob recalled, "I used to worry all the time about doing the right thing at the critical moment. There were so many unknown factors, and I worried about what I'd do when the chips were down. I spent many a sleepless night planning the next day's work. But after that first winter's flying in the mountains, I found that experience had taught me the right reactions. I automatically made correct decisions in crucial moments. So — I quit worrying."

The winter of 1932-33 Bob described as "the greatest winter of my life." He was doing what he wanted most to do — giving service and building up a profession. What's more, Valdez was beginning to feel like home. When he had bought his Fairchild, Bob had insisted on "everything," and had both wheels and skis for his plane, as well as extra motor parts. "I even had spare wings." Whatever he lacked he "scrounged around the Territory" and picked up from wrecked Fairchilds. Although he had no hangar at the little Valdez strip, "I had the largest hangar in the world — the wide-open spaces!"

He built a little wooden shop for his parts and tools, and loved nothing better than to putter around, working on his plane in his spare time. "One of the sights in Valdez," said Noel Wien with a smile, "was Bob out there on the field in his greasy coveralls, with airplane parts and tools spread all over the ground."

Bob always rented a cabin close to his plane's pasture, and when the wind howled off the glaciers at night his sense of ownership gave him little sleep. Many a night he pulled on his trousers and parka and hurried out to the field to see how his pride and joy was weathering the high winds. He learned to "quarter" the airplane at least two-thirds angled from the wind, to destroy the lift of air so the wind wouldn't tip the plane over. "I had enough ropes on that Fairchild to have held the steamship *Yukon* to the docks at Valdez!" he said with a laugh. And yet the williwaws that sped down off the ice cap at the head of Valdez Glacier could defeat the most careful plans. Once, when he had just landed and stepped out of the cockpit, a sudden burst of wind lifted the plane and it started to fly. Bob jumped on one ski as it sailed past him, and was carried up with it "just like a balloon," 50 feet into the air. It flew along about 250 feet, then let down, gently, without injuring the plane. One night, when we went out to check his plane in a 50-mile glacial wind, Reeve heard a "swish" through the air, and looked around to see a piece of sheet metal, which had torn loose from someone's roof, whip by his head, missing decapitating him by inches. It actually came so close it tore the edge off his parka.

Wherever he landed, one of Bob's immediate chores was to keep the plane's skis from freezing fast. If he were to make a stay of any length he cut a pole and jacked the skis up on it, then scraped off what snow and ice was already frozen on. When it came time for takeoff, if the skis couldn't be cleared by scraping them with his fur mittens, Bob got out his firepot and melted them free. In the winter, many of Alaska's air-minded citizens kept long poles out on their local landing strips so that ski-planes could taxi right up on them when they first landed.

The workhorse of "Glacier Pilot" Bob Reeve was the Fairchild, alternately equipped with wheels, skis, and pontoons — whichever the season or mission called for.

U.S. Air Force Photo

Shown here is the Eaglerock, the type plane that Bob Reeve took up into the gla-cier-dotted Chugach Mountains on his first Alaskan flight.

U.S. Air Force Photo

Reeve learned to carry a supply of black-dyed gunnysacks in the back of his plane, so that he could throw them out over any area where he wished to land, and mark a runway. Miners who were expecting him to come in to their sites sometimes scattered lampblack along the snow to mark out a landing field. The lampblack, however, was not a reliable landing aid, since, wherever the sun hit, it melted down into the deep snow, forming great potholes. Black flags were perfect for sunless winter days, orange flags most effective in bright spring sunlight.

But even after he had made several landings at a particular site and had his landing field well marked with a row of flags, Reeve found that the glacier landings never ceased to have a strange, eerie quality. Making a gliding approach to one of his glistening, cloud-land fields, Reeve could see all his flags. "When they looked like one straight ahead, you were down." (The lighted slope line used on approaches to modern airports is the present-day version of this homely landing aid.) "But the only way I ever really knew I was down for sure was after the motor had idled for awhile." When the plane sank onto its feather-soft cushion of deep snow, it was often difficult for Bob to convince himself that he was really down, and he sat in the cockpit for minutes with the engine running before he could make himself open the door and get out. The day Reeve hauled Charlie Elwood into his claim on the Columbia Glacier, Charlie was lying on his belly on top of a load of freight when Reeve glided gently down onto a blanket of fresh snow, opened the cockpit door, and started to climb out of the plane.

"Don't leave me!" Charlie screamed, clutching Reeve's shoulder.

"But we're here, Charlie," grinned Bob. "This is your claim and we've got to unload."

"Holy smoke!" Charlie grunted in awe. "You sure gave me a scare. I thought we were still in the air and you were bailing out and leaving me up here all by myself!"

"Fledgling airman" Bill Egan, the most regular of Bob's helpers, described what it was like to make an airdrop. They would load the plane, take off with the door off the plane and a rope around Bill which was secured to the interior of the cabin so he wouldn't slip out with the barrels. Then Bob would fly in over the mine site and bank the plane so that the wing and stabilizer were up and out of the slipstream and the floor of the cabin was almost centered over the mine site. When Bob was satisfied with the position of the plane, he yelled "Now," and Bill either shoved or kicked the stuff out the open door. If the plane was not in perfect aiming position, Bob yelled "Hold it," and made another run. Reeve kept his attention on aiming his airplane, and never turned around to watch or instruct his helper. "If Bob ever once put faith in you," explained Bill Egan, "he never questioned what you did."

Once, when they had an order for a load of timbers, the lumber was so long that it actually extended over Reeve's shoulder, up into the cockpit, so that he had to hunch down in his seat to avoid hitting the planks with his head. Egan was terrified that, when the time came to shove the timber out, he would accidentally hit Reeve's head in so doing and shear an ear or give him a knockout blow. "But all the time I was handling that stuff, Bob never even turned around."

Bob took pride in his aim — was able to plunk down the stuff just about where his customers wanted it. (Unlike some flyers who landed supplies that it took three days' digging in the snow to uncover!) He dropped a Diesel engine, dismantled and wrapped in a bed mattress, by parachute, into the *Big Four* — and the engine was running within four hours' time! When miner Ted Johnson ordered a 50-pound sack of flour, Bob obligingly flew over his mine, looked down, saw where Ted had placed a stick in the snow for Bob to aim by, and let her go. The sack of flour plummeted down on top of the stick and split open, and flour spilled out all over the snow. Next time Johnson saw Bob he remarked, rather wryly, "I knew you were good, Bob. But I'm damned if I thought you were that good!"

One of Reeve's near crashes during this fateful year of numerous accidents had little to do with factors of decision or ability. Making a landing at the Bremner Mine in blowing snow, in a 30-mile downwind, Reeve could barely see the snow-shelf runway, nor, as it happened, could those below him see him coming in to land. He had just touched the runway and was moving along at about 60 mph when a miner driving a caterpillar tractor suddenly crossed directly in front of the plane. "Only thing I could do was give it a hard left rudder and ground-loop off the shelf into a gully."

Reeve dove 20 feet off side into the soft snow of the gully, emerged without injury to himself or the plane. But it took a day's work to dig the Fairchild out of the snow and make a runway up out of the gully. Then the cat (fitted with "snowshoes" — boards bolted onto the treads, for snow work) was hitched onto the plane by a rope, and pulled it up onto the landing shelf.

"While the average pilot spent his life on wheels," explained Reeve, "my flying was almost completely with skis on snow and ice." It was a special type of flying, with no known rules nor special equipment — and it received a great deal of attention. Actually, one of Bob's problems was how not to allow the interest and admiration his flying received to influence his good judgment. "I kept warning myself: 'Don't get overconfident. You may think you're good but you're not. Never forget that the country is stronger than you are. Luck is stronger than you are.' It is easy," he said soberly, "to become a victim of your reputation." Reeve attributed Gillam's eventual death to the fact that he had built up a reputation, and he couldn't back down, although its demands were past human ability. "One time," said Bob, "I was flying along, thinking I was pretty good, believing what folks had been saying, and I became so hypnotized by my thoughts that I looked up to find I was about to crash into a mountain! It was a good lesson. It reminded me that anything can happen — anytime."

Flying in the Alaskan bush country is not much different now than it was in the days of Carl Ben Eielson, Noel Wien, and the other early pioneers. It is true that now there are regulations to be obeyed, electronic aids to navigate by, and better landing fields, but the snow and the ice, the fog and the wind, and the mountains are still there. And it still takes a special kind of intestinal fortitude to make the unscheduled flights off the traveled airways to the places where there are no navigational aids and no airfields. In Alaska the ground people still depend on the airman to bring their mail and supplies and emergency aid when it is needed. In short, there is still a need for the bush pilot who will fly anything, anywhere, anytime. Here is the story of one of these modern-day bush pilots.

Busiest Pilot in the Bush

Lawrence Elliott

IN THE PAST 15 years Alaskans have come to believe there is nothing Don Sheldon can't do with an airplane, nor anywhere he won't try to fly one. He has come down in dollar-size wilderness swaths to snatch up a downed flyer or a sick child. He has kept isolated homesteaders in mail all winter. Summoned to the aid of frostbitten mountain climbers, he has fought through blizzards, landed on minute patches of ice, and got the men out. Once, speeding an about-to-be-mother to the hospital, Sheldon found himself in a losing race with the stork, and he was forced to help deliver the baby at 4,000 feet.

In a land that has produced quite a clutch of airmen who have passed into legend, Sheldon is a living legend, successor to those seat-of-the-pants pilots who only yesterday were heaping mail, mining gear, cows — it never mattered what — into rickety biplanes and punching air trails across the uncharted land. "Sheldon isn't just good," said Bob Reeve, president of Reeve-Aleutian Airways and one of that original breed. "That boy is the best."

A lank, leather-skinned bachelor of forty-one, Sheldon operates out of Talkeetna, a way station on the Alaska Railroad some 80 miles north of Anchorage. He has participated in many search-and-rescue missions, like the one in 1954 when a C-124 was missing nearby in a raging blizzard. Military helicopters swarmed over to Talkeetna, but every time they tried to go up to search, severe icing forced them down. At last Sheldon rolled his Piper Super Cub out of the hangar. "OK if I have a look?" he asked, and took off.

Flying low over the flatlands 40 miles to the north, he spotted the wreckage and bounced in for a landing. He found the survivors badly hurt. Knowing he couldn't take off from the brush-pent clearing with any extra weight, he flew out alone. In an hour he was back with a doctor, medical supplies, and sleeping bags. Next morning, as the storm abated, he guided the helicopters in.

Don Sheldon grew up in Montana and can't remember a time he wasn't hanging around some airfield. At sixteen he went west with the peach harvest, packing bushel baskets clear to Seattle. There he boarded a ship for Alaska, where he cut firewood, mined gold, hauled garbage, and trapped beaver. Then he got a job as a mechanic's helper with an airline and took part of his pay in flying instruction. No sooner had he earned his pilot's license than he was in the wartime Air Corps, en route to England as a B-17 tail gunner.

To fill in the hours between missions, he started a bicycle-repair shop, and by mustering-out time he had enough cash for a down payment on an airplane. But back in Anchorage he couldn't generate enough flying business to keep up the payments on his plane; he finally signed on as a driver for a chain of laundromats.

The laundromats were owned by a good-natured soldier of fortune named Stub Morrison. He, too, was sky-happy, and when he learned that his new driver could fly an airplane he determined to sell his business, buy an airplane, and start an air service with Sheldon. Timorously Stub broached the scheme to his wife, Lena. "Might as well," she said succinctly. "Your heart sure isn't in dirty laundry."

Stub and Sheldon settled on Talkeetna for a base, bought an ancient Piper, and started to fly hunters into the game-rich Susitna Valley. In slack times they shot wolves from the air for the $50.00 bounty. Before long they had three planes, and neither had ever been happier.

Then, in the fall of 1950, Stub was flying to Anchorage when a fog bank rolled in. At eleven next morning Sheldon spotted his plane. Its nose was driven five feet into the ground.

Lena decided to stay on. "It's what Stub loved," she said. "I'll stay and run the radio for you." And she did. When Sheldon was in the air, she was never far from the powerful receiver that sat in her living room and periodically crackled with a report of his whereabouts.

Not long after Stub's death, Bradford Washburn, director of Boston's Museum of Science, came to Talkeetna. He was in the process of mapping and photographing Mt. McKinley, he said, and Bob Reeve had suggested that Sheldon might do some flying for him, including a number of glacier landings.

Mighty McKinley is 20,320 feet high. Winds of 100 mph and temperatures of 20 below zero are not uncommon, even in July. Sheldon and Washburn flitted through McKinley's canyons and around its crags, and between them polished up the glacier-landing techniques that have been adopted for virtually all northern mountain flying.

To make landings in a "whiteout" — a milky shimmering whiteness through which a pilot can see no horizon nor gauge the airspace between his plane skis and the snow — Sheldon flew over the glaciers as low as he dared while Washburn threw spruce boughs from the window. Plunging into the snow like darts, the dark boughs provided the essential ground reference point.

When Washburn's map was finished, Sheldon knew McKinley better than any other flyer. His new knowledge brought him additional business. Once it had taken climbers weeks to get within striking distance of the summit. Now Sheldon could fly them to a 10,000-foot base camp and supply them by airdrop.

In the last five years, 21 expeditions have set out to climb McKinley. All but six have entrusted their fate to Sheldon. As they move upward, he becomes their sole link with the outside. There is a suspicion that Sheldon secretly considers mountain climbing a monumental foolishness. But whatever his private skepticism, when he takes on a climbing party, he shepherds its members like a nervous mother hen.

Not long ago he paid $1,100 for a long-range transmitter which he presses on each group so they can be in constant touch with him. Said the leader of a recent British climbing expedition, "You have the distinct feeling that Sheldon is only lending the mountain to you, that he's always flying around to make certain you don't mess it up by getting yourself killed up there."

One of Sheldon's most audacious flights was a lifesaving mission in 1960. It began when a climbing party radioed that Helga Bading in attempting to become the second woman to ascend McKinley, lay near death from dehydration and lack of oxygen. In Talkeetna, Sheldon was soon on the long-distance phone with Bradford Washburn, trying to reconstruct the scene where Mrs. Bading clung to life. Wasn't there a snow basin not far away? Mightn't a landing be attempted there?

Sheldon took off, was soon following the Kahiltna Glacier up to 15,000 feet. Flying directly at a gaunt pyramid of pink stone, he cut his engine, turned at the last split second — and was over the hidden basin. A moment later he had dropped to the snow, not 300 feet from the rendezvous. He was at an elevation of 14,200 feet, higher than an airplane had ever before touched down on Mt. McKinley.

Mrs. Bading was carried aboard. What followed, she says, was the most terrifying time of all: "We dodged peaks everywhere. It was like riding a truck without brakes down a mountain ledge. Then we were flying right at an ice face — I thought: 'This is the end!' — but as we rushed through the clouds, there was a tiny opening and Sheldon slipped through it and we were safe."

One day last summer, I took the train up to Talkeetna to talk with Sheldon. In his barn-red hangar nine members of a mountaineering expedition were crating their gear after a successful climb. I stared down the bumpy dirt strip where he has probably logged more landings and takeoffs than any other active flyer in Alaska. When Sheldon appeared, a cluster of men swarmed around him. One wanted to fly to Anchorage; another had some gear to be delivered to an oil survey crew; a third was trying to arrange for a hunting trip. Sheldon listened to them all, nodding agreeably. Later, in her neat white house near the airstrip, Lena Morrison worried aloud: "He's trying to be a whole danged air force. One of these days he's going to fall asleep up there, and I just hope his guardian angel is flying copilot."

Sheldon does everything himself, it seems. He has tried hiring a mechanic to maintain his fleet of planes (the number fluctuates: it stood at 11 the day I was in Talkeetna), but invariably spends so much time peering critically over his man's shoulder that they soon come to a mutually agreeable parting. I asked why he didn't take on another pilot to share his staggering work load. "Did once," he said with distaste. "The guy tried to land on top of a mountain. I fetched him out all right, but there's still $18,000 worth of airplane up there."

Sheldon himself has had his share of accidents, but hates to talk about them. About as far as he'll go is to concede, "I've owned 37 airplanes in my time and they didn't all die of old age." When he does clobber a plane, he usually walks out before anyone even knows he's missing. He hasn't the semblance of a personal life; his day starts at earliest light, and in summer he has been known to spend 20 hours a day in the air.

Once in a while his mood deepens. He will brood about the fleeting years, the fact that he has no family. Then, characteristically, he will break the spell with a yarn: "Did I ever tell you about the time I got lost in a storm up in the Arctic! It's a fact, I was down so low to the ground that I saw a fox on an ice hummock — and darned if he wasn't higher'n I was!"

No account of Alaskan flying would be complete without a report on the dedicated "week-end warriors" of the Alaska Air National Guard who have become such an integral part of not only rescue, but also normal day-to-day aerial operations in the frozen north.

Located at Anchorage International Airport, the Air Guard's 144th Air Transport Squadron is a close-knit, busy group of men, many of whom are bush pilots in their civilian pursuits and know Alaska and the Arctic like the back of their hands.

Approximately 90 per cent of the 150 officers and men of the squadron own their own homes and are homesteading under Alaskan laws that provide the men their land free of charge in exchange for clearing the property and building a home there. A number of the men are what the Air Guard calls "technicians." These are men who are full-time Guardsmen, employed steadily to keep the planes and facilities operating at the standard of perfection demanded of a land quite unforgiving of carelessness and mistakes.

The Air Guardsmen's flying is both varied and interesting. One day they'll make a spectacular rescue like retrieving the downed scientists and Navy men. Another day they'll work with the Federal Fish and Wildlife Service transplanting moose calves from Central Alaska to the Southeast "panhandle" in the hope of establishing a new herd. The next day, they might aid the Forest Service in hauling men and equipment to critical fire areas.

They are on constant call to fly the rescue and mercy missions, which have become so frequent that the Air Guardsmen regard them as routine. A hunter is lost, a miner is injured, a bush pilot is down, or a remote village is choked off from supplies. Under any of these circumstances, the Air Guard moves into action. The following story is typical.

Alaska Air Guard in the Arctic

Maj. James C. Elliott

WHEN THE big Navy transport touched down on Arlis II, a large ice island off Alaska, the scientists let go with a rousing roar of approval. The group, from the University of Alaska, had been conducting scientific research on the ice island for days, and the subfreezing temperatures, lack of comfortable facilities and the loneliness of the frozen Arctic were coming to an end. As soon as their remaining supplies and gear were loaded aboard, they'd be heading back to Point Barrow and to the comforts of home.

Although the weather was reasonable, temperatures were far from comfortable that November afternoon in 1961. At that time, daylight, or twilight really, lasts only about two hours a day. And that twilight had long turned into Arctic darkness by the time the scientists and crewmen crawled shivering aboard the aircraft. Using their landing lights to penetrate the darkness, the plane's crew turned the aircraft into the wind, pushed the throttles open, and roared off across the ice. Soon, the aircraft was in the air and headed for Barrow.

From outward appearances, the scientific adventure appeared to be over. As the crewmen settled down to their cruising altitude, the passengers unbuckled their seat belts and talked jubilantly of what each was going to do his first night back in civilization. Quite a night lay ahead!

Suddenly, however, the plane shuddered. First one engine began to cough, spitting defiantly and belching long torches of flame from the engine exhausts. Then, the other engine choked, too.

The crewmen moved swiftly in the cockpit. But the manifold pressure fell on both engines. Both were quitting! Impossible, one thought to himself silently. Both engines just don't stop like that! What were the odds? A thousand to one? A hundred thousand to one? Maybe, even a million to one. It didn't really make much difference. Whatever the odds, they had just caught up with the Navy and a small band of dedicated scientists.

An Alaska Air National Guard C-123J on Taku Glacier during a resupply mission.
Alaska Air National Guard Photo

In the darkness and without power, the plane began to descend. Landing without power even under the best of circumstances is no picnic. But landing without power and in darkness! Well, how rough can the odds get? Fortunately, however, someone spotted the ice floe.

The next question was obvious. Is it large enough to land on?

Yes, someone estimated excitedly.

OK, then, there was only one other problem.

Is it smooth, so we can slide in safely, or is it jagged and rugged, so we can't possibly land safely?

But why worry with frightening questions. There were no alternatives. They had to land on the ice floe.

As they approached the floe, not a word was spoken. Except for those silent prayers to God, everyone simply held their breath and braced for the impact. Without the roar of the engines, the descent was eerie. Then came that loud scraping noise, the plane shrieking ominously as it skipped along the frozen waste and finally came to a halt.

Perfect! That's what it had been — a perfect landing. And all 11 souls on board were safe. Or were they?

Now, they were floating aimlessly in the Arctic, hundreds of miles from anywhere. Communications, for all practical purposes, had gone dead with the engines. Indeed, someone would miss them and come looking. But that might take time, particularly if the weather decided to join the forces that already had plagued the unfortunate scientists and their Navy crew.

The crew had little trouble finding the difficulty that had caused their embarrassing and harrowing experience. It just had to be fuel. And sure enough. Someone, instead of pouring aviation gasoline into the plane's fuel tanks, had put in diesel fuel, 110 gallons of it, and the engines just refused to run on that strange new diet. It was a case of Murphy's Law, indeed. Murphy's Law holds that if something can happen, no matter how tenaciously one tries to prevent it, that something is, sooner or later, going to happen.

As the downed scientists prepared to make the best of their circumstances, the Alaskan Command received word that the plane was down and dispatched search aircraft. For 19 hours, no one spotted the downed Navy aircraft. During the twentieth hour, however, a C54 piloted by Maj. Fred Kinsel sighted the distressed group. Kinsel radioed his "find" immediately.

Now came the question of actual rescue. Helicopters were out. The ice floe was too far away. Many suggestions were made, but, in the end, reason always pointed to the Alaska Air National Guard. The Air Guard's 144th Air Transport Squadron at Anchorage was equipped with C123J aircraft; in fact, the outfit had the only jet-augmented C123's in the Air Force inventory. Some of them were rigged with skis, also.

When folks from the Alaskan Command phoned Lt. Col. Bill Elmore, the Air Guard base commander, they found not a second of hesitation.

"You bet," answered the tall, rugged-looking Air Guardsman, "we'll go get 'em."

Maj. Dean L. Stringer and Maj. Thomas Norris volunteered as pilots for the flight, while M/Sgt. William A. Christy agreed to serve as crew chief/engineer.

Because of all the unknowns involved, such as landing conditions on the ice floe, etc., the crew planned to arrive over the downed scientists between 11:30 and noon. Daylight — such as it is in the Arctic at that time of the year — would just be breaking, and they'd have about two hours before complete darkness fell over them.

With the ice floe located 500 miles from land, the Air Guard crew would not have the easiest time in the world finding one ice floe, Stringer realized. There were no radio aids to help them, and the navigation equipment aboard the C123's left a lot to be desired. Major Kinsel and his crew aboard the C54 would help steer the C123 for the rendezvous, they decided. And luck was with them; the weather looked good.

It stayed good, too, When Kinsel led Stringer and his crew over the ice floe, visibility was as good as one could expect in that twilight. Circling overhead, Stringer and Norris checked out the terrain on the floe and chose their landing path. Above the C123, Kinsel and his crew circled in their C54, dropping flares to help the rescue.

As they approached the touchdown, Norris lowered the skis and switched on the landing lights. Down came the flaps.

"You've got her made," Norris told Stringer as he leveled out. And a few seconds later, the C123 slid noisily but smoothly onto the ice.

The Air Guardsmen, of course, couldn't hear the scientists and Navy men. Their reaction undoubtedly was the loudest, most enthusiastic, ever heard in those isolated parts, however.

Stringer taxied his C123 to the Navy plane, his landing lights still burning. Crew Chief Christy opened the huge cargo compartment doors and hopped out.

In the bitter cold, Christy made his way to the scientists and explained that Stringer would leave the C123 engines running. In those temperatures, Stringer reasoned, there was no sense in taking a chance on frozen oil. Besides, they didn't want to be slowed down by having to drain out the oil and heat it up to restart the engines.

The scientists couldn't care less about that matter. The Air Guard had come to get them, and they were more than ready to leave. The sooner the better.

In only a short while, the gear had been transported across the ice from the Navy plane to the C123. The Navy crewmen and the scientists crawled aboard the Air Guard plane, the doors were shut, and Stringer, with both his jet engines roaring and his conventional engines pulling full power, roared off the ice floe for Point Barrow.

A few hours later, 48 hours after they had gone down, the group was back in Barrow, relieved and grateful. Another chapter in Air National Guard Arctic adventure had reached a successful conclusion.

PART FIVE

FLYING THE ARCTIC TODAY

Already contrails mark a traveled highway across the top of the globe, and passengers sip cocktails matter-of-factly over the North Pole and complain to the stewardess that the cabin is too warm.

—BERNT BALCHEN

Introduction

FOR ALL PRACTICAL PURPOSES, polar exploration ceased during World War II. Astute students of the international situation realized afterward that an opposing ideology — communism — was a new enemy which, like the one recently abolished, also had an avowed desire for world domination. Free world strategy became focused on the top of the world again. Governments of both sides of the Iron Curtain sent teams of scientists to study the weather, geology, oceanography, and every other possible aspect of the northern latitudes that would be of either peacetime or wartime use. The main reason was for defense. A giant radar "fence" and airfields were planned and built rimming the Arctic Circle. The United States Air Force was charged with the aerial defense of the nation against the growing might of the Soviets. If an attack should come, the most likely path would be the Arctic.

Bernt Balchen, famed Norwegian-born Arctic pilot and explorer, now a retired United States Air Force colonel, once remarked that "The Arctic is to us what the Mediterranean was to the Greeks and Romans, the center of the world. We have to push out there for our defense." The United States has done just that and in girding for defense, useful by-products have been improvement of polar navigation methods and aids, increased reliability of equipment, and an ever increasing accretion of knowledge for aircrews. The world has grown appreciably smaller as a result. It was inevitable that this would be so. It is the story of aviation; indeed, it is the story of human progress.

Ever since the discovery of America, men have sought to "saile by the West into the East" through a Northwest Passage to the Orient. Sebastian Cabot is believed to have tried first in *1508*, saying, "If I should saile by way of the North-west, I should by a shorter tract come into India." Many brave men followed Cabot in search of that magic route but never found it. The dream persisted and in *1906* Roald Amundsen's small sailing sloop entered Davis Strait on the Atlantic side of the continent and emerged three years later in the Bering Sea on the west.

The success of the airplane brought a new desire for a northwest passage to gain greater speed and accessibility to the Orient. Many an airman had found that if a string were stretched between New York and Tokyo, the "Great Circle" Route so traced will represent the shortest distance beween these two points and will go through Canada, along the shores of the Arctic Sea, and down the Kamchatka Peninsula.

In July, *1931*, Charles A. Lindbergh, first man to span the Atlantic alone from New York to Paris, decided to make a survey flight along this route to Japan and China, with his wife Anne acting as radio operator. Mileage and time would be saved — both important factors in planning future air routes between America and the Far East. But like his Atlantic flight, this trip had its inherent dangers. The route was new and untraveled, conditions along the route were unknown, maps were unreliable.

In spite of the possible difficulties, the flight into the unknown had a fascination for the intrepid pair. As Anne Lindbergh wrote, "There would be those austere and breath-taking moments when, looking down on inaccessible territory, one realizes that no one has seen that spot before. It is as fresh, still, and untouched as the night's new-fallen snow. Unchanged from the day it was made."

After careful planning, which is so typical of the man, Lindbergh bundled his wife into the rear seat of his single-engine, pontoon-equipped Lockheed Sirius and headed north from Washington, D.C., to New York and North Haven, Maine. From there the famous pair flew to their northernmost point, Point Barrow, Alaska, via Ottawa, Moose Factory, Churchill, Baker Lake, and Aklavik. The following account by Anne Lindbergh shows the effect of another polar phenomena on the Arctic flyer — prolonged daylight or darkness — while attempting the leg of their flight from Point Barrow to Nome. Their enemy was the darkness as they descended the latitudes away from the land of the midnight sun. The result was an unscheduled landing at Shishmaref, a small fishing village on the Bering Sea. . . .

257

North to the Orient

Anne Morrow Lindbergh

"WHAT TIME does it get dark at Nome?" My husband pushed a penciled message back to me. Dark? I had completely forgotten that it ever was dark. We had been flying in the land of the midnight sun, though actually its period was over in August. The sun set, but the sky did not darken on either of the flights, from Baker Lake to Aklavik, or from Aklavik to Barrow. But tonight — for it was about eight-thirty in the evening — the light was fading rather fast. Streaks of the remaining sunset ran gold in the inlets and lagoons of the coast. We had turned the corner of Alaska after leaving Point Barrow and were flying south to the little mining town, Nome, on the Bering coast. An unknown route, an unknown harbor; we must have light to land.

"WXB — WXB — WXB," I called back to our friend at the Barrow radio station. I had tried in vain to reach Nome. "Nil — hrd (nothing heard) — from — WXY (Nome) — or — WXW (Kotzebue) — what — time — does — it — get — dark — at — Nome?" His faint signals traced dim incomprehensible marks on my brain, then faded away. It was no use; I could not make them out. I would have to let go of that thread and pick up another.

"Can't — copy — ur (your) — sigs (signals) — will — contact — NRUL (the *Northland*)" I signed off. There was no time to lose. Again I tried, "NRUL — de — KHCAL — nil — hrd — from — WXY — what — time — does — it — get — dark — at — Nome?" No answer. The sparks from the exhaust flashed behind us in the growing dusk.

Was it really going to get dark? It had not been dark since Baker Lake, since that evening when we set out recklessly at seven to fly all night. It had seemed, I remembered, a kind of madness to start at that hour. It would soon be dark, or so I thought, and to fly at night, in a strange country, through uncertain weather to an unknown destination — what were we thinking of? Spendthrifts with daylight, we who usually counted every coin; who always rose early to fly, at three or four in the morning, not to waste a second of the precious light; we were down at the field, the engine warmed up and ready to start with

258

the first streaks of dawn, in order "to get there by dark." Dark — that curfew hour in a flyer's mind, when the gates are closed, the portcullis dropped down, and there is no way to go around or to squeeze under the bars if one is late.

But that night at Baker Lake, we were going north, into the land of the midnight sun.

"And it will be light all the way?" we had asked incredulously. (Though of course we knew it to be so.)

"Sure — it won't get dark at all — going north like that." The game warden had nodded his head. "Light all the way."

Going into that strange world of unending day was like stepping very quietly across the invisible border of the land of Faery that the Irish poets write of, that timeless world of Fionn and Saeve, or the world of Thomas the Rhymer. It was evening when we left Baker Lake, but an evening that would never flower into night, never grow any older. And so we had set out, released from fear, intoxicated with a new sense of freedom — out into that clear unbounded sea of day. We could go on and on and never reach the shores of night. The sun would set, darkness would gather in the bare coves, creep over the wastelands behind us, but never overtake us. The wave of night would draw itself together, would rise behind us and never break.

But now — going south — my husband switched on the instrument lights. We were running short of fuel. Our gasoline barrels were on the icebound *Northland* and we had not refueled since Aklavik. There was no chance of turning back. We must land before dark.

"NRUL — NRUL — what — time — does — it — get — dark — at — Nome?"

At Barrow, I remembered, we had even wanted the dark. When I went to bed the first night, I had pulled down the shades, trying to create the feeling of a deep black night. For sleep, one needs endless depths of blackness to sink into; daylight is too shallow, it will not cover one. At Aklavik, too, I had missed night's punctuality. It was light when we went to bed and light when we rose. The same light shed over breakfast and lunch and supper and continued on through bedtime, so that I hardly knew when to feel tired or when to feel hungry.

But now, seeing signs of approaching night — the coves and lagoons took up the light the sky was losing — I was afraid. I felt the terror of a savage seeing a first eclipse, or even as if I had never known night. What was it? Explorer from another planet, I watched with fear, with amazement, and with curiosity. . . .

259

"WXY — WXY — WXY — what — time — does — it — get — dark — at — Nome?"

Suddenly an answer: "WXN — WXN — Candle — Candle — " One of the relay stations on the coast had heard us, "Will — stand — by — in — case — you — don't — get — WXY," came their message. At last someone to answer.

"What — time — does — it — get — dark — at — Nome?"

There was a silence while he relayed the message to Nome. I looked out and caught my breath. The sea and sky had merged. The dark had leaped up several steps behind me when my back was turned. I would have to keep my eye on him or he would sneak up like the child's game of steps. But the radio was buzzing. My head went down again.

"The — men — are — going — to — put — flares — on — Nome — River," came back the answer, "it's — overcast — and — getting — dark." Then, continuing, "When — u (you) — expect — arrive — so — they — no (know) — when — lite — flares?"

I passed my scribbled message forward. The lights blinked on in the front cockpit. I read by my own light the reply, "Arrive in about 1½ hours — don't lite flares until plane circles and blinks lites."

An hour and a half more! It would be night when we landed! Turned inland, we were over the mountains now and there were peaks ahead. It was darker over the land than over the water. Valleys hoard darkness as coves hoard light. Reservoirs of darkness, all through the long day they guard what is left them from the night before; but now their cups were filling up, trembling at the brim, ready to spill over. The wave of night climbed up behind us; gathering strength from every crevice, it towered over us.

Suddenly my husband pulled the plane up into a stall, throttled the engine, and, in the stillness that followed, shouted back at me, "Tell him there's fog on the mountains ahead. We'll land for the night and come into Nome in the morning."

"All right, where are we?"

"Don't know exactly — northwest coast of Seward Peninsula."

Without switching on the light I started tapping rapidly, "WXN — WXN — WXN — fog — on — mountains — ahead — will — land — for — night — and — come — into — Nome — morning — position — north-west — coast — Seward — Peninsula." I repeated twice.

"Hurry up! Going to land," came a shout from the front cockpit. We were banking steeply.

Charles Lindbergh was not only a pioneer in transatlantic flight, he was one of the first to realize the importance of flying the Great Circle Routes to Asia and Europe. He is shown here with his wife, Anne Morrow Lindbergh, before his famous flight to Tokyo via Alaska in 1931.
Wide World Photo

The Lockheed *Sirius* flown by the Lindberghs is shown at Churchill, Manitoba, being refueled before the takeoff for Baker Lake. Lindbergh performed all maintenance and refueling of his plane himself. His wife acted as radio operator and navigator on the epic flight. The plane was exhibited in the Air Force Museum for several years, and is now in temporary storage awaiting its permanent home in the National Air Museum.
U.S. Information Agency

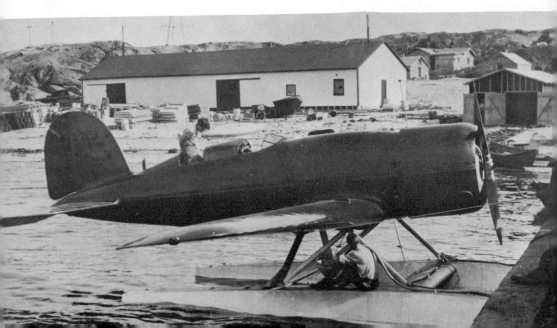

No time to try again. No time to listen for reply. I did not know if they had received it, but we could not wait to circle again. We must land before that last thread of light had gone.

Down, down, down, the cold air whistling through the cowlings as we dived toward the lagoon. I must wind in the antenna before we hit the water. The muscles in my arms stiffened to soreness turning the wheel at top speed, as though I were reeling in a gigantic fish from the bottom of the sea. One more turn — *jiggle, snap,* the ball-weight clicked into place — all wound up, safe. Now — brace yourself for the landing. How *can* he see anything! Spank, spank, spank. There we go — I guess we're all right! But the ship shot on through the water — on and on. Must have landed "downwind." Now it eased up a little. There, I sighed with relief. We were taxiing toward that dark indistinct line ahead — a shore. About half a mile off my husband pulled back the throttle, idled the engine for a few seconds, then cut the switch. In the complete stillness that followed, he climbed out on to the pontoon.

"Think we'd better anchor here." He uncoiled the rope and threw out our anchor. Splash! There it stayed under about three feet of water with the rope floating on top. Heavens! Pretty shallow — thought we had more room than that. Well, we were anchored anyway. We were down — we were safe. Somewhere out on the wild coast of Seward Peninsula.

When World War II was over, interest in commercial air routes to Europe and the Far East via the Great Circle Routes was resumed. In May, 1949, Bernt Balchen was commanding the Air Force's Tenth Rescue Squadron in Alaska. He requested and received permission to fly from Fairbanks to Thule, Greenland, via the North Pole. He had not seen Thule since 1942 when he had made an aerial survey and reported that that remote outpost could become one of the main ramparts of defense in the Arctic. Seven years later, this conviction was stronger than ever in his mind and he wanted to see the site once more. Flying over the Pole had become routine for the Air Force and Balchen reflected on how far man had progressed in the Arctic because of the airplane, what the future promised, and his part in making polar flying so commonplace. . . .

True North

Col. Bernt Balchen

WE TOOK OFF from Ladd Field in one of the four-engine C-54's assigned to Tenth Rescue for our long-range search program. Air Force B-29 weather-profile ships called Ptarmigans were flying regularly over the Pole now, and our squadron was extending its rescue operations in case of a forced landing on the polar ice. It was a beautiful spring evening when we left Fairbanks, and the scattered lights of the gold camps pricked the twilight as we crossed the Tanana Valley and the winding Yukon River and climbed over the Brooks Range, packed with clouds. We broke out on top at 12,000 into the full rays of the midnight sun. Below us the tundra was shrouded in darkness — still two hours until dawn down there — and in a few moments we picked up the sleepy lights of Barter Island.

We took a heading of true north, across the unbroken whiteness of the Arctic Ocean. East toward Herschel Island the ice was solid, but 40 miles out we came on the first open leads, and 100 miles from the coast were giant ice floes on which a C-47 on skis could set down safely. From here on there was a low cloud layer a couple of hundred feet high, covering thousands and thousands of square miles. This is a common condition in the Arctic during the summer, and I made a note that our search planes would need reliable radar for rescue operations here. The undercast extended from 76° to about 80° north latitude, and from then on we had good visibility all the way to the Pole.

Spread out before me, as I sat at the controls, was an ever moving ocean. North at 85° the ice was definitely drifting toward the Greenland Sea, looser to the east of us, with more big leads than on the Alaska side. Even at the Pole itself I could see patches of open water, the floes grinding together and throwing up pressure ridges, constantly shifting as the ocean currents carried the pack over the top of the world. This ice is getting thinner each year, as the whole Arctic grows warmer. Since Dr. Nansen's ship *Fram* drifted across here in 1896, it has decreased in thickness more than 20 feet, and in the same period the level of the Atlantic Ocean has risen 9 inches. Cod and other fish of temperate regions are moving steadily northward into the milder waters, and leading scientists like Professor Sverre Petterssen and Hans Ahlmann predict that if the present rate of warming up continues for another 30 years, we shall have an ice-free ocean over the North Pole in the summertime.

I looked north as I flew, and beyond the north to the future, and in my mind I could picture commercial vessels plying some day over this vast new sea, opening up the riches of all the hitherto inaccessible lands within the Arctic rim: Prince Patrick Island and Grant Land, and the whole Canadian Archipelago. Perhaps a gold strike bigger than the Klondike would be made here, or the greatest oil sinks of the northern hemisphere would be found where now ice covered all. We should have a shortcut to the Far East that would alter our present steamship routes and create new industrial areas, with incidental population movements. More important from a military standpoint — and my mind kept turning over and over the little remark that Colonel Grigge had made to me at Kirkenes at the end of World War II — we should have another ocean to defend.

I banked a wing and circled the Pole, flying around the top of the world in two minutes, and then set a straight course for Thule, where a joint U.S.-Danish weather station had been established. We landed on a gravel strip at the base of the mountains, but not in the same area I had recommended to General Arnold for a runway. As I was filling out my Form I, a sergeant of the crew scratched his head. "Look, Colonel, weren't you pilot on the South Pole flight, too?"

I nodded absently as I was writing. "Ja, sure. Why."

"Well, then, don't that make you the first man who ever piloted a plane over both Poles?"

"I guess it does," I said. It hadn't occurred to me until that moment.

It is extremely difficult to achieve a "first" in polar aviation any-more. The North Pole has been overflown so many times in recent years that air traffic control has become a problem. This was not so in 1951. Although the North Pole had been conquered many times by military pilots, very few commercial or private pilots had yet made the attempt. There was one airline captain, however, who did. His name was Charles F. Blair, a veteran of 18,000 hours' flying time as a U.S. Navy and airline pilot. Flying for American Export Airlines in 1942, he conducted the North Atlantic survey flights which preceded the airline's inauguration of scheduled service in June, 1942; and commanded the first commercial nonstop flight across the Atlantic.

Blair's flight in May, 1951, was particularly noteworthy, not because he chose to make the flight at all but because he chose to do so alone and in a single-engine, obsolete World War II fighter plane. With all of his experience and knowledge of navigation, it should have been a routine flight. But it still takes a certain brand of skill and daring to be first to do anything in the Arctic.

He Beat the Sun from Norway to Alaska

Francis and Katherine Drake

ONE SUNNY DAY in May, 1951, a bareheaded man in tweeds streaked across the rooftop of the world in one of the great flights of history. High over that wilderness of polar ice Capt. Charles Blair risked his neck to explore a matter of international importance: Are nonmilitary transpolar flights feasible?

Only very-long-range military planes, with special navigating aids, fuel for 10,000 miles, crews of a dozen men, fly across these frozen wastes. At the North Pole the earth spins like a gigantic football. No destination stays put, no magnetic compass registers correctly, no radio can reach the earphones. The floating ice cap is in ceaseless turmoil, breaking up, refreezing, cracking again. There is no place to land in safety, and a navigational error of a few degrees can spell the difference between Alaska and Siberia.

Why, then, did quiet, serious, 41-year-old Charlie Blair draw out his savings and transform himself into a one-man polar expedition? Blair's record didn't mark him a stunt man; he is a master airline captain, with 3 million miles and 450 Atlantic crossings in the log.

Headshaking began when Blair bought an Army surplus Mustang F-51, vintage 1943. It was a museum piece as fighters go, but it was fast and strong. Revamping this propeller-driven jalopy into an aerial hot rod capable of distance flying monopolized months of Blair's spare time. But by January, 1951, the Mustang was ready. She had a new 1,700-horsepower Rolls-Royce Merlin engine and a staggering new fuel capacity. She had a new name, too — *Excalibur III* — though around the hangars she was called "the Flying Gastank."

Blair's idea of a warm-up flight provoked more headshaking. He proposed to ride the winter winds from New York to London, 3,479 miles nonstop — astride a "jet stream." These jet streams are westerly winds of superhurricane force that boil around the upper stratosphere, reaching a peak of 250 mph or more in winter.

January 30 provided the right setup and Blair had three days' leave. With the wind barreling down the runways, he lifted *Excalibur* from Idlewild International Airport and disappeared into an overcast of snow and ice. Seven hours and 48 minutes later he set her down alongside London's sooty chimney stacks. Blair had traveled faster than any distance flyer before him, at an average speed of seven and a half miles per minute. And his record still stands, jets notwithstanding.

Landing in London with ample fuel reserve convinced Charlie Blair that he had licked *Excalibur*'s distance handicap. Another important obstacle remained: navigation over the polar ice cap. His solution of that problem — "prepackaged" navigation — made aviation history and blueprinted a method by which passenger liners may soon be following his trail across the Pole. He figured out a way of doing the complicated work *beforehand* and boiled down flight procedure to a simple routine.

First he set a precise day, hour, and minute for his takeoff. Next he plotted on a chart his roadway through the sky, a beeline from Bardufoss, Norway, to Fairbanks, Alaska. He chopped it up into hours and established from navigational tables the angle the sun would make to each of these time intersections at a specific minute. Thus the sun would give him a route marker for almost every mile of the trip.

Getting a sun bearing, or angle, in flight is a simple operation, like looking down the peepsight of a rifle. Blair would need a sun compass, or angle measurer, and a bubble sextant to help him determine

Capt. Charles Blair waves from the cockpit of *Excalibur* just before taking off from Oslo.

Blair's triumphant arrival at New York's International Airport after his amazing flight. The obsolete fighter plane in which he made it, a converted F-51 Mustang, appears dwarfed by the Stratoclipper in background.

whether or not the wind was drifting him off course. With these two instruments and a preplotted course, all he would have to do en route would be to read off sun angles and compare them with corresponding readings on the chart. If they did not agree, he'd have to yank *Excalibur*'s nose around until they did.

Blair selected May for his flight, a time when Arctic weather is normally at its best. On May 29 the sun and moon would be almost at right angles to the Pole, a phenomenon which offered opportunity for a navigational doublecheck. At Bardufoss, his departure point just inside the Arctic Circle, Blair checked his plane with Lindbergh-like precision, set his three watches, and reshot the sun. The airport personnel were filled with misgivings. The picture just refused to add up to a polar exploration — the bareheaded man in tweeds, that tiny plane, daring to challenge the harshest wilderness on earth! And all this American had checked aboard was a four-leaf clover, a letter from his small son addressed to "Santa Claus, North Pole," and the first polar airmail — 3,000 postcards to be auctioned off for the Damon Runyan Cancer Fund.

The airport clock clicked to departure time. Blair waved and closed the cockpit cover. It was a heavy takeoff — the tail, glutted with gas, dragged like a meal sack. Spectators held their breath, then, *hallelujah,* up came the tail at last . . . and *Excalibur* was airborne.

Blair adjusted his oxygen mask and set up the sun compass. From now on, this was his routine: Every ten minutes take bearing, check with packaged plan, adjust course as necessary. Every hour doublecheck with sextant. For the rest, watch fuel, nurse engine, check oil, check distance run, keep on being a human calculating machine.

Below, the sea was like plate glass. Beneath its unlined face rotted a thousand unsung polar expeditions. At Spitsbergen, the most northerly habitation in the world, Blair had a date with a radio signal — atmospherics permitting. Luck was with him. The signal, streaming in high and clear, indicated the island passing just where it should have been. *On course — on time.* Blair's spirits soared. Next call, Alaska!

Now he hoisted *Excalibur* to 22,000 feet, his thriftiest cruising altitude. For nearly an hour he flew on without any sense of progress. Time and distance counted for nothing. He felt like an insect trapped between cloud and firmament. The midnight sun, blazing into the cockpit, made him swelter.

Abruptly, the clouds thinned out below him, and Blair caught his breath. There stretched a sight few men have seen — the soulless, silver-plated panorama of the polar ice cap. Blair stared down in awe, from four miles up, at the floating crust that helmeted the world, the legendary realm without a sunset or a dawn. The chart indicated that he was passing the area where, 25 years before, the Amundsen-Ellsworth expedition had been forced down. Theirs had been the first attempt to reach the Pole by air. Blair recalled Ellsworth's description of that landing on a frozen sea, "choked with a chaotic mass of floating ice . . . it was like trying to land in the Grand Canyon." It sent a shiver up his spine. *Excalibur*'s landing speed was 145 mph!

Nearly five hours after takeoff now, and the moon should be popping up above the starboard skyline. It would be one degree above the earth at the North Pole. He strained his eyes, but the intensifying haze obscured the moon — if it was there.

Approaching latitude 90 degrees north — that theoretical pinprick on the ice where compass points dissolve — Blair fumbled in his pocket for his son's letter. He raised his sextant, preset it for 90 degrees north and squinted at the sun. And there it was, dead center in the bubble. . . . He had reached the North Pole!

Out of the sliding window zipped the letter to Santa Claus, and a wave of emotion swept over Blair. That penciled scrawl was going to land close to the spot where, locked in ice, reposes one of history's milestones, a monument to human courage. Almost half a century ago six swaddled figures had stood there, planting the Stars and Stripes, while one of them, through cracked and bleeding lips, said, "I . . . formally take possession . . . in the name of the President of the United States." It had taken Robert E. Peary 23 years of successive effort to cross that last 400 miles of ice cap.

Now came the test of tests for Blair. At the precise moment when he crossed the Pole everything in the world, all oceans, countries, all humanity, lay south. It was like sitting above a maypole, faced with one's pick of countless streamers. Just one led to Point Barrow, Alaska, on the way to Fairbanks. Its neighbors streamed off to Siberia, to Greenland, to wastes of sea and land. Until Point Barrow's radio signals could reach him, the sun remained Blair's only guidepost.

As the earth had turned, the sun had crept from behind Blair's left shoulder and now was slowly moving up toward the bow of his plane. It had begun to glaze the blue-gray mist, making it difficult to see ahead. He rose to 25,000 feet, where the glare was less, and bored on.

Two hours from the Pole, the sun reached a point immediately above *Excalibur's* nose. Blair was now flying in a globe of shining haze which shut off visibility in all directions. With every hour the glare increased and the cockpit seemed to shrink. He felt he was the loneliest human in the world.

Then he flicked a switch, setting the radio direction finder for Point Barrow. The needle quivered into life, swung, steadied, came to rest. *Dot-dash-dash-dot* — the faint, intoxicating music of humanity. Point Barrow calling.

Blair passed over Point Barrow one minute ahead of flight plan. Less than two hours later postal authorities at Fairbanks, Alaska, began to stamp hour-of-arrival on the first polar airmail. Those 3,000 postcards had flown across the rooftop of the world so fast that they had beaten the sun from Norway to Alaska by more than half an hour. Actual flying time was 10 hours 27 minutes. Blair, ten pounds lighter after 3,300 miles of sweating inside an oxygen mask, was aching and weary, but exultant. His one-man charge against the ice cap had nudged the goal of shorter, cheaper air routes over the Pole nearer to reality.

Just a few years ago, only a few men had ever flown an airplane above the Arctic Circle. Today, hundreds of pilots, both military and civilian, have made thousands of flights in the northern polar region. Every day jet airliners take off from airports in the United States and Europe and head for this once forbidden land because it is the shortest route to their destinations. The pilots and crews are in their shirt sleeves and fly above the weather; their passengers relax in nonchalant comfort, unaware of the altitude, the outside temperatures, or the speed of their craft. There is no doubt that the airplane's years of trial and error are over.

The efforts of those early Arctic pioneer flyers have been rewarding and have transformed a strange, mysterious land into a new frontier that can be traversed in complete safety. The following excerpt from a book by William S. Carlson, former chief of the Air Force's Arctic, Desert, and Tropic Information Center and now president of the University of Toledo, has captured the story of modern flying in the region beyond the Arctic Circle. . . .

To Keep Them Flying

William S. Carlson

NAVIGATION TROUBLES, rather than weather, used to be the chief limitation on Arctic flying. Ordinary compasses on early aircraft had little value in high latitudes. Among the corrections made by science was a new method of navigation called the "grid." In these days, however, when vast scientific advances are everyday news and the launching of satellites may be bumped off the front pages by other newsbreaks, there are startling prospects ahead for navigators.

The new satellites that are being launched by the armed forces in increasing numbers can spin around the earth almost indefinitely, sending back information that will soon make commonplace an all-weather and precise navigational system for ships and planes, and eventually spaceships. The navigational satellite, Transit II-A, had an accuracy when launched of well within one-quarter mile, far better than any instruments now being used can obtain by traditional methods.

It is true that air navigation in the polar regions will always have problems not found on other world airways. There aren't very many conspicuous landmarks for a navigator to pick up from the air, and those that do stand out can be quickly blotted from sight by driving snow, the peculiar vagaries of Arctic sunlight and darkness, or even the deadening monotony of most of the barren landscapes. The navigator must also stay alert to the extreme convergency of the meridians in the high latitudes. He finds that ice floe and sky are often uniform in color. He experiences the perilous whiteouts, and his radio acts up because of ionospheric disturbances. The great distances between ground stations also makes him work constantly at his instruments.

Some of the wartime techniques of Arctic aerial navigation were passed on to the Scandinavians by U.S. Air Force personnel, and one of the results was a great step forward for commercial aviation. In 1952, Scandinavian Airlines System took delivery of its first Douglas DC-6B four-engine aircraft at the factory in Santa Monica, California. Rather than use the conventional Atlantic route to get the plane home, SAS decided to take the shortcut. The plane flew by way of Edmonton, Alberta, and Greenland to Copenhagen. The trip took less than 24 hours. The new Northwest Passage of the twentieth century was opened.

The pilot of that first SAS plane was a Dane named Povl Jensen. This was not his first experience in the north. Eighteen years earlier he had visited Greenland when Pan American Airways had employed him to survey a northern route connecting the United States and Europe.

Immediately after Scandinavian Airlines System's historic flight, SAS negotiated with the American government for a permit to make regular flights via Greenland and Canada to California. The route was officially opened on November 15, 1954. Colonel Balchen, who continued to be the inspiration behind so much of our Arctic activities, was a passenger on the preliminary experimental flight from California to Copenhagen in 1952, and November, 1954, he was at Los Angeles waiting to receive the first scheduled plane to fly from Denmark to California. In less than a year, the Great Circle Arctic Air Route was established as a commercial success. The schedule was extended to three flights a week, and in November, 1955, a tourist class was introduced. Sondre Stromfjord was selected as an intermediate base, and there Scandinavian Airlines System built a modest

A far cry from the days of pioneer polar flights are these F-102 Delta Daggers, responding to requests from aircraft control and warning stations throughout Alaska.
U.S. Air Force Photo

hotel for overnight guests which, with increasing traffic, had to be expanded.

Transpolar air service between Scandinavia and western America is proving of great importance. This has been recognized by two of our carriers, Trans World Airlines and Pan American, both of which fly a route from the West Coast of the United States via former Air Force Base "Crystal 2" in Frobisher Bay and over the Greenland ice cap to Europe. They do not use Sondre Stromfjord. The Danish government also actively promotes local air activity in Greenland, as does the Canadian government in its own Arctic, and our government in Alaska.

Danish transport flights are made for the Greenland Department from Copenhagen to the airfields at Narsarssuak and at Sondre Stromfjord. The Danes have constructed a landing strip at Mestersvig in the lead-mining district on the east coast. Helicopters have operated for the mining company from this base since 1955 and they are being employed elsewhere in Greenland in geodetic surveys.

The first scheduled Europe-to-Japan airliner of Scandinavian Airlines, bypassing the bases of northern Greenland and crossing near the Geographic North Pole to Alaska and then on to the Orient, landed in Tokyo on February 26, 1957, fifteen minutes ahead of schedule. A sister plane which took off from Tokyo over the same route was delayed by head winds and landed in Copenhagen an hour and a half behind schedule. The two big aircraft missed a carefully planned rendezvous over the North Pole by only a few minutes.

Today the Arctic is a superhighway for commercial flights between Europe and the Orient. Six airlines — KLM Royal Dutch Airlines, Trans World, Pan American, Scandinavian, Air France, and Canadian Pacific Airlines — now use the Great Circle Route across or near the Pole for long-distance intercontinental flights. The new route shortens the journey from Copenhagen or Amsterdam to Tokyo for propeller-driven aircraft by 24 hours compared with the former route via the Near East, Pakistan, India, Siam, and Hong Kong to Tokyo.

The polar route between northern Europe and the far Pacific cuts 15 hours from another conventional route, the one across the Atlantic and America. This great advantage in time cannot be ignored, for in 26 hours, after taking off from Oslo, one can be almost halfway around the world in Tokyo, with stops made in Alaska and, if necessary, in the Aleutians. The distance is about 7,500 miles. From London to Tokyo via Rome, Cairo, Calcutta, and Hong Kong the time is more than 40 hours, including stops. The saving in time for jet aircraft, which fly at greater speeds, is correspondingly less.

Not so obvious and well known as the time factor are the safety advantages of favorable weather and smooth operation on the polar route. Precipitation in the Arctic and sub-Arctic is heaviest in summer, but surprisingly light for year-round average. Fifteen inches of precipitation, corresponding to semiarid parts of our Midwest, is common to the northern area. Sections away from the coast have very little moisture from December to March.

Arctic zone temperatures vary much less than those of many areas of interior landmasses in the temperate zones. Water acts as a stabilizing medium with its ability to retain heat. The natural tendency for temperature to decrease with an increase in latitude is offset in the Arctic by the sea around the Pole. (This is in sharp contrast to the

274

Antarctic, which is a continent of ice-covered mountains.) Water acts as a radiator in the winter, preventing temperatures from falling extremely low, and as a refrigerator in the summer, keeping temperatures from getting very high. Therefore great extremes of temperature are found only in areas combining high latitudes, low elevations, and a considerable distance from the sea. The coldest spot in the northern hemisphere is around Oimekon in Siberia, inland about 200 miles south of the Arctic Circle. Temperatures there drop to 90° below. The coldest temperature recorded in Alaska and Canada is 79° below at Fort Good Hope, 20 miles south of the Arctic Circle and about 280 miles south of the coast.

To have high summer temperatures, a landmass must be away from the moderating influence of the water. The extreme heat record for Alaska, 100° in the shade, was observed just north of the Arctic Circle, at Fort Yukon, near the center of Alaska. Fairbanks, 100 miles south of Fort Yukon, has recorded 99°. Days with 90° temperature are not uncommon, and wheat grows regularly north of the Arctic Circle in lowland areas far from the cooling sea.

Counterbalancing the cooling effect of the sea in summer is the warming effect in midwinter. This comparative warmth comes both from the two currents — the Japanese and the Gulf — and from the radiation of some heat from the Arctic waters, even through a film of ice. It is unlikely that the temperature could fall much below −60° to −70° at the North Pole. The lowest temperature ever recorded on the Beaufort Sea coast of Alaska was 57° below zero. This is uncomfortably cold, of course, but 250 miles south of the ocean in the mainland of Canada it goes 30 degrees lower than on the shore; in Siberia 600 miles south of the Arctic Ocean it also drops 30 degrees lower than on the coast.

There are violent local gales in areas of the Arctic, but, in the main, the northern sea is one of the most placid areas in the world. Near land, and in areas where plateaus descend to the sea level as on the coastal area of Greenland, there are strong gales, and along the north coast of Canada and Alaska there are fierce autumn and early winter gales.

A midwinter sun that hangs over the horizon in sub-Arctic latitudes will not dissipate fog or low cloud. In some places, during periods of calm, layers of this mist start at 100 or 200 feet and remain through the day. Generally such mist is quite thin. The orientation of crystals makes horizontal visibility poor, while vertical visibility is good. Pilots have had the weird experience of seeing a landing strip clearly from overhead but being unable to make a landing.

The spring and summer periods are neither as long nor as warm as we are accustomed to in southern latitudes, but they do have much more light than ours. Men on the DEW Line can read without artificial light at midnight from mid-June to mid-July. The number of hours of sunlight does much to make up for the shorter frost-free period.

Pilots prefer the Great Circle Route over the far north because low temperatures and dry atmosphere are deterrents to engine and airplane icing. Turbulence is rare, and flying weather is consistently stable throughout the year. The safety record of the Air Force has been excellent. Commercial operations over the northern route have been free of casualties and even damage to aircraft. Fixed schedules have been adhered to closely. Although the Arctic routes cross thinly populated areas, there are many emergency fields adjacent to DEW Line installations, Hudson Bay Company posts, Royal Canadian Mounted Police posts, and weather stations that now dot the Arctic wastes, and no plane is ever more than two hours' flying time from a landing strip.

Even with the advances made in Arctic flying, costs remain high. All maintenance materials, supplies, and gasoline must be sent by ship to northern bases during the limited summer season and by air, at heavier costs, during the remainder of the year. There is need for continuing studies of weather, navigation, mapping, and magnetic surveys, as well as selection and care of personnel, including problems of their morale and adaptation to an inhospitable environment.

The Arctic is not a region of nameless terrors where miracles are needed to survive. The man who tackles the north country for the first time must remember that winter cold can kill; that a single fire in camp can mean disaster; that Eskimos have been lost in blizzards within a snowball's throw of warmth and shelter.

Exploring parties, however, have crisscrossed Arctic lands and seas for hundreds of years, and long before the establishment of military air routes during World War II, bush pilots and small commercial airlines successfully served a number of isolated Arctic communities.

Civilization is moving closer to the top of the world, but tourist traffic by air will not boom for remote regions. The few attempts that have been made to attract tourists to Greenland have ended in failure. Much of the Arctic probably never will be popular among tourists who are seeking excitement, but rewards exists for flying over the northern route. The flight within the Arctic Circle gives every traveler a thrill.

The settings of the airfields at Sondre Stromfjord, Narsarssuak, and Thule are beautiful. Sondre Stromfjord and Narsarssuak are at the head of long fjords which empty into Davis Strait; each airfield is only a few miles from the great ice cap which dominates all the scenery. In summer the approach to Sondre Stromfjord by air from the ice cap to the east or the fjord to the west is breathtaking. Narsarssuak can be approached only up the fjord from the west. In winter, of course, the areas are dark, but winter is the season of the brilliant northern lights. Winter temperatures do not encourage outdoor activity. The air base at Thule, much farther north, is restricted to military operation. If it ever is open for commercial use, it will rival Sondre Stromfjord and Narsarssuak.

This is an air age, and long-range aircraft have changed our world. Places that are farthest apart by ordinary geography are much closer by air over the Pole. We can no longer overlook blank spaces on our maps. All military targets in the populated part of the globe over 35° are reachable. As Bernt Balchen has said, "the Arctic is no longer a cold spot, but the hot spot on this planet."

During simulated rescue exercises, a YH-21 "Work Horse" helicopter hovers over a temporary campsite set up on the Greenland Ice Cap, near Thule Air Base.
U.S. Air Force Photo

The name of Col. Bernt Balchen has been mentioned many times in this anthology. This is because he ranks as one of the greatest authorities in the world on polar aviation. Holder of transport pilot's certificate No. 941, he has logged more hours over ice and snow than any other pilot.

When Balchen completed his duty with the Amundsen-Ellsworth Relief Expedition to Spitsbergen in 1925, he came to the United States and a year later was copilot for Floyd Bennett on a round-the-States flight. In 1927, he was a member of the Hudson Bay Expedition. Later, with Bert Acosta and others, Balchen piloted Byrd across the Atlantic Ocean to France. In 1928, he flew a Ford mercy supply plane from Quebec, Canada, to Greenly Island, Newfoundland.

Balchen was chief pilot on the Byrd Antarctic Expedition in 1928-30. Lost in the mountains during the last Antarctic trip, the sturdy Norseman was rescued by Byrd in 1930. He also participated in the search for the sealing ship Viking, *which had been destroyed by an explosion off the Newfoundland coast.*

A native of Norway, and a former member of the Royal Norwegian Air Force, Colonel Balchen joined the United States Air Force from which he retired several years ago. He is much sought after for advice on polar aviation problems. The following questions about flying in the Arctic are answered by the man who is the best qualified in the whole world to do so....

An Interview with Bernt Balchen

Q. Colonel Balchen, are there advantages to winter and cold weather flying?

A. Yes. The cold, heavy dense air makes for better airplane performance; this is especially important for jet plane operations. The cold will materially reduce the required field lengths due to the denser air during winter seasons.

Smoother flying conditions are also a general rule during the cold season. More often cold weather is accompanied by clear weather with good visibility. The weather is usually characterized by less severe frontal passages without the accompanying high winds and precipitation. Convectional activity is uncommon in the cold regions.

However, when an intense frontal activity takes place, one can expect weather of much more severity than in the temperate zones, with severe turbulance and high winds over 100 mph and more. These are, however, local and rare in occurrence.

Q. Colonel, do you personally have as much confidence flying in the far north as you would in the tropics?

A. Naturally I have more confidence in flying in the far north — where I have spent most of my life — than in the tropics, of which I know very little. I know just about as much about the tropics as an airman returning from his first tour of duty in the Arctic knows about that region and its problems — very little.

Q. What would be the principal difference between flying in the far north today, and when you flew the Arctic in 1926?

A. There has, perhaps, been more of an improvement in the flying in the far north since 1926 than there has been in the temperate zones for these reasons: the equipment we were flying in those days in the Arctic had very little provision for cold weather operation. Whatever winterization was made, was more or less based on the personal, limited experience of the operator, or pilot.

I was then a pilot in the Norwegian air force, where we at that time had a winter flying program calling for ski operations and cold weather flying. During the winter of 1926-27 I flew in Canadian bush operations, in the Hudson Bay region, where we experienced temperatures down to 67° F below. We encountered a lot of troubles and slowdown in our operations due to inadequate winterization of equipment.

Q. In the cold north, are there any unusual weather conditions?

A. Yes. There are unusual conditions which are mostly functions of visibility or light conditions. We have one deceptive condition due to blowing snow along the ground that easily can get one into trouble. From above, the visibility seems fine, the vertical visibility is very good.

For example: a wind of 25 to 30 mph is blowing and you are attempting to line up with the runway before landing. You can see all features of the runway lights from an altitude of 500 feet. But it will all be obscured as you get into the swirl of blowing snow, which will reduce your forward visibility to only some hundred yards at the ground level.

Another condition is called a "whiteout." This occurs on overcast days when there are no shadows to break the uniform white light from the sky and the snow-covered ground. There is no perceptible horizon and nothing upon which the eye can focus at a distance. One has no visual impression of the height above the ground. This has caused the untimely end of many an Arctic pilot — flying into the ground.

Q. Are landings and takeoffs from snow and ice different?

A. Taking off from ice and snow-covered runways of operational airfields where there is proper snow removal is not much different from normal wheel operations. However, landings and takeoffs from unprepared or temporary landing strips on ice and snow require experience in judging those surfaces with respect to snow depth, compactness, ridges, ice thickness, and a lot of other factors. Such surfaces require skis or ski-wheel combinations, and these demand special training. The same is true when learning to fly a big flying boat. There is no substitute for experience and seasoning in this kind of work. It takes several years to become a satisfactory ski pilot.

Q. Do you have any tips along these lines?

A. Yes. Pilots should be assigned to cold weather operations for extended tours of duty.

Q. What is the biggest danger when flying in the far north?

A. Unpreparedness and improper knowledge of environment.

Q. What about the man? Do you have any suggestions for him?

A. Every man should have proper indoctrination in cold weather clothing usage, nutrition, survival, and living outside in the cold.

Q. What is the greatest single improvement in anti-icing, or de-icing equipment in the last few years?

A. The heated wing, in my opinion.

Q. Do you have any special tips for winter flying?

A. See to it that cold weather operations procedures are rigidly adhered to. Avoid getting your aircraft cold-soaked. Be very careful during preflight to check prescribed operating temperatures and pressures before takeoff. During letdowns and landings avoid overcooling of cylinder heads.

Q. Do you have any suggestions for survival in the far north?

A. See to it that your survival equipment is all aboard the aircraft. Check your own personal equipment to see that you like it and it fits you; that it is clean and in first-class condition.

If you go down in the Arctic, stay with your aircraft so you can

Col. Bernt Balchen is, without doubt, the most experienced polar aviator in the world. He has flown over both poles and participated in many expeditions. He is shown here in the cockpit of Lincoln Ellsworth's Lockheed Vega monoplane.

U.S. Information Agency Photo

be located. You have shelter and fuel in your aircraft, and both are primary factors for survival in the Arctic.

Q. Is navigating in the far north a great problem?

A. Not any more, with our well-developed techniques in high-latitude navigation,

Q. Is there any advantage to using jets in the far north?

A. Jet operations in the Arctic are simpler than piston-powered planes. They do not require any warm-up period and are not as much affected by cold-soaking as conventional aircraft.

Q. Drawing from your experience in both the Arctic and Antarctic, what is the principal difference between those two regions?

A. The principal difference is that the flying weather in the Antarctic is more severe. The season of good flying weather is usually much shorter there than in the Arctic.

Significant Events in
Arctic Aviation

1897   Andrée made his disastrous attempt to guide a balloon, *The Eagle*, from Spitsbergen to the North Pole.

1907   Walter Wellman made his first attempt to fly to the North Pole by dirigible.

1912   First airplane built in Alaska but did not fly.

1914   Lieutenant Nagurski, a Russian, made the first airplane flight in the Arctic regions from Novaya Zemlya in search of Sedow.

       First flight made in Alaska.

1920   First formation flight by Army Air Service airplanes made from Washington, D.C., to Alaska.

1924   Carl Ben Eielson carried first airmail in Alaska from Fairbanks to McGrath.

1925   Amundsen, Ellsworth, and Riiser-Larsen flew in Dornier-Wal flying boats from Spitsbergen to about 88°N., within 136 miles of the North Pole.

       Richard E. Byrd flew over Ellesmere Island and Greenland during MacMillan's expedition to gain experience preparatory to a north polar flight.

1926   Byrd flew from Spitsbergen to the North Pole and return in 15½ hours on May 9.

       Amundsen, Ellsworth, and Nobile flew in the airship *Norge* from Spitsbergen over the North Pole to Nome, Alaska, in 70 hours.

       Sir Hubert Wilkins and Eielson made a 150-mile reconnaissance flight over the Beaufort Sea.

1927 Wilkins and Eielson made a 550-mile reconnaissance flight from Point Barrow over the Beaufort Sea. They made several landings on the sea ice. Finally, after a forced landing, they sledged to the coast.

Canadians made an aerial survey of Hudson Bay.

1928 Wilkins and Eielson flew from Point Barrow, Alaska, to Spitsbergen in 20½ hours.

Nobile flew in the airship *Italia* to the North Pole from Spitsbergen. The airship was wrecked on the return flight.

1931 Arctic cruise of the *Graf Zeppelin* to Franz Josef Archipelago.

Wolfgang von Gronau of Germany made the first airplane flight over the inland ice of Greenland from east to west.

Parker Cramer and Oliver Paquette made the first flight from west to east but were lost at sea on their way to Europe.

Charles A. Lindbergh made a survey flight to the Orient via the Arctic route. His wife Anne accompanied him as radio operator.

Donald MacMillan used airplanes to map the unknown interior of Labrador.

1932 Aviation was introduced in the Soviet Arctic.

1933 Lindbergh surveyed the northern transatlantic air route. He flew over Labrador, Greenland, Iceland, the Scandinavian countries, and the Soviet Union as far east as Leningrad and Moscow.

1937 First airplane landings at the North Pole made by the Schmidt Expedition.

Two successful flights made by Russian planes from Moscow to North America via the North Pole.

1942   Alaska-Siberia (ALSIB) route opened for the ferrying of aircraft between United States and Russia.

Significant Events in Antarctic Aviation

1902   Captain Robert F. Scott made the first and only balloon ascent ever made in the Antarctic.

1928   Carl Ben Eielson and Sir Hubert Wilkins made the first successful airplane flight in the Antarctic from Deception Island.

1929   Richard E. Byrd made the first flight over the South Pole with Bernt Balchen as pilot.

Wilkins returned to Antarctica and used airplanes extensively equipped with floats.

1940   Byrd used seaplanes for the first time in guiding ships through the Ross Sea pack ice.

1946   *Operation Highjump* begins. The U.S. Navy, with a task force consisting of an aircraft carrier, submarine, icebreakers, cargo transports, and a command ship, conducted the largest exploring expedition ever organized.

1947   Six C-47 cargo transports made first takeoff from deck of a carrier using JATO in connection with *Operation Highjump*.

1956   R4D transport of the U.S. Navy made first aircraft landing at the South Pole. This same type aircraft had made a landing at the North Pole in May, 1952.

1957   First commercial airplane landing in the Antarctic. Pan American World Airways Stratocruiser landed at McMurdo Sound on a charter flight.

Index

Riiser-Larsen, 18, 26, 28, 31, 32, 46-55
Ritscher, Alfred, 135
Robbins, S. E., 236
Rockford, Illinois, 69
Rodebaugh, James, 233
Ross, James C., vii
Ross Ice Barrier, Antarctica, viii, 108
Ross Ice Shelf, Antarctica, 161
Royal Dutch Airlines, 274
Rudolf Island, Franz Josef Land, 90, 99
Russian and Soviet exploration, viii, 16, 78-103, 139
Rymill, John, 115

Sabine Island, Greenland, 204-207
San Jacinto, Calif., 92, 101
Saskatoon, Sask., 222
Satellites, 271
Scandinavian Airlines System, 272-274
Schmidt, Otto, 88-90
Schofield, E., 213
Schwabenland Expedition, 135
Scientific observations
    Graf Zeppelin, 83-85, 87
    IGY, 139, 155, 161-162
    Rymill expedition, 115
    Schmidt expedition, 89-91
    University of Alaska, 250
    University of Michigan, 69-70, 161
Scott, Robert Falcon, viii, 108-111, 131, 134, 149
Scripps Island, Antarctica, 117
Severnaya Zemlya, 84-86
Seward, William H., 217
Shackleton, Ernest, 108, 111, 112, 118, 131
Sheldon, Don, 244-247
Shetland Islands, Scotland, 75, 211-212
Shevelev, M. I., 88
Shinn, Gus, 141-148, 153
Shirshov, 90-91
Siple, Paul, 161
Smith, E. H., 204
Smith, Harry L., 194-199, 201-202
Sondre Stromfjord, Greenland, 272-273, 277
South Geomagnetic Pole, 139
South Pole. *See* Antarctica
South Pole Station, 149, 150, 154
Speed, Harvey, 141-143
Spitsbergen, 5-7, 16, 33-36, 39, 43, 45, 46, 57, 64-68, 77, 210-213

Stefansson, Vilhjalmur, 57
Stefansson Strait, Antarctica, 117
Stoltzman, Ray, 182
Streett, St. Clair, 221-224
Strindberg, Nils, 6-15
Stringer, Dean L., 252-253
Sun compass, 39, 40, 47
Susitna Valley, Alaska, 245
Svea, 5
Sweden in Arctic exploration, 4-15

Taimyr Peninsula, Siberia, 86
Talkeetna, Alaska, 244-247
Temperatures, polar, 22, 27, 31, 99, 161, 162, 264, 274-275
Terningen, 8
Texie Doodle, 176
Thule, Greenland, 263, 264, 277
Ting Mayuk, 218
Trans-American Airlines Corp., 74
Trans World Airlines, 273, 274

'Untin' Bowler, 73

Valdez, Alaska, 238-239
Vancouver, B.C., 92
Vodopyanov, M., 90

Wakeham Bay, Que., 74
Washburn, Bradford, 246
Webb, D. W., 195-197, 203
Wellman, Walter, 16
White Island, Arctic, 9-10, 14
Whiteout, 160, 279-280
Wien, Noel, 233-236
Wien, Ralph, 233
Wilkins, (George) Hubert, 57-68, 77-78, 112-117, 135
Williwaw, 172-173, 239
Wilson, R. H., 194-195, 199, 201-202
Wisting, 47-49
Wood, Robert, 73
Wordie, J. M., 118
World War II, 165-213
Wrangell, Alaska, 224-225

Young, Ed, 236
Yumashev, 94, 96, 98-101

Zeppelin, Ferdinand von, 16, 77, 78

289